W9-CSR-748

THE
WORLDS
OF JAZZ

Other works by André Hodeir
Published by Grove Press

CLEOPATRA GOES SLEDDING

JAZZ: ITS EVOLUTION AND ESSENCE

SINCE DEBUSSY: A VIEW OF CONTEMPORARY MUSIC

TOWARD JAZZ

WARWICK'S THREE BOTTLES

THE WORLDS OF JAZZ

ANDRÉ HODEIR

TRANSLATED BY NOËL BURCH

GROVE PRESS, INC., NEW YORK

LIBRARY
WITHDRAWN WESTERN OREGON COLLEGE
FRANCE AND M. OREG97Z850

Copyright © 1972 by Grove Press, Inc.

All Rights Reserved

ISBN: 0-394-48023-6

Library of Congress Catalog Card Number: 74-155132

No part of this book may be reproduced,
for any reason, by any means, including any method
of photographic reproduction, without the permission of the publisher

First Printing

Manufactured in the United States of America
by American Book–Stratford Press, Inc., New York

Distributed by Random House, Inc., New York

The translator wishes to thank
JACQUES HESS for his precious assistance

To the B-flat blues

CONTENTS

PART FOUR

ETHURE AND CULTICS

PART ONE

THE
MAN WHO
PLAYS JAZZ

1

For Tuning the Instrument

Forgotten. Had you forgotten? Could you possibly have forgotten? The green hours of initiation, the intoxication, and that feeling of certainty, that sweet feeling of certainty; that whole interior inner web that had once been your life. Forgotten? That wasted youth that slipped through your fingers, forgotten? The man you once were, with his naive infatuations, the man you want to cast aside forever, forgotten? The man you have cast aside forever. His myths, lost? His fetishes, destroyed? Is everything he left you like a remote heritage still throbbing at the bottom of the pit into which you hurled it? Forgotten?

She gazes down at the notebook lying open before her on Frank's desk that lovely blue-tinted paper that he had made to order by S.B.

& S. he hated the store-bought yellow paper used by most arrangers if he couldn't have a sensual contact with the paper nothing happened in his head a mysterious operation writing music where does it come from she could understand better when he began trying things out on the piano but at night he didn't want to disturb the neighbors so he concentrated sitting motionless staring at the sheet of paper not even sucking at his pipe and it seemed to go on forever sometimes she even doubted that he was still awake but she didn't dare talk to him and then hesitantly he would pick up his mechanical pencil the little black-and-red mechanical pencil that she had given to him he was never without it and would begin to write laboriously at first as if it actually hurt him rotating the pencil between his fingers for minutes or even hours on end the pencil never left the paper its rotations growing gradually faster how many revolutions it was as if a machinery had been set in motion that would not stop until the whole section had been written with its notes values dynamics ties notations then he would put down the pencil and begin to read it over smoking in little puffs she would feel his body relax she would bring him a cup of coffee taking care not to set it down too near the paper otherwise he would be sure to spill it across the page and then he would get so angry for such a gentle man to calm him down she would tell him that Beethoven's manuscripts were stained too but he didn't like Beethoven she would glance affectionately over his shoulder at the open notebook still blank on the right but already covered on the left with those incomprehensible hieroglyphics rather pretty on the whole like everything that comes down from the past what is more beautiful than Japanese writing isn't it strange she said to him that the same system of notation used in the works of the past can serve to write down the most modern things even jazz it's not true it can't he answered with a smile and he picked up his pencil and set it rotating again she would watch him write toward the end she succeeded in imagining merely from the look of the page how the arrangement would sound when she heard the tape or record she would recognize it right away I took that one over to Locki's place a few Sundays ago and seeing it so black he made a face at all those sixteenth notes as though nobody but Frank ever wrote sixteenth notes and those chromatic passages all those sharps and flats and Frank got mad if even one was left out and those time changes I won't be able to sleep again tonight my poor eyes and those piano chords they never seem to stop they go all the way up to the sky and was this a B-natural or a B-flat

*　*　*

and the announcer introduced a Charlie Parker record, one of the Charlie Parker records you knew best of all, one of those records whose grooves you could have counted. Then there rose within you, with that irresistible force that unexpected things have, a prayer, the phrasing of which startled you. *Fool! Try to play the way you used to!* You wished that silent plea addressed to a dead man would be immediately effective, would act on the record's contents, revive the scrap of life that was crystallized there forever. For ever? You would soon know. You might soon know.

The tape recorder is running. Monk looks down at the keyboard open before him and for the seventh time this week launches into *Crepuscule with Nelly*. No one could say how many times the same tape recorder has captured the same piece in almost identical versions. Some were erased; others still exist buried away in a pile of boxes in one corner of the room. Some day, perhaps, a musicologist will study those tapes, will try to grasp the slow transformation that occurs from one to the next, a transformation so gradual that it may be as imperceptible as the erosion of rocks under the steady lapping of the sea. They will be dated, incorrectly, no doubt; or else, erased; or then, again, numbered arbitrarily and stacked away on the highest shelf of some record archives.

Too high. The air conditioning has been set too high. The chill has affected the instrument's strings. The A-string has reacted even more than the others; it is almost a B-flat now; therefore its vibrations must be faster and tighter; yet this is not apparent to the eye, only the ear can tell the difference. The eye would regard this string as identical to the other three—same length, same silver color—if it did not know that they differed by a single detail. When the eye takes in the four strings as they issue forth from the nut, they seem to be parallel; however, as it moves down the fingerboard toward the bridge, it becomes apparent that their paths are divergent. Beyond the bridge, the eye loses sight of the strings, only the huge round bottom of the instrument remains visible; then the floor of the bandstand appears, the strips of carpeting that run around the room and, still farther out, the many-shaped heads turned in various directions.

When the piano began to rumble in a certain way, it would be the crucial moment, the first stage of a never-changing progression. Beside him, Ken and Teddy would be waiting with expressionless faces. They would know what piece this introduction was working up to, whereas the public would still be in doubt. The uncertainty of the people out there would give him pleasure; that was the reason why he liked to play in concert. Holding in his hands the immediate fate of a thousand people who were all looking at him. . . . One moment more! And then after another sudden twist, he would finally come out with the theme that everyone would immediately recognize with a feeling of pleasant surprise, the murmurs of a satisfied crowd would be wafted up to him like a reward. Perhaps things wouldn't happen exactly that way in the soft lights and subdued atmosphere of this nightclub. A small audience does not make such an open display of its satisfaction. Yet he would sense it, gauge it by the way the faces and bodies around him would relax.

Walls! made of good stonework, strong, proudly standing, built at a time when things were meant to last, enfolding in their sturdy arms the delicate beauty of an Italian-style concert hall. Until this evening, until the first short blast from those seven brasses in staggered formation at the back of the stage, they have had reasons to believe themselves immortal. So far as everyone is concerned, they are still immortal. The attack of the brasses was sudden; the walls' long memory failed to recognize that perfect simultaneity. They felt the pain of an inconceivable wound. The shock reached the audience, too, but the sound waves passed between the heads, and though it may have caused an impression upon thousands of ears, it was against the walls that it finally spent itself. Horns! Gentle horns of Weber's overtures, your caress was never like this; nor yours, sparkling trumpets of the Jupiter Symphony. The music of that period in which the walls came erect loved and respected architecture. Beethoven's storm raged within the temple built to house it; never did it harm these walls; even the deadly kettle-drum passage in the last first movement could not shake them. The walls have sheltered Niccolò Paganini's diabolical violin, the walls have witnessed the resurrection of the old Cantor, the walls have mourned the gentle Schubert, Clara knew them, and they vibrated to the sound of that same piano under her fingertips, sumptuous chords probing at their innermost resonances, ferreting out the secret harmonics of the stone, that same piano which the little round man hardly dares touch (is it really the same one, the walls don't recognize it, they don't know anything any more). . . .

He knew that the tastes of his audience would be perfectly attuned to his own; no need for evasive tactics to please it; no need ever to do it violence. Actually, what they would want him to play would be whatever he himself felt like playing. He would keep that Gershwin tune under wraps a few seconds more, then, when he felt they wanted it badly enough out there, he'd let them have it. He knew that all their pleasure lay in the frustration he would inflict on them. A passing frustration; the tension would soon be resolved. With the cunning of a playwright building a scene for a famous actor, he would take pains to delay the entrance of the theme. Like sweet Juliet, the melody would appear only after the artfully protracted digressions of an initiatory prologue; but once the moment of revelation had come, it would not slip away again; everyone could lose himself in it, forget himself in it, sing himself in it.

You are sitting in your favorite armchair leafing through a newspaper and taking from time to time another sip of coffee; now and then your gaze wanders to the wall, but this is immaterial; nothing can happen to you, you are immortal. Then suddenly that thing that's been running stealthily in the background stops chanting nonsense and the announcer introduces a Charlie Parker record. You might easily have missed it if the write-up on the tennis match had been just a bit livelier, but at that very moment you turned the page and the announcer introduced a Charlie Parker record. *Fool!* There was no drama in the announcer's tone; he just said it the way he might have said: here's the latest Paul Anka record, or: the President lunched with the Chinese ambassador, or: General Motors has gone up one point, or again: the Bermudas are going to beat Italy at bridge; and yet what his voice announced with steady neutral detachment was a Charlie Parker record. Was this a statistically probable event? Was it frequent for Charlie Parker records to be announced just like that, out of the blue? Perhaps that particular announcer had never had to face this responsibility before. Or perhaps, on the contrary, he had already reflected on the fate of those who live, tranquil and uncommitted, in an unchanging world, *fool!* with its well-defined values, perhaps until now he had managed to skip certain titles, certain names, pretending not to see them whenever they turned up on his list. Jazz magazines are silent on the subject, but law magazines are rich with controversies over the contradictory verdicts rendered by the courts of various countries against announcers dismissed for either failing to announce a Charlie Parker record or for having announced it; and the appellate courts of the world spend most of their time sifting through the reasons adduced by the lower courts. Was the announcer awed by the idea of all that, or was it merely out of sheer absentmindedness that, just when your radio was tuned to his station, no sooner had his eyes scanned the title of the Charlie Parker record than his voice announced it? *Fool!* Now that it was done, now that he'd announced it, was he sitting speechless behind his dead mike, aware of his helplessness, not daring to ask the engineer to put him back on the air so that he could make a correction, or was he waving frantically at an engineer who wasn't looking his way, was he screaming a warning that none could hear?

The eye does not linger on the variously shaped heads turned in various directions; it merely notes their steadily declining number (seven this evening; there were eleven last night, thirteen the night before, and seventeen the first night), and their variable but always asymmetrical layout along the points which radiate out from the bandstand, alternately red-and-black wedges of carpeting that form a star-shaped pattern on the floor of the room. As the eye slides back up the instrument, it sees other colors: the brown of the bandstand floor, then the mahogany of the instrument, the whiteness of the bridge, the gleaming silver of the strings, the black of the fingerboard (very different from the black in the carpeting).

She would watch him write all day long and when an urgent commission asked for an all-night sitting he told her to go to bed but she knew where her place was what could she do during all that time he'd suggested she learn copying Locki was overworked some day he'd go blind but she didn't want to lose her critical independence better to know nothing than just a little she was happy when he sat down at the piano she would call to him from the kitchen no Frank not that chord generally he trusted her women's taste is more reliable they can't do anything but they can appreciate when he sat down in front of his blue paper alone absolutely alone she knew he was in spite of her own attentive presence his appreciation had to come before anyone else's she would hear him swear between his teeth struggling trying to tame those forces inside him fortunately he had a practical mind a phrase like that's for Jay Jay he's the only one who can play it the way I feel it but he's not in New York phone his agent maybe he'll be back before the recording date but before she could get the information he'd already thought up another phrase the most imaginative arranger around Sonny said he also called him my little treasure chest no taller than a boy but so attractive and a glutton for work capable of sitting eighteen hours with pencil in hand only asking for coffee now and then that was how he'd made his way up as famous as an arranger could get to be in those days the reporters were always after her Mrs. Costello this and Mrs. Costello that Shelley listen to me tell me what about this what about that and now who cares about Shelley Costello how many of them still remember Frank Costello even Locki has stopped phoning has he changed jobs the piano keyboard Frank always wanted it left open always open till the day he died as long as I'm alive it will never be closed he declared he thought he'd live forever she glances at it now it's closed she deliberately mislaid the key nobody will ever open that piano again he didn't use it much he relied on what he called his inner ear on the little red lamp that lit up in his head when he'd just written a risky progression when that happened he'd never hesitate to erase the whole thing it hurt him though especially when he was dead tired but above all he was a conscientious craftsman none of this will stand up in front of a jury he would say and start over again she would look up from her book and see him crossing out whole pages with a blue pencil a fat indelible one because anything he wrote with the mechanical pencil could always be rubbed out that was what his eraser was for he called it Scruple but when he crossed something out it was final hopeless a whole painstakingly constructed section would sink back into nothingness.

Something emerges. Where has it come from? As Monk makes his way through the exposition, an obscure concern is growing at the back of his mind. Is he going to find that chord again, the one he discovered the other day and which ought to fall into place a bit further on, in the twenty-second bar? Sometimes a lover makes a rendezvous without knowing whether the beloved will keep it. Monk must be starting to realize that his only reason for choosing *Crepuscule with Nelly* today was that new chord. He is still intrigued by his discovery; confusedly, he senses that it can modify the meaning of the harmonic progression on which the channel of the theme is based; and yet here was a theme he thought he had completely explored. *Dialectics:* If he had not played the theme so often in recent days, he would not have made that all-important change in it; but if he had not made this discovery, he would not be playing the same piece over again today. *Aesthetics:* Does his relentless playing of his own themes over and over again mean that he wants to play them as well as possible, does it mean he is trying to perfect the themes themselves, or is it his way of developing, in himself, their improvisational potential? *Psychology:* Is he trying to recapture the joy of his discovery, savor it just once again (even though he knows that this is impossible), or is he worried, is he afraid that he has forgotten the chord?

How strange: the knowledge you once had of that record has slipped away from you. The record that you owned, the record that you watched merrily spinning, unable to read a word of the printing on the label, not even the company, that was the only detail you didn't know by heart, records are tamer now, they revolve so slowly that you could even read the bass player's name if it were there to read *fool!*—you watched it and listened to it, even though it had nothing left to teach you, you anticipated its every surprise and yet you loved it, and you loved possessing it, it had been made for you, Charlie Parker, you knew, had recorded it just for you, he had *given* it to you—and right now you don't know that record any more, you can't even remember how it begins—have you lost it or has it lost you?—which instrument is going to play first.

This he knew: once the audience had reacted and he had enjoyed their reaction (he still enjoyed it, he wasn't blasé yet), appearances would gradually change. His accompanists would come in at just the right moment in the tempo he had been building up with his usual perfection, now they would give him their support, Ken and Teddy, his old faithfuls, almost too faithful, in fact, following him all over the world (he'd better give them a raise pretty soon if he didn't want trouble), and he could start to overlay the Gershwin tune with his own portrait. The audience wanted nothing else: it wanted his hallmark, his inimitable style—it wanted *him*. Success! How could his records have sold a hundred times, a thousand times better than those of any other pianist, no matter how talented, if he didn't have some kind of trade secret? Success! He had always been rolling in success and he always would be. His success lay in his style; in the quiet badgering movement of his left hand that suggested the throb of a guitar, in that subtle rubato which he would use a bit later (not until the third chorus, though) and which would set the chairs rocking under the ladies' buttocks, in the sound he could get out of a piano, any piano at all, in those orchestral effects, those changing colors, in those arpeggios that he would drape like so many sweeping garlands around a carefully chosen ballad, one of the audience's old friends, one they had come expecting to hear and which he would know how to make young again. Since the whisky would be more expensive tonight on account of his appearance—

success: not a single empty table—he wouldn't stint on the thrills, they would go home full and happy.

Now the instrumentalist's right hand comes into range of the eye, holding the bow and letting it slide over the strings, close to the bridge. Outside the field of vision, the left hand, with a deft movement that no longer needs the supervision of the eye, grasps the peg that controls the A-string, and turns it slowly; the sound lowered in pitch. Effortlessly the glance crosses the separation of the stage and the room; it stops at the party in the red-and-black background. The heads are as before; their arrangement is the same; only the orientation of each has changed. The eye comes to rest on the third string which the bow is still stroking. The third finger (on either side of this ruby-studded digit, the others are not symmetrical) grazes the string exactly in its middle, producing, as the powers of mathematics ordain, a note twice as high: one hundred and twelve vibrations per second instead of fifty-six.

The rendezvous. It's coming. The appointed place. The time and the place. Occasionally time and space confess their basic identity. Only in music are such confessions possible. Only in music is it possible to arrange the kind of rendezvous Monk has with his chord. He is on its trail; he will catch up with it on the very first beat of the twenty-second bar. Is the slightest hesitation going to appear in Monk's playing? No sign of panic, however fleeting. The man is calm. Still, he has been wrong in the past, he has made mistakes and even wrong mistakes; but in those overhanging structures which constitute Monk's themes and his developments of them, a mistake can always be brought under control, taken in hand, it can become the key to a chance creation. Mistakes are part of Monk's system. Accepted and integrated. Except when some wrong mistake disrupts the continuity of discourse. Then Monk stops; he gets up with his unsteady step and starts pacing the studio. I made the wrong mistake. Or: I forgot a chord. But Monk has not forgotten this chord yet. He's at home, sitting at his piano, playing, playing.

At home, between four walls, you find yourself in a ridiculous situation: sitting in this armchair, in the center of the red carpet on which you used to like to loll, choosing a record from the stack spread out voluptuously around you, black naked vibrant living bodies, your right hand holding a cup of coffee that you can't set down anywhere. Your left hand, in which a newspaper trembles ever so slightly, is too far from the radio to reach it, and you haven't time to get up: the past is just outside the door and the hinges are about to give; you'll have to submit.

The walls, the wounded walls, the humbled walls, the suffering walls uneasily watch the little round man sitting placidly at the piano and flinging lone metallic sounds into the air. Are the seven archangels in staggered formation, sitting at the back with their instruments on their knees, waiting for his orders? Is it in his power to have them unleash the lightning which they undoubtedly hold in their hands? Will one of those calm, regular gestures of his be a signal that the walls won't notice, has he already made up his mind, has he decided to assume responsibility for the ghastly undertaking, isn't that how those things happen, he must be imagining that the deed is already done, he must be weighing the horror of it, savoring his triumph, laying out a future for himself as irrevocable as the past. Yet perhaps the little black witch doctor is quite harmless, perhaps the fate of the walls is simply written in the parts in front of the seven men, perhaps he is not the chief of state who presses the fatal button, perhaps the missiles blast off all by themselves to carry out a plan every detail of which has been worked out in advance, including the end of the world. Is this the end, the inconceivable and necessary end of an existence the course of which the walls have always regretted? How could they have possibly foreseen the fate which the gods of the world of sound, the gods to whom they are dedicated, held in store for them when space was filled with Italian nightingales and their endless modulations, when the huge compact mass of the Romantic orchestra rose into the air, when the black-and-white concert piano, a marvel of craftsmanship, rang out with its deep basses, or when there issued forth from the back of the stage the icy notes of the organ with its invisible officiant, or even when the heavy Wagnerian fanfares blared out? The walls remember, the walls will not forget.

Monk will remember the chord. This is a certainty. He cannot help it. Perhaps his mind will have nothing to do with it. His fingers, then. Like well-trained animals, they will spread themselves of their own volition over the black-and-white keys at just the right time, forming the only geometrical figure capable of embodying, in the world of sound vibrations, the idea buried in Monk's unconscious. The fingers are aware of these correlations. They are readers of symbols, whenever they happen to break free. Free for a moment. Back to the wild state. Monk relies on his wild fingers. He knows they'll find the chord again, even if it escapes him. True, Monk might search for it. The chord does not exist only in himself, it is there, close by, somewhere on one of this week's tapes. All he would have to do is listen to them one by one. But Monk (too lazy, perhaps, for this kind of research) prefers to rely on his fingers. He watches them scamper, curiously splayed out on the keyboard before him, the wide-open keyboard.

She doubts whether the jazz-world remembers him Prez yes of course or Bix on account of his legend but Costello still the musicians liked him there was warmth in the way they said hello Frank when he came into the studio with his eyes shining he loved that it was the moment when he could relax and yet deep down inside an obscure sneaking anxiety was buzzing away how would it come off all those notes packed onto the blue-tinted paper from S.B. & S. what was their relation to the fifteen young men who greeted him with a smile she knew he would be satisfied with what he'd written a job done a job well done so would the musicians they would launch into it confidently the arrangement was Frank's he'd written it personally Frank never hired ghosts he preferred to turn down a job altogether that time he said no to Sinatra that was just like him what a pity too much work that month twelve arrangements a week and Frank wasn't the kind that wrote his arrangements four at a time setting up a music stand in each corner of the room and going from one to the next when you're tired of number two you go to number three for a change and so on she'd seen Bud Higginson work that way what a businessman Frank said he had too much know-how he could write badly on purpose when it paid schlemiels they don't deserve their names on the labels Frank wanted people to respect him look at the way he defended his music against band leaders and singers with their bright ideas cut out the trombones here nothing doing if I wrote them in there it's because they're necessary cutting them out would unbalance the whole band it would all have to be rewritten persuading always persuading that was part of the job the musicians too say Frankie I can't play what you wrote here not you Don don't say that I had your legato in mind when I wrote that I said to myself what a treat that will be if only Don's free otherwise I'll have to make it simpler honestly I'd hate to give that up couldn't you just try okay man I'll try generally Frank got his way in the end anyway he seldom wrote anything difficult without first making sure it could be played how many times had she called up Harry or Sandy about some instrumental problem then Frank would take the receiver and start to sing in that voice of his that sounded like a eunuch's and yet God knows that voice made everybody laugh his friends even made fun of it in front of her but absolutely true to pitch said Joe to the nearest comma no to the nearest savart said Frank correcting him he was right to be proud of that it was the symbol of his integrity.

The coffee shivering at the bottom of the cup, black with white reflections, is no help; neither is the rug, which has slyly kept the imprints of your old records in its red fibers, imprints which your footsteps have avoided effacing. You have no idea what dark disaster is about to engulf you. One moment more! If only you could travel back over all those years and suddenly *be* that man lolling on the rug, listening to the music of that moment, a music ageless like yourself, just a parcel of the universe madly whirling. . . . But your armchair refuses to vanish and the two of you remain riveted together.

All the way back at the beginning of his career—he remembers—he had faith in the future—he had never doubted that he would succeed—and yet he didn't know that he would find that gimmick of his—playing in tempo but a little behind the beat—syncopating the whole phrase—displacing what others would play "four-square"—he didn't know it would be the key to success—that it would last—that he, the inimitable pianist, would become the one most imitated—all over the world—because in Madrid—or in Rome—or rather Paris—there's supposed to be a character whose whole career has been built on an out-and-out plagiary of his technique and style—what mimics those Frenchmen are! another one became famous imitating General de Gaulle—as plagiaries go, it was a thorough job, they say this character took everything from him—even his first name—in fact the squares over there got them mixed up—but for a jazz-sensitive ear, when it came to swing and imagination it was not exactly, not quite exactly the same thing—Paris—he didn't much like Paris—maybe the Place Vendôme at noon—ungenerous people—no sense of hospitality—when they came to see him after the show, it was still part of the show—what's he like when he's not playing—they tried to outdo each other in friendliness but they never came back—always different faces—waiting at the hotel for somebody to call him but nobody ever did—two weeks in Paris are worse than a lifetime of tours—he preferred giving one-nighters —at least you got to travel—and anyway Paris was linked in his memory with

* * *

Whumpf! This time the blast was even shorter, but more incisive, sharper and louder. It contained a kind of density which the walls had never known before. Space was filled with a mad tremor; the walls shook. Seven black men in staggered formation under the orders of one black man, seven lords sitting in judgment at the back of the stage with more black men beneath them, subordinate figures hunched over instruments that look hunched themselves (queer horns, circular skins, plump hips strung with wires): this is the oddly assorted phalanx which is producing the volcanic activity that worries the walls. It is true that the walls, in their walls' lifetime, have seen countless combinations materialize on the stage in their midst, and more than one evil geometric figure has appeared there since the day when a faun as false as Don Giovanni stealthily let in barbary in every form: the huge, multicolored mass of spring and everything else that has come after and which no longer lives in harmony with the walls, which clashes with them—but the clashes had been glancing ones; whereas this evening the shock has been head-on, a tremendous slap with nothing to break its force (the walls had failed to foresee this attack or they would have protected themselves, reinforced themselves, shored themselves up). . . .

Perfection. Governed as it is by the powers of mathematics that divide the string into two equal parts producing a perfect harmonic, the world of sound is a manifestation of absolute order. Complex though it may be, the instrument's architecture expresses in appearance—the eye knows that it is only in appearance—that self-same organic symmetry. On either side of an imaginary line dividing it down the middle, the two flanks of the instrument swell up, expand, blossom out in identical shapes until they meet the slender ribs around the edge of the belly cut with sound holes. All the wooden veins converge toward the sound post, that soul of the instrument, hidden under the bridge, past which the strings seem to come together in a bunch before plunging into the tailpiece. On the near side of the bridge, over the fingerboard, the strings form a barely open fan, as regular as the shape of the instrument itself, only one detail of which belies its perfect symmetry.

Does Monk have doubts? Is he suffering? A drop of sweat oozes out of a pore in his forehead just as he plays the last note of the twenty-first bar. He knows the rendezvous is almost here. Where? Has he already overshot his mark? He mustn't panic. When? He brings all his willpower to bear. Here it is! The sforzando! Dramatic accents! Aaaaaah! *Coup de théâtre!* Monk didn't play the chord. Another combination came to him. His fingers and himself, in a single burst. And it's a beautiful combination, one that meshes so perfectly with the accentuation of the phrase as to make one thing clear at once: that other chord, the one Monk was looking for, was only a preliminary stage, a suggestion of the one he has just discovered in all its overpowering truth. Monk opens his mouth and lets out a wailing shout of triumph. *I've got it! I've got it!* What a relief! Freedom! Monk glances at the tape recorder. No, the spools are still turning. The green gaze of the magic eye stares back at him. The chord has been taped. Monk won't forget it now.

He can't forget those two weeks in Paris. Buried in a vaudeville program, *en vedette américaine*—"the American star," that's what they call you over there when you've got second-billing—he can't forget—he wouldn't want to have to go through that again. The horrible feeling when the euphoria goes away, when the witch doctor realizes that his hocus pocus is useless—the rain isn't going to fall—what could he have done, keep on going through the motions —the audience was ice-cold—it didn't work in Paris—he should have been satisfied with a recital—his fans would have filled a hall— the people hadn't come there for him—they didn't know the pieces he was playing—and even if he'd played *La Vie en Rose* it wouldn't have helped—those people weren't familiar with his style—they hadn't learned to love him yet—he couldn't make love with the audience.

How slow the ceremony! How long the anticipation of the sacrifice to come! Each moment may be the last, at any moment the blow may come that will bring down the walls. The walls know it; but each passing second is a promise of life, more agonizing than death itself. This long delay before the ritual is consummated seems to come down from ancient times, from long before the walls were built, when men knew how to wait, liked to wait, a feeling which the walls have never known, designed as they were to resonate to sound structures in motion. The flute holding forth now in the center of the stage is nearly as suave as Orpheus'; yet hidden in its deceptive gentleness is the threat that looms behind it. Strange, that flute: what is it doing alone among all those brasses? Its frail voice is reminiscent of the strangely caressing tones of an instrument which may have been imaginary, for the walls never saw it, but whose ambiguous charms they once experienced: drawn-out, tenuous, diaphanous sounds floating through a dream in which moving shapes appeared upon the walls' surface. They remember the most remarkable of those weightless, immaterial pictures which did not sink in but slid over them without leaving a trace. Was it a prophetic dream? It showed a procession of gondolas, a funereal rite—dire presage?—accompanied by a slow unobtrusive music that was quite the opposite of tonight's; and yet the walls sense a distant kinship, a subtle bond between the ceremony that rose out of the sea-green hues of the Canale Grande and the one they are witnessing now. A warning from the gods? The walls are afraid.

You've forgotten it, that's why you're afraid of that thing locked up in the grooves that you can already hear scratching under the sapphire (it must be a seventy-eight, if they still exist), you're afraid, you've forgotten, you've betrayed that teenager who sent away for Sidney Bechets and black-and-red Armstrongs. Look at John Hammond: time hasn't robbed him of anything, Fletcher Henderson still means something to him; or that old Negro who told you all about a contest between Bean and Prez: the one with his big sound, the other with his gags, it seemed to him like only yesterday, *fool!* but you, so full of your development, what's the value of this privileged here-and-now of yours, what will its value be ten years from now? Will you be forgotten, you also?

The eye has long ago grasped that tiny detail. In order for the instrument to be perfectly symmetrical, the thickness of the strings would have to increase on one side of the dividing line and decrease on the other. As the eye sweeps across the instrument from right to left, it sees the strings grow steadily thinner, as if the instrument had no middle. The eye knows that other, profane eyes might fail to notice such a minute lack of symmetry; but for this eye, it exists. The eye strays for a moment into the carpeted area and considers the faces that people it. They are not arranged in any particular order; and if the eye lingers to examine each in turn, the dissymmetry which it discovers there is far more apparent: noses bent to one side, eyes of different shapes, mouths that pucker irregularly, wrinkles of uneven depth, bumps peaking through misshapen bald spots. . . .

She leafs through the old scores that she liked to classify proud of the cataloguing system she had thought up Frank if you ever need your fourth version of *Lover Come Back to Me* yes the one with the French horns well I can find it for you in less than a minute yes she could have found that score instantly among the thousands that

lay piled on the bookshelves but Frank just laughed that's perfectly
wonderful and wonderfully useless it was true there never had been
an example of one of his score's serving twice and yet Frank didn't
want them thrown out he liked to know they were there around
him you never know Pettiford good old Pettiford this one was
written on his request Frank admired him so much he always took
his side defended his odd-ball antics once right in the middle of a
recording session O.P. put up his hand to stop an eighty-piece
orchestra because he had just stressed a top G against the fingerboard instead of bowing the harmonic G as indicated on the part
Frank had yelped for joy that's conscientiousness for you and
Pettiford gave him his friendship in return a friendship that
deepened when he found out that Frank wasn't like other arrangers
didn't write the double bass part last what couldn't those two have
done together if and this package here yes there's still a note pinned
to it a list of musicians that old habit of Frank's some names crossed
out and replaced by others Keg Chuck Red Yank Bing Bull Rod
Babe Cub Hal Hank Skip Tex Mel Mert Lou Truck Stu Buck Pops
Dick Don Doc in other words all his favorites Erschienen ist der
herrliche Tag except for Pettiford who wasn't there any more to
play the double bass part the easiest to perform but the hardest to
write in Frank's whole career those were his very words you see he
went on these arrangements are the only ones I really care about
and yet I contributed nothing to them but a bass part it was *his*
record he had personally supervised the pressing Herz und Mund
und Tat und Leben the only scores he took the trouble to copy out
in ink Hilf Gott, dass mir's gelinge put a jazz feeling into it Durch
Adams Fall ist ganz verderbt while scrupulously respecting the text
except for a few transpositions Ach wie nichtig, ach wie flüchtig
even classical musicians had praised his transcriptions admirably
performed a model of discretion that's what a famous egghead critic
had written Frank showed that article to all his friends Mit
Fried' und Freud' ich fahr' dahin in spite of that the record didn't sell
it came too soon like all masterpieces later others did the same thing
and made big hits that's the way it goes Frank could take things like
that in his stride he joked about it and sometimes he even claimed
that he deserved that failure as punishment for his vandalism but
whenever he would put the record on for other people he demanded complete silence how do you like it as background music he
would ask them insidiously is it good enough to chintz up your
conversations Locki was more philosophical about it you can't keep
people from talking that's what records are for some you talk above
others you talk about Frank got mad then me too when it's an

Ornette Coleman I talk but when it's my arrangement of the great Johann Sebastian I listen and if I can spend time listening to something I know better than anything else in the world then other people can listen with me.

The eye lingers for a moment on the black fingers studded with red as they press the string against the slightly blacker fingerboard; then, moving down again, it takes in the colors: silver, white, dark mahogany, brown, another red, a still blacker black, and finally the white, faintly pinkish heads. It knows that in a space beyond its scope of awareness the harmonics are multiplying: perhaps they form an inverted pyramid whose tip coincides with the fundamental tone produced by the fifty-six punctual vibrations. In this setting, the exploring eye—which cannot identify itself with any other eye—discerns no pyramid. Black is not the harmonic of white; black is the harmonic of nothing.

Monk can no longer pursue his former objective. Trivial objective! The sudden appearance of that unexpected chord, of that beautiful chord, has swept away the landscape through which he was slowly making his way. A new world has been revealed to him, forcing upon him a genetic mutation. He has changed species. Run. Jump. At times his fingers get ahead of him, at others he guides them; he runs too fast, loses his bearings, reels with happiness; and at the same time realizes that his chance has died. A drop of sweat falls on the keyboard next to one of his fingers as it ceases to move. He realizes that he has stopped, that he is no longer playing. A lone note, a decapitated, drawn-out B-flat resounds in the returning silence, hardly ruffled by the humming tape recorder busily recording it. Unfinished. Lost on the way. Not quite. This time Monk will listen to the tape. He knows that he will have to make his way painstakingly back to the breaking point, figure out what happened, and then start to drill, drill relentlessly down the tunnel which will lead his thought patterns (through what suffering he can guess only too well! and yet at the same time he yearns for it) to a final result. Monk does not argue with himself. He knows that he will do it. In spite of his laziness. Monk groans. His joy has left him. Blindly, he gropes along the top of the piano for the glass which he knows is there. He takes a drink.

The cup is still ten inches from your mouth: there's no time left for you to drink. As you listen to the needle scratching in the groove, this is what you are wondering. What is forgetting? The condemning of a past moment. But in the name of what? In the name of perennity; because that moment has not lasted, because its echo has not reached your ears. Perhaps that moment was unique? That moment died, it died and left no posterity. But what if you loved at just that moment, what if your madness was complete at just that moment, what if you forgot yourself at just that moment? *Fool!*

What would he do if he were ever forgotten—the chilliness of that Paris audience might spread across the world—an epidemic of chilliness—what would become of him—of course all his needs would be provided for—twenty years of success are a paying proposition—but isn't success a kind of need too—all the big name old-timers who make their farewells now and then but can't make up their minds to step out of the spotlight—people make fun of them—sometimes he wonders whether success can die—others before him have been abandoned—do they still talk about the old-time pianists—the ones he idolized—Fats yes but he's dead—Tatum too but toward the end he didn't have any success, just a reputation—does Teddy Wilson give lessons—does Fatha Hines still play that endless trill, is it still enough to drive an audience wild—and he himself with his rubato and his arpeggios—what if it didn't work any more—he imagines himself saying to Ken and Teddy it's all over this is where we part—but before it came to that—all the efforts he would have had to make just to survive—how could he conceive of such a thing: him playing with all his heart sweating panting humming what his right hand was going to play in order to guide it better desperately pulling out all the stops and the audience refusing to respond like in Paris! No!—Impossible!—It's im-pos-sible!—Perhaps as he grows older he'll find he can't do it any more—do you really lose your faculties—will his left arm that wonderful pendulum grow less precise—like an aging jaguar with a heavy leap will he miss his prey—can power die?

In staggered formation—is that the secret of their power? A magic arrangement? Wasn't that taboo word arrangement spoken a while ago by the little man? The walls didn't notice, the walls can't remember—in staggered formation, the seven indifferent-looking men who work hard to produce trills whose restrained quality does less to hide their violence than to reveal it, the seven men are waiting, the walls know, for the first crack in them to appear. Then it will be all over. No longer will the walls shiver with happiness to the rounds of applause. No baton will ever again wave before them, sending the chords of a symphony to echo through their stones. They knew that one day they were bound to see the last of that revered old maestro whose hair had grown white before them, and of the lovely singer with a voice as deep and smooth as themselves, who was his protégée. Are they also fated never again to watch the hair of another maestro whiten? Will no young contralto launched on a brief dazzling career ever sing before them again? Was this strange concert their requiem? Who said that? Immortal! There are no such things as ruins, no hand ever wrote menetekelupharsin on a wall, no wall has ever had to appear before minosaecusrhadamantus no magic arrangement can bring down walls made of good strong stonework, proudly standing, secular, air-proof, providence, density, televisiontologirationally! Liars! Liars! She knows that all these memories are lies and that things were different more beautiful and at the same time more sad in dulce jubilo all that reality she had put together during the endless nights next to that pile of useless scores that will never be played again never think about that again Paris never think again Monk closes his eyes he wonders whether that final achievement will slip through his fingers whether he has the means to attain it all you have to do is lift your hand but do you still have time how many dead grooves dead rest at last requiem and those spools spinning away *fool!* that turntable everything that's spinning stupidly in your head the heads out there his head grows empty around him the lights have been lowered he can no longer see the audience he is beginning to feel it the presence of a multiple being hemming him in Farewell! the Parthenon too will fall he fell slowly over on his left side the doctor made a face worked too much that man did judged! who can claim the right to judge who *fool!* Wir danken dir, Gott, wir danken dir do values flash by like those lying pictures in their dream one chasing away the other elusive red and black the lines converge toward the instrument located in the center of the bandstand with the wooden veins a single fasces which the eye follows to the center where the sound post lies invisible soul where is his soul Gottes Zeit ist die allerbeste Zeit she prefers to gaze endlessly at the hieroglyphs listening to records is exhausting starting over is exhausting Monk looks at his inert fingers one hand two hands the spotlight coming on punches out on the keyboard an order that cannot be disobeyed it is still possible to run away you cannot you are a wall buried in the earth like him can he run away now the moment has come to go into a trance an emptiness appears inside him he is nothing but a pair of hands moving toward the keyboard Monk has long since created an emptiness within him he is no longer present to the world Poet! she

LIBRARY
EASTERN OREGON STATE COLLEGE
LA GRANDE, ORE. 97850

wished he had been a poet he'd have written for her *fool!* and would still speak to her instead of these hieroglyphics as if they were carved on walls brachycephalic dolichocephalic what are they waiting for standing there always standing it's time to stand up prevent that how can it be done Aus tiefer Not schrei' ich zu dir survive and the piano begins to rumble in a certain way *fool! fool!* what are you waiting for she wishes he were there Oh! come back! come back! the man I used to be!

Wait. It is no longer possible to wait! The walls resign themselves, the walls accept the inevitable. Let them be destroyed since the gods have so decided! They have had their hour of glory, it is only fair that they should suffer now. Let the end come quickly. If death throes last beyond a certain point, they lose their nobility. What hope was left for them? That all this be merely a sham, the little black man a false witch doctor, the staggered formation a harmless trap. Are they impostors, those seven high-ranking personages, are their hunched, hollow-chested slaves the same? Are they rising now to punish the walls or is their barely suggested dance still only a warning, an endlessly repeated prophecy of coming destruction? Are they putting their trumpets to their mouths so that all will be consummated? No? Can it be that this is a commonplace gesture that has lost its magic power in the disenchantments of daily routine? Have the walls nothing to fear from those balding Samsons, condemned to remain forever inferior to themselves, unable to keep their promises of wild destruction? Nothing to fear from a music whose explosions are those of an already half-extinct volcano? Are the walls safe? Can they pride themselves on having lasted longer than men, longer than the dreams of men?

Longer than the works of men?

It's over. Just as the last dead groove scratches to an end, your right hand made the necessary move. The operating instructions were simple, you knew that. Just twist the red-and-white knob a quarter turn to the left. True, this act did require a small sacrifice. Ridiculously small. Was it really a record by? The remains of the white cup, at your feet. Ludicrous. The rug is no longer your enemy. Regretfully, affectionately, you watch it (here it is no longer red) slowly drink, drink the Lethe. Once more, you wrap yourself in forgetfulness.

2

Truthful Account of a Journey to Jazzinia

(ANNOTATED EDITION)

Our spaceship's computer was abnormally emotive. Thus it was, after a sequence of events whose narration would be tedious, that we came to be stranded on Jazzinia. During the early part of our stay, our only concern was to be sent home again as soon as possible; we longed to breathe the air of our native planet. However, while formalities followed their natural course, as circuitous there as elsewhere, the extraordinary mores of that world began to arouse our curiosity and we undertook to set down a faithful transcription of them for the use of those who, unlike ourselves, have not been unfortunate enough to spend part of their lives among the barbarians.

We are quite aware that the customs described in this document are so strange that they are bound to raise doubts in the minds of our hypothetical readers or even elicit their sarcasms. In the past, other returning voyagers have met with smiles of disbelief from the untraveled. For every Ulysses who managed to hold the ear of the wise Alkinoos, how many Marco Polos, Gullivers, or Careris had to live ever after in the midst of universal incredulity! Though we feel that we can predict how our tale will be received, we have not omitted a single detail but give it to the world just as it was written, and we beg that the reader will regard it as nothing more than the conscientious description of a society whose most remarkable features are the importance ascribed to language and the aptitude for renewing it.

The Jazzinian language involves words, music, and dancing. It is not only vocal, but instrumental[1] as well. In Jazzinia it is all language, whether it be spoken, played, or mimed. What does this language express? Nothing, as a human being would understand it. Jazzinians have only one passion: the will to power. Language is a pure product of their ego and has no communicating function attached to it. (Only the congregations, whose reforming zeal will be described later, are concerned with communication.) Whenever an individual Jazzinian displays, by his use of language, unusual power or originality, he arouses in others the desire to imitate him if they are weak, or to annihilate him if they are strong.

Jazzinian society is based upon a two-fold hierarchy. A rigid caste system guarantees its structural stability; but the highly flexible relationships which exist within each caste maintain the social scale in a perpetual state of upheaval. There are two castes. The upper or "active" caste corresponds to the nobility. Its members express themselves mainly through music: the Active Ones have the right to bear instruments. The lower or "passive" caste corresponds to the plebes. Deprived as they are of instruments, the Passive Ones speak; occasionally they dance, although this form of language is now somewhat archaic. In the past there were rebellions; the commoners tried to seize the instruments which would have brought them titles of nobility and, they thought, the means to wield Power. These uprisings, however, were put down ruthlessly. Now the two castes coexist; seemingly they ignore each other; not until one has acquired some familiarity with Jazzinia does one realize that they are necessary to one another. The real power is in the hands of a secret oligarchy. No prestige or popularity can outweigh the subtle,

---

1. The author refers to musical instruments which are similar, it seems, to those used on Earth. As we shall see, however, they fall into a system of classification quite different from our own.

powerful influence of the priests, whose task it is to organize the public meetings, or that of the companies, whose privilege it is to convene the language recording conventions and to appoint their presidents.[2]

Bearing an instrument, as we have said, is the sign of nobility; the lack of one identifies the commoner. However, within each caste an unstable situation prevails which is subtly expressed in Jazzinian dress. This is fairly similar to our own, except for an odd opening found either on the side, at the level of the pelvis, where it has the shape of a spindle, or on the chest, in the middle of the bosom, where it has the shape of an equilateral quadrangle. When we appeared before the official in charge of Law and Order, his first act was to cut open our clothes, jackets, or blouses at the neckline. The cut had a quadrangular shape, which, as we soon learned, placed us at the very bottom of the social scale.

In Jazzinia, Haunch outranks Quad. As foreigners, we were the only ones who wore the latter sign constantly. To our amazement, we discovered that Jazzinian clothes had openings on both chest and pelvis, but that an ingenious device[3] made it possible to conceal these openings as one would close a trouser fly or a back pocket. This alternate baring of chest or flank is so frequent that clothing wears out only in these places: we saw people throwing onto refuse heaps sumptuous greatcoats[4] for which we would have gladly traded our own shabby garments, had we been allowed to do so.

When a Jazzinian appears in public, he carefully closes both openings, thereby exhibiting a well-bred neutrality. Leaving one or the other open would be a breach of morals; leaving both open could only be a sign of insanity. The ritual of the openings begins whenever a meeting takes place between two Jazzinians of the same caste. In contrast with the customs of primitive tribes, the set phrases of greeting in Jazzinia are brief and most often monosyllabic.[5] As soon as the conversation proper begins, it reflects the

---

2. The analogy with the covert power of the Church in the Middle Ages is obvious; we are dealing with a medieval type of society.

3. The author does not tell us whether this device was a sartorial adaptation of the trombone slide or whether it was more like the zipper used in certain areas of our own planet.

4. The ostentatious luxury of the privileged caste cannot conceal the poverty of a world which in certain ways, we fear, may be underdeveloped.

5. Indeed, this feature is typical of a highly developed civilization.

Jazzinian's inborn aggressiveness. Tempers start to rise until the stage of the insult has been reached. In Jazzinia, this is one of the basic forms of language. Each party does its best to innovate in this field. Some have a lyrical bent which produces a quasi-Homerical style; the natural subtlety of others calls for the art of understatement. It is not in good taste to overstep certain limits laid down by tradition. A sequence such as "Moron!"—"Vermin!"—"Abortion!" —"Sewer rat!"—"Curate!"—"Cretin!"—"Crritic!" would be unacceptable, on account of the last term.[6] An exchange of insults is actually a verbal joust in which speech may be supplemented by singing when it involves two *vocalists*, notables who do not have the right to bear instruments but are allowed to imitate vocally, by means of the syllabic technique known as *scat,* the sounds of the instruments played by the Active Ones.

The rule has it that the joust, whether spoken or sung, ends only with the defeat of either of the antagonists. This occurs when one of them is nonplussed by an unexpected insult which he is incapable of parrying. At this point, eloquence is no help at all; it is best to know a few secret thrusts. The disciples of a dreaded dualist named Hornet often won by using the magic word *pitch* invented by their master, the exact meaning of which no one knows (not even Hornet, his enemies say).

As soon as the exchange of insults is over, the winner proudly opens the slit in the side of his clothing—he is said to be "showing his haunch"—while his less fortunate opponent is obliged to "show his quad." These gestures are not simply a matter of custom: to the Jazzinian mind, the one has really become quad, and the other haunch. The winner is granted moral rights over the loser. He may inflict upon him countless petty annoyances; he may, for example, among Active Ones, make him carry his instrument, or even—but this would require a streak of sadism—force the other to learn one of his own airs by heart.

The loser, however, does not give way to despair. He knows that his condition, unfortunate though it may seem, is only temporary. Another occasion will arise on which someone who has just shown his quad may prove haunch by comparison with another interlocutor. There may even appear, as among the gallinacean species, three-cornered equivalences (A dominating B, B dominating C, but

---

6. Whether the author implies that the critic's function is held in small repute or, on the contrary, that it is too highly respected to be referred to in such circumstances, is debatable.

C unexpectedly getting the advantage over A). A Jazzinian proverb sums up the matter thus: "You are always someone else's quad." These, it is true, are exceptional situations. In the ritual of language, which is the Jazzinians' sole concern, the most skillful exponents have acquired a technical mastery in the handling of insult which is ill-suited to triangles.

Out of respect, out of devotion to language as such, a Jazzinian will show his quad just as soon as he ceases to understand. He would rather admit defeat immediately than endure the shame of the joust's turning to his discomfiture and his being made a fool of in public.[7]

Verbal jousts are mainly practiced by the plebes. Among the Active Ones, insults are rare. The slightest display of arrogance in voice or attitude causes smiles to vanish and eyes to shine with anger. The challenge is obvious: a duel is the only possible resort. Unless the heavenly constellations[8] are very unfavorable, it is then customary to organize one of those festivities which gave the planet its name. In Ancient Times they were known as "contests," but in modern usage they are called "jazz." They are in fact musical combats in which the instruments play a preeminent role. Here the Jazzinian gives magnificent vent to his aggressiveness; here the very

---

7. Among his more amusing memories of the war, Lord Mountbatten quotes the following story: Surrounded by the Japanese, one of his generals had to communicate at all costs by radio with the main body of the British forces, and although the enemy was listening in, he managed to do so daily, with the help of two officers, both of whom had studied French in the same English schools and who spoke that language with such a strange accent that not even a Frenchman could have understood them. They were thus able to transmit, with full knowledge of the helpless Japanese, a great many messages. In this case, the Englishmen were haunch and the Japanese quad; the latter were being fooled and knew it, but could do nothing about it. We have reason to believe that if this had happened on Jazzinia, the armistice would have been signed forthwith; the besieging troops would have surrendered to the besieged.

8. The fact that astrology plays a part in Jazzinian customs confirms indeed the fact that we are dealing with a medieval type of society. The location of Jazzinia is not known precisely enough to allow us to study the constellations seen in the planet's sky (this would provide us with priceless data). All we can do is point out that the symbol of the Quad—whose astrological origins are indisputable—is considered, as it is on Earth, as a sign of disfavor.

meaning of a people's language is sublimated in a huge variety of rhythmic passes and melodic touches.

It is generally agreed on Jazzinia that the small instruments, such as the trumpet or saxophone, are signs of paramount power. History tells us that these instruments were once sacred; according to legend, the Spirit blew through them. Hence the deep-rooted notion that they are by essence superior. (Hence, also, the current though improper use of the verb *to blow* as a synonym for the verb *to play*, even with reference to instruments that have nothing to do with the breath. Unconsciously, the instrumentalist is alluding to the Spirit that "breathes" his inspiration to him.) In order for the jazz to be held, however, the main opponents, the "soloists," must be attended by the seconds or "accompanists," Jazzinians of noble blood, who are kept out of the highest offices by their heavier, more cumbersome instruments. In bullfight terms, the accompanists are the picadors. When a duel begins, all those who are in the arena proudly show their haunches. Jazz makes this mandatory; it determines the beauty of the struggle as well as its moral qualities. For this reason, duels are never marred by irregularities. An accompanist who favored one party or the other would be held up to universal contempt. A duelist may object to this or that accompanist but only on the grounds that he belongs to a conflicting sect: later we shall see that there can exist incompatibilities of language.

It is customary for a jazz to take place before an audience. The nobles are all invited. The presence of members of the lower caste, who are eager for these spectacles, is tolerated in return for an admission fee collected by a manager-priest.[9] Free access to the arena is allowed only for minor bouts, involving protagonists of doubtful fame. An aristocrat's retinue may come in at any time without paying; in fact this is the only advantage that goes with a condition involving no small share of servitudes and even humiliations.

In the Middle Ages, the crowd had the right to say which of the duelists would remain haunch at the end of the bout. As Jazzinian society developed, new rules were necessary. The lower caste no longer has any say in the matter. Generally, the loser will, of his own accord, put down his instrument and lay open the front of his doublet; at other times, the struggle ends before either antagonist

---

9. Possibly the most famous duelists were bound by some oath to the more influential priests. The author does not mention this particular, but his premises allow us to make room for such an assumption.

has agreed to show his quad. (We were told—but this seems too paradoxical to be true—that now that the final decision belongs to the combatants, the duels are much shorter; in the past, it seemed, only dawn could end them, and it was the audience that begged for mercy.) The gathering then breaks up in confusion. Each one, according to his own beliefs, keeps repeating the name of his champion. Discussions ensue, but none of the arguments set forth have any real weight. During the first days of our stay, the *aficionados* watched their champions triumph through the use of "swing," a magic word that actually seemed to cover many things— for if someone proclaimed in the name of swing that A was the winner, someone else immediately used the same grounds to claim that it was B.

There is nothing surprising about such variable criteria in a country which does not even have a set inheritance procedure. One belongs to the caste of the Active Ones by parentage, but this expression does not mean the same thing on Jazzinia as it does on Earth. Anyone who claims to be the son of a lord actually is the son of that lord provided his peers acknowledge his legitimacy. Thus, no one can deny that Satchel is the son of Qing; and everyone agrees that Sonnie's father is Yard. Sometimes, of course, conflicts do flare up. Just let a young saxophone-carrying nobleman go counter to public opinion and maintain that Praise is not his father at all: duels have been fought for less. We even heard a statement that would have been unthinkable in the mouth of our most Romantic heroes: "X is no longer my father; henceforth, my father is Y." A new blood relation completely annuls the previous one and even the very memory of it. A Jazzinian is allowed to challenge and defeat his first father, provided he has forgotten that he was once his son.[10]

The first Jazzinians lived within a small surface area: the Delta. Their society was fairly simple in those days, although the outlines of the hierarchies already existed. Later, when the Jazzinians had invented the big paddle-wheel boats which enabled them to explore the canals of their planet and colonize it, trouble broke out. The nation's rapid growth was achieved only to the detriment of its political unity. In the Middle Ages the first sects appeared. Originally, they were small social cells. A group would form around a famous chief in order to cultivate new ideas, generally subversive

10. The author says nothing of the sexual customs of the planet. Should the haunch-quad duality be regarded as a sexual symbol, *haunch* signifying *virility*?

ones, and new forms of language. This was the beginning of modern Jazzinia. True, the intense activity of the most thriving sects and their endless conflicts tended to accentuate the ideological Balkanizing of the planet; however, the sects managed to reconcile the spirit of individualism with the Jazzinian's communalistic propensities, while at the same time furthering the development of his natural aggressiveness. This explains why the movement was so tremendously successful.

Founding a sect implies giving it a language, and this language reflects the merits and ambitions of the founder and his disciples. Thus, the language of many a minor sect is merely the development of an already established language, or even the outgrowth of a particular accent. It is at its very inception that a sect's activities really constitute an innovation; as time goes by, its language tends to become stable. However, a sect is all the more powerful and respected as its language is the less easily understood by outsiders. During the Fifty-Second Street Century,[11] a young lord named Dix founded a sect called the Beep-Hop which soon became very famous. The Dixians displayed an overwhelming superiority in the art of phrase-coining. Added to this was their remarkable speed of execution. They were so nimble that in a given space of time they managed to emit twice as many sounds (or *scat* syllables if they were vocalists) as the customs of the day allowed. Thus even the most courageous duelists avoided them for fear of having to show their quad.

During the following century, a pianist—in other words a parvenu[12]—named Theo, who had taken part in the founding of the

---

11. The author gives no explanation of this curious denomination. On the other hand, a bit further on, he mentions that a lord who became famous during that same century founded, during the next century, a rival sect and came into conflict with another lord, "who, a few centuries earlier, had founded" a third sect. Thus, Jazzinians, whose historical activities cover several centuries, seem to enjoy a much longer life-span than humans.

12. In view of the author's previous observation that the smallest instruments belong to the higher aristocracy, the term *parvenu*, here applied to a famous sect leader, can be explained by the discrepancy between the eminent social position that he holds and his over-sized instrument. This sheds light on the Jazzinian hierarchical system: the piano, organ, bass, and drums, all heavy instruments, are suitable for accompanists (similarly, the trumpet is a nobler instrument than the trombone, the baritone

Beeb-Hop and had even been made its high priest, broke with that sect and created the sect of the Sphere. Rejecting the speed of the Dixians, which he had never entirely approved of, Theo came out in favor of a moderate tempo, which he brought back in fashion through his own airs; however, these involved a structural system of such complexity that only he and a few privileged members of the Sphere could grasp its functioning.

The adepts of the Sphere sometimes consent to speak of the mishap that befell an especially famous duelist named Chili, who a few centuries earlier had founded the sect Corpo e Anima. Invited to a recording convention at which Theo was presiding, Chili had such confidence in a capacity for assimilation (which his own disciples described as unlimited) that he agreed to play a treacherous spherical air, around which he expected to spin out with accustomed ease the majestic coils of his arpeggios. But he got himself so mixed up that for the first time in his career, he, the haunchest of the haunches, had to lay down his instrument. Every Jazzinian historian has recounted and commented upon this historical event, but their conclusions vary according to the sect to which they belong and should be subjected to careful analysis. Contrary to the asseverations of the Corpoeanimists, who regarded the convention as a deliberate trap, it seems that Theo had never intended to humiliate his glorious elder, but rather to pay tribute to him.[13] At that time, it was not yet known that the mechanism of institutions is stronger than the will-power of individuals: Theo might have thought he was in control of the situation when actually he was not. However, it behooves us to recall the malicious way in which that same Theo, under other circumstances, ridiculed a famous air by Surpaunch, another parvenu who, having spent his own life making fun of the best-loved airs and bringing out the quad on many a wealthy author's chest, certainly could not have imagined that he would be the posthumous butt of a similar insult aimed at his most famous air, the one most played throughout Jazzinia, and that it would all be the fault of a sect leader who nonetheless enjoyed finding resemblances, not to say a family likeness, between himself and a defunct lord,

---

less noble than the alto); and anyone who climbs above these subordinate tasks to reap the honors of the solo is a parvenu.

13. Considering what the author says about Jazzinian aggressiveness, his interpretation of this incident may cause doubts in the reader's mind. Although he exposes the excesses of the Spherists, it is not impossible that he may himself have come under the influence of their doctrine.

Jemz 0031416, who was none other than Surpaunch's own father. Several interpretations of this incident have been suggested; some regard it as a fresh sign of the Sphere's omnipotence and others as a sacrilegious violation of the traditions of filial respect.

Similarly, the duel between Theo and Lord Mice during a historic recording convention presided over by the latter, gave rise to endless controversy. Mice's friends and followers naturally accused Theo of underhandedness; they claimed that after refusing to act as accompanist as custom demanded, he tried to confuse the other participants by making them lose count of the measures, but only succeeded in losing count himself, so much so in fact that, had it not been for Mice, who had the kindness to intervene in his solo, Theo would not have gotten back on the track at all, and that this outside intervention was so humiliating for Theo that he should have had the honesty to show his quad. The Spherist version is quite different. Overstepping his rights as president, Mice, they say, began by forbidding Theo to accompany him. Theo took a fitting revenge by accompanying, as only he knows how—that is, by glorifying himself through the expression of his ego—another guest, Lord Sacring; then[14] when his own solo came, by launching into one of those structural games at which he excels and which so disconcerted Mice that he panicked and lost count of the measures[15] which was immediately re-established by Theo with such strength and sureness that were it not for Mice's hypocritical attitude, only one combatant would have been left standing in the arena. Remarkably enough, each thesis has its upholders, whereas the main subject of debate (the counting of the measures) is an objective fact, about which only inexperienced duelists really argue. Other commentators, it is true, maintain that the controversy was invented by the disciples and their followers. This would partly explain its incoherency; but the various interpretations will seem equally credible

---

14. This confirms that large-sized instruments, though they have won the right to solos (denied them in the Middle Ages), cannot ignore the rule of precedence which demands that the small instruments be heard first. In spite of his being a sect leader, Theo has to let Mice and Sacring pass ahead of him.

15. It would have been interesting to study the kind of numbers used. However, it is practically certain that an evil omen is attached to the numbers of the second power and consequently, that four-beat measures and periods of sixteen measures or sixty-four beats are excluded from Jazzinian grammar.

to anyone who is aware that on Jazzinia reason comes after passion.

In any encounter, the choice of arms is vitally important. A duelist has gotten off to a bad start if the language at which he himself excels is not immediately recognized as intrinsically superior. Certain syntactical constructions which are at a premium within a given sect may turn out to be serious mistakes if the customs of another sect prevail. The rules of Corpo e Anima or the Benneese, two hedonistic, pre-Dixian sects, incite the duelist to invent subtle modulations and make the most of them. This is precisely what is banned under the rules of the T.N.T., a new and powerful sect whose influence, based on terrorism, is steadily growing. With the help of Jazzinia's fast-moving history, which tends to devaluate things of the past,[16] the outcome of a duel between a member of the Benneese and a follower of the T.N.T. leaves no room for doubt; in any case, the disproportion of the forces in presence— Polonius *vs.* Hamlet—would *cause it to be canceled before it began.* Only the exceptional prestige of the Archduke of E. makes it possible for such encounters to take place at all; however, the old Archduke is more cautious than the over-confident Chili, and when he agrees to face some lusty representative of the new sects, he is careful not to venture onto ground with which his young adversary is only too familiar.

In the past, the jazz was merely a form of entertainment which the hedonistic sects sought to discipline. The duelists fought for the fun of it. It was not until the last century that mysticism appeared with the sect of the Sole. Placed under the protection of the gods of the city, dueling gradually became a ceremony. The epicurean tendencies of earlier eras fell into disrepute and major sect leaders such as Train, Ming, and Roc replaced them with an austere mythology. It was now considered that the loser's symbolic sacrifice could open the gates of immortality to the winner. Did the great duelists thus hope to escape the common fate? The most obvious result of these paganistic practices was the creation of a great many

---

16. If we are to believe Michel Foucault, it was Bopp, at the beginning of the nineteenth century, who introduced the notion of historicity into the field of language. The very name of Bopp has a suspicious ring for informed readers. It is no longer possible for the author of *Les Mots et les Choses* to reject the hypothesis that *Über das Konjugations-system der Sanskritsprache* was the work of an author alien to our planet. It does seem in any case that an awareness of the relative value of language came very early to Jazzinia.

intolerant sects, which spent their time excommunicating one another and turned the planet into a Babel of confusion. The divinities which the young sect leaders worshiped under the names of Choice and Freedom—not daring to call them Luck and Chance—were mockingly dubbed by their elders Bluff and One-Upmanship; but these, deep in their hearts, were furious at their inability to tear down those detested idols.

It has been pointed out that this modern paganism coincided with the appearance of mental illness. There are many kinds of mental illness and we cannot describe them all. The most spectacular form is soliloquy, a disease which strikes once-famous sect leaders late in life when they have fallen into oblivion. They cannot accept this fact and their despair drives them to withdraw from society altogether. They refuse all contacts with others and give up dueling except, perhaps, with their own shadows; their only desire is to talk to themselves. They may be seen wandering around alone, playing endlessly; sometimes people come to listen out of curiosity.

The harmless wanderers are joined in their lonely ravings by other mental cases who have traded their instruments for pens and indulge the strangest of all aberrations in this land where the word is king: writing.[17] They are called arrangers or, when they are incurable, composers. They all want to be sect leaders, but each is the only member of his lodge. The companies, however, in their impenetrable ways, sometimes single out one of them for the presidency of a convention; some of the most literate Active Ones are chosen to come and read the queer signs that the madman has spent months or years laying out on ruled paper. Possibly this is an exorcism of some kind; it is said that in some cases, the patient stops writing.

It may also come to pass that the companies, in their providential generosity, bring to light a previously underground sect, or send into the arena some obscure duelists who have yet to reach maturity. Aiding and abetting madness with the one hand—for he who lives without folly is not so wise as he seems—the companies further with the other a revolt in which their wisdom and experience may detect the first blossoms of a future order. Thus, like chess players working out several patterns of attack at the same time, they cater to both right and left without diminishing in any way the support which they traditionally give to the reformed congregations that

---

17. Thus, in Jazzinia, writing seems to be a *disease of language*.

constitute, along with the caste system, the principal factor of social stability on Jazzinia.

The activities of the congregations or *bands* as they are called, tend to inverse the order of values implicit in the Jazzinian nature. Leaving to the sects the task of renewing the language with no concern for the mass of Passive Ones, the congregations claim to address themselves only to those masses. The poor outcasts who are born without instruments and who never have a chance to shine in the verbal jousts are collectively sanctified by the band under the sacred name of Public. In the seminaries where the reformist doctrine is taught, the would-be congregationist, after doing cruel penance to detach himself from worldly things—Evolution, the Ego, the Jazz—goes on to study the altruistic goals of language[18]; he cultivates everything that can be immediately grasped by the Average Listener, who represents the ideal portrait of the Passive One; and his basic precept is "Thou shalt not Conquer, thou shalt Convert."

On Jazzinia, the congregations retire into their convents only as long as is necessary for the spiritual exercises or *rehearsals* prescribed by the rule. When this period is over, they travel far and wide, spreading the good language and doing their share to edify the public. Unlike the duels and soliloquies of the underground sects, the official ceremonies sponsored by the manager-priests take place in temples whose size is proportionate to the fame of the visiting congregation. The Viscount's Congregation officiates in the Palace before two thousand Passive Ones; the Congregation of the Quartet in the Opera House, before a flock of three thousand; and at the Winter Garden, there are five thousand faithful to attend Satchel's sermon. These figures must be respected at all costs, otherwise the

---

18. Superficially, it may indeed appear that the altruistic goals of language run counter to its real goals by means of an oversimplification which would fail to take account of dialectics. In a first phase, language is expression and communication; it must therefore be comprehensible. In a second phase, it becomes obvious that one must be one-up; language must then become incomprehensible, through a kind of short-circuiting of expression. This second phase presupposes the first; but when it in turn is done away with—as among the reformists—one wonders if the result is not, with respect to custom, a far subtler short-circuit? Considering the Jazzinian nature, is this not an indirect form of aggression, a horrible frustration?

congregation will disappear. Moreover, the manager-priests are seldom mistaken in their estimates. How can the audience disappoint those who are waiting for it, when it knows they will give it what it expects? Indeed, no matter how great the enthusiasm of the crowds gathered to hear it, each congregation scrupulously follows the all but immutable ritual or repertoire that has come to be associated with it.

Many a famous duelist who has been converted to the truth of the band after a rampageous youth is advised by the priests and the companies to take the leadership of a congregation. He is fully aware that when he dons the band leader's robes, he is laying himself open to the scorn of the younger Active Ones. They will suspect that his only reason for shirking the noble adventurous life of the duelist is his fear of their forthcoming successes. Only recently they still admired him; now they avert their gazes to avoid watching him communicate—the word, for them, is as obscene as the act—or deny his origins through such servile gestures as the *bow*—another filthy word—which his new functions oblige him to execute before the public while it gives demonstration of its faith. However, there is a figure whom the young Active Ones hate even more than the band leader: the despicable *sideman*, who, without a word of protest, puts up with the unbearable paternalism of the band and its host of coercions and mortifications. This hatred and contempt are experienced all the more violently by the young Active Ones as they have no way of expressing them openly; indeed, Jazzinian law protects the congregations and insulting them is prohibited.

Thus, the bitterest protest against the established order rose from the catacombs in which the underground revolutionary sects had found refuge. Their leaders constantly predicted that the temples would soon fall, burying beneath their ruins congregations, priests, and public alike. It seems that this prophecy, of which we heard many rumors during the last part of our stay, actually came about after our departure, and that its fulfilment was even more tragic than was expected, since, as our space ship carried us back to Earth, her astronomes lost all trace of Jazzinia, giving us reason to believe that the planet had disintegrated. Thus we must once again ask for the reader's trust, since henceforth he has only our word to vouch for the truth of the facts related in this document.

3

Playing—Dora

Monday

Must it be? It must be. The early muffled clamor from the marketplace under my windows dispels my dreams, in which the greatest part, no doubt, has always been played by a kind of auditory voluptuousness. In a normal man, visual memory is predominant; it feeds his dreams with erotic images. But what resurgings can be expected by a man possessed by his sense of hearing? What obsessions will decorate his nocturnal ceremonies? I have long been familiar with the sounds that people my sleep. I have learned to tear off their masks and discover behind their infinite diversity a single source. Dora. Only their order of appearance varies. Usually the vibrating, trembling sounds come first, opulent or furious; the trade winds of the bass suddenly give way to the cutting blast of the treble, so shrill at times that I can't help waking. As soon as sleep returns, I move through a neutral zone that is either writhing with slurs which leave dirty wet marks, or crowded with shapeless, heavily stamping accents which oppress me. The feeling of passive discontent, of resigned helplessness that comes over me then, gradually becomes one of masochistic satisfaction. A thirst for ugliness plunges me into hellish pits full of gratings and raucous screams. But I know that the atrocious and the sublime are one, and that in the depths of this horror lies a savage beauty. Then everything turns inside out and upside down. I relish nasal twangs like dashes of vinegar; a fitful cataract of mocking laughter arouses within me a desire for revenge; a spray of stridencies intrigues my ear, vigilant even in sleep, for this is when it learns to distinguish between subtly tangled dynamics and timbres. Finally, the night ends on a metaphysical meditation inspired by some huge crescendo which opens my mind to the perception of Time, or else by some sustained note with no beginning and no end, the first step to Eternity. I then enter a state of bliss which nothing can spoil: the sound within me is diaphanous, Dora's very soul is alive within me and would belong to me forever were it not for the muffled clamor of the marketplace that dispels my dreams at first light of dawn. For a moment, the balance is achieved: Dora is in the market, the market trembles around Dora. Then Dora fades away and I hear only the tradesmen calling out their wares.

Must it really be? Walking aimlessly, I let the crowd carry me along the alleys of this buzzing labyrinth. If some movie camera could follow the black dot of my skull through that uniform motleyness, it would be seen to describe complicated geometrical figures. Absurd course, strange itinerary, considering my actual destination. I don't want to meet Pierre. Pierre is in the market; at night, Pierre never dreams. I wander or pretend to wander some more. I'm waiting for the heat of the day; I'm waiting for desire to draw me irresistibly down that dark alleyway which hides the even darker stall of the respected merchant. No ray of light need make her shine. She is there. Ready and waiting. Secondhand, little used. I approach, gazing at her slender curves; I hold out a still hesitant hand; my fingers graze her, touch her, feel her, gently press her joints, testing their silent sensitivity. The merchant is watching me; he sees me bring Dora to my lips, press my lips to Dora, weld my mouth to hers. . . . He knows that I won't give her up.

Tuesday
Dora is mine. Training has begun. Dora is stubborn; Dora bellows

when my rod is too severe; Dora does not want to do what both of us were made for. From the marketplace, I hear only a confusion of noise; I no longer hear the tradesmen's cries. Do they hear Dora's? Her suffering is my only concern. She suffers; I am her torturer. In my clumsiness, I dream of other sobs and wails that would be due not to my incompetence, but to my skill. Desire conjures up before me the image of our hymen consummated at last: all the life that my breath will blow into that inanimate body, all the molecules of air which that body will in turn set in motion around my body. May the memories of my nights come to my aid—for the daylight hours are cruel.

Must I first educate myself, must I take a course in training? There are excellent schools, Pierre jeers in my ear. They teach "natural" training methods, which would enable me to establish a satisfactory relationship with Dora, to play with less effort and possibly to survive; for if Dora is incorrectly trained she will become dangerous and eventually kill me. I won't enroll. I'm not interested in husbanding my strength. My life may be a short one, but Dora will owe nothing to anyone else and everything to me. Moreover, Pierre's example, and what he has done with his mate, can hardly prompt me to listen to his advice. The experience of others is not to be neglected, I'll grant that; but I would like to be sure that it is in keeping with my aspirations. Dora doesn't have time to outgrow scholastic reflexes.

Night has fallen; the day's work is done. Dora has nothing more to learn. My will to tame and subjugate her has overcome her resistance. She has let herself be persuaded. Around noon, her sobbing became a voice; as the sun declined, her voice became music; by evening, that music had become song. To know that song and take my pleasure from it, the night will not be too long.

Wednesday

I have exhausted the joys of our tête-à-tête. One cannot play on oneself. I play on Dora; Dora plays on me. She plays, I play: henceforth there is no difference. It would be impossible for me to feel that *we* play: I have done away with the distance between us; our tête-à-tête is a kind of solitude. Dora is my solitude. In order to move beyond this phase, I must face other men who have had the same experience. With a thrill of emotion, I go out to meet them. Lying quietly in her box, does Dora share my excitement? Her song has never mingled with another song. Must it be?

Playing with others is a strange adventure. Dora in society side by side with other doras: how like them she is, and how different! We go from one discovery to the next; we lack familiarity with the customs of others. Dora lacks so many things. Her song must be organized in order to fit in, it must become language. I realize that a world of conventions lies between Dora and the world and that it is up to me to teach them to her. There are scales that fence in the notes with invisible bars and set up hierarchies among them—but this is something which Dora's morphological structure accepts. There are chords whose composition and rigorous succession my ear can grasp: she must not ignore them. There is a rhythmic discipline which rules out the free frolics in which she once indulged. It is Dora's turn to learn that she cannot play on herself.

What has become of my dreams? Are they lost beyond recall? I shouldn't have gone into the market; I shouldn't have bought Dora; I shouldn't have led her this far. Now we must go on to find a new ease, a naturalness that will prevent our being intimidated by others. We had learned to play on one another; now we have to learn to play on others. Self-knowledge is predicated on one's knowledge of others. The difficulty lies in achieving the kind of dissociation which is necessary if we are to rise above the entity which we call the group and, at the same time, remain within it, since its life depends in part on the nature of our participation. We should be capable of filming ourselves; for when we play on others, our behavior is no less important than theirs.

What does "playing on others" mean? Do we not form a communal society in which each individual plays for the benefit of the group? True, but the prevailing equality is fragile indeed. We play by turns; this succession in itself constitutes an inequality. If we all play together, and Dora's voice, which is fuller than the others, stands out among them, then this is another inequality. As soon as we stop drawing on our common fund of memories for the themes of our inventions—in other words, as soon as one of us, having invented a theme, persuades the group to use it—our beautiful balance is threatened, and it will be near the breaking point when the arrangement, that other means of appropriating the personality of others, appears on the scene.

Despite my sincere wishes to comply with group discipline, I can hardly accept the position in which I am placed by the arranger. It seems to me that I detect, behind his avowed objective—the enriching of our collective experience—an ulterior design to dominate. Dora learns a theme all by herself, but she needs a computer to decipher an arrangement. I fulfill this function. My mistakes cannot be blamed on Dora. The arranger derives an advantage from this. I can sense that he is depriving me of my freedom; later, he will deprive Dora of hers, requiring of her a fidelity which she owes only to me. He is worming his way into our intimacy.

Pierre submits daily to this tutelage, eyes glued to the baton which controls his every move, but I did not expect to find it here, not even in attenuated form. It would be easy for me to throw it off: there are other groups in which arrangements are unknown, but this would be limiting the scope of our experience. Wouldn't it be better to restore the balance by working up my own themes and arrangements? Deep in my eyes would shine that same defiant gleam that I cannot bear in the eyes of anyone else: "What are you playing, just what are you playing?"

"I'm playing me."

"No, it's me, me, me!"

These thoughts recede as soon as Dora and I are alone again. What foolish schemes! I owe myself entirely to my capricious slave, my possessive slave. Difficult Dora, fascinating Dora. Constancy is not her forte. She is changing and uneven; suddenly I feel that she's farther away from me than on the very first day. Will the hours and hours and hours that I must spend just to make her smile or to quell her jealousy finally exhaust my love for her? I don't know what to do, I can't stand it any longer, I'm on the verge of despair: then she stops slipping away from me and is once again the pleasure-giving good fairy whom I thought I had trained. Chained to her as I am, subjected to such painful alternations, how could I find the strength to assume responsibility for the group? In the past, the poets published the utterings of their Muses: I could transcribe the imaginings of Dora and give them to the group to feed our collective celebrations; but would this be the way to pay her the tribute she expects? Wouldn't she regard these as unnatural relations of some sort, as the perversion of an intellectual?

Thursday

Everything I wrote yesterday is true. The life of a group does involve that spirit of competition, that will to channel the energies of others and subordinate them to personal objectives. Everything I wrote yesterday is useless. The real drama of the individual and the group is not acted out on that stage at all.

True, your vanity is satisfied by having reduced others to a state of dependency; but what about your pride? It might be thrilling to know that all the resources of a group are being applied to a single goal: the fulfillment of your own dream. But your pride asks, what is that dream? Is it just another arrangement? Is it the crystallization of a solo played over and over again a thousand times, shabbily illuminated by wretched holding chords?

Under what conditions would I accept one man's deliberately seizing power over all the others? His dream would have to rise up from depths deeper than I can begin to imagine, it would have to be a poet's dream and a technician's dream, and that technician would have to abstain from working everything out in advance and leave his performer leeway for exercising judgment and even taking personal initiatives; his thinking would have to be neither too complex nor too difficult to understand, considering the limited amount of time that I can devote to someone else if I am not to lose sight of myself; lastly, he would have to convince me and direct me. Then, for a few hours perhaps, I would be his Dora. But not Pierre, no. I will never be Pierre.

If I never meet a man of that caliber—and how could I meet him?—my own abdication in someone else's favor, or his in mine, seems unthinkable to me because the advantages to be gained by it, if any, will be paltry. The tyrannic nature of the symphonic society in which Pierre lives has reduced him to slavery; yet at least the standard of living there is fairly high. In our world, where there are no Beethovens to rule, despotism would soon lead to poverty.

A man whose genius urges him along the paths of spontaneous creation must not try to dominate the group around him but adjust himself to it unreservedly. Dora knows this: the first thing I expect of her this evening is to abdicate her sovereignty. Once this indispensable limitation has been placed upon our powers, those of the group will increase tremendously. These are the united states which we must establish; they will provide us with a tool for broader, firmer, and more authentic artistic creation.

Every art has rules: the group is my discipline, its rules are those of my creative act. I divide them into two categories: the rules of the game and the rules of the art. The first are of a mechanical nature; their function is to organize the combined voices so that anarchy will not take over. The second set of rules derives from the first and is an interpretation and extension of it. This second set defines the aesthetic orientation of our game. (We must never forget that we are *playing*.)

The rules of the game are, by their very nature, precise. They draft the social contract that binds the members of our community and, above and beyond us, links our community to the collectivity which constitutes the sum of all the communities similar to our own that follow the same rules. They establish order in both time and space.

Pierre chaffs me: "You're an overgrown child playing at making music. The momentary excitement which you derive from your naive games renders your rigorous rules inoperative since they're too restrictive in some respects and not enough in others. The temporal sequence of events, which we know to be the very foundation of musical art, is left by you to the mercy of impromptu imagination. Your schemas (unless you are playing an arrangement, that bastard form of musical composition) are subject to unpredictable changes with no other excuse than that of sheer momentary fancy. On the other hand, you claim to possess creative imagination and you use only spiral schemas. Yours is a Nietzschean game indeed! There is all the time in the world to admire the eternal return of the same thing, on the microcosmic as well as the macrocosmic level, since from one piece to the next the same type of schema recurs (only the number of episodes varies) and each turn of the spiral is a replica of the last, with a few minor differences. But while your outlines are vague, your structures are rigid. The spiral is invariably divided into patterns which set you a series of regular appointments that you cannot fail to keep: the rules of the game force you to carry on a constant embroidery work (which you pompously call variations). You embroider on the patterns and you embroider on them again; and your neighbor does the same, though you can't really say he's imitating you. Your technique is a function of your situation in the group (which group, in spite of that "unity" which you are so proud of, is merely an association of two subgroups). Your accompanists make use of accentuation, spacing, inversion, etc. (You see how well I've grasped the mechanics of your game!) If you're a soloist, your job is to produce a melodic substance whose tonal function is in accordance with the harmonies or, if you prefer, in harmony with the chords. This type of embroidery is more delicate work, no doubt. I admit that I couldn't do it; and when you're at the peak of condition, as an athlete would put it, I'm impressed by some of your exploits and have to confess that your embroidery work involves some degree of inventiveness. But one confession deserves another: won't you confess that in your normal state you have no qualms about resorting to clichés—discreetly, I'll grant you that, otherwise I'd say you were cheating—

but so naturally that I suspect each of you holds in reserve a sizable stock of clichés? But then it is only human to take out insurance against the accidents of the game, and one can hardly be blamed for packing a lunchbox before hitting the road."

What bitterness, what envy is revealed in these gibes that are just a bit too pointed! Pierre has given up all joy; it's been years since he has played at home; his play on the marketplace spells work. In the name of a higher form of beauty, a conductor whom he did not choose robs him of his personality. He was raised in a tradition which authorizes such thieving practices; but in exchange, the classical composer had to let his performer feel that he had a share in the process of creation; whereas the division of labor introduced into the modern orchestra enslaves the desk-man and reflects the contemporary composer's contempt for his anonymous servant. Pierre is the most scorned man on the marketplace.

Pierre cannot forgive me Dora's youth, nor the pleasure I take with her. Our rules are what they are. No one can say our formal solutions are weak: we simply don't concern ourselves with the problems of form. We haven't the time: we are too busy harvesting the fruit of the present moment. A more or less propitious combination of a certain frame of mind and a set of precepts—the rules of the art—determine whether we harvest it well or badly. Since they constitute an interpretation and extension of the rules of the game, the rules of the art imply a choice, a personal one, we like to think, but History probably makes it for us. I say "choice"; Pierre might say "preconception." I'll accept the word; it seems to me rich in implications. A preconception is the result of a vision. Just as in a certain type of dream narrative, the obsessive persistence and reappearance of *images* (in the cinematic sense) calls for a descriptive realism that bars the image (in the metaphorical and literary sense), so too, Dora's rejection of vibrato is the result of my deliberate intention to eliminate from my playing everything that smacks of rhetoric. Is this a preconception? It certainly is, and so is our soaring melodic phrase which pays no heed to the caesura of the cadences and sails boldly over the gaps produced at regular intervals by the four-bar pattern. We do not play alone and must therefore accept the rules of the game; but the game would be senseless if, in making our choice of the rules of the art—a choice which elevates our technical experience and gives each of us the creative strength of ten—we did not strive to approach some vaguely glimpsed beauty. Moreover, the fact that each of us has accepted a set of common rules gives us back our free will. I maintain that a thorough assimilation of the rules of the art makes it possible to play alone in the midst of the group, and that because of them the couple Dora-and-I is more closely united today, functioning for the community, than we were the day before yesterday alone in our room.

Some day the accumulated weight of these preconceptions will weigh too heavily; the rules of the game will break down. Things that are now taken for granted will vanish. Am 7 will no longer be followed by D 7; multiples of four will lose their cabalistic powers. It is not determinism that will triumph, as Pierre would have it—for in the dark of his soul, he wants me to be like him—but, on the contrary, the indeterminate. Pierre is right in one respect: our game involves a hunger for the irrational, for raving madness, its structures must writhe and its joints crack. We will no longer refer mechanically to our themes but expand upon them indefinitely; better than that, all pre-existent material will be done away with. The game will become a psychodrama, the theatricalization of an emotion. New rules of the art will institute a ceremony suitable for invocation and incantation. A new kind of solitude will be discovered. And Dora will come to know free love.

Friday

The circle of our connections is enlarging. Today, we played in public. Another great experience. Dora is an Albertine who enjoys sequestration; however, for her first venture into the outside world, she let herself be polished up. The prettiest debutante.

As I went on stage, I wondered what use the audience was, why did it exist. It is there; I tolerate its presence; this is a right which it has bought on the market, but it mustn't think we play for it.

Women. Many women (as though Dora did not sum up the essence of femininity!). What do you and I have in common? The prettiest of them all is looking straight at me. Shall I put charm into my playing just to please her? In the past, it seems, this was the thing to do. But we have built an austere society.

Strange, those bygone days, when they played for people to dance. . . . They say that at times the women's fancy steps stimulated the blowers' zest, though they also say that the blowers kept their eyes shut. It is unlikely that this could have created a give–and–take, an interplay, an exchange, if one refuses to accept the idea that the sexual phenomenon of dancing can correspond to music on the level of the libido; but at least the audience's presence was justified. Even if the band's functionalism was a one-way affair, at least there was still a relationship between band and audience to explain that indecent presence. You pay us to make you move your legs: it is possible to find meaning in this. But what of this motionless audience that *pretends* to listen?

When we play, is there really anything to listen to? It's true that Pierre listens to us: he takes note of our technical flaws. But what about nonprofessionals? Are they buying pleasure? Isn't all the pleasure for the man who plays and for him alone? Listening to us seems to me as stupid as watching a basketball game (and here, at least, the spectators are often former players who experience the game vicariously). Pierre admits to hearing only a slender fringe of the works he performs: the entire symphony is focused on its conductor and beyond him at the audience. But if Pierre could play here, he would be the center of the universe.

Strangely enough, Dora's first voice tonight sounds unsure. It is as if she were reacting to some outside phenomenon. She knows that she's being listened to. Is she afraid? A thousand stories, terrifying and ridiculous, come back to me. Can the audience really affect her and distort our playing? I gather Dora, I plead with her. Gradually, the malaise fades away. Her song finally bursts forth as pure as ever. Dora's path was only momentarily perturbed by the proximity of the fat dead star.

Once this petty incident was closed, the audience could have no more effect on Dora. The meaning of its presence (since there must be one) cannot be expressed in terms of action. Perhaps the audience is a conscience: the conscience of the couple that we form, a mirror that shows me what lies beyond Dora, forcing me to wonder how those people out there see Dora, how they hear her. They can't possibly see or hear her as I see and hear her. Do Dora and her song have an objective reality for them which I must discover, whereas hitherto I was concerned only with knowing the essence of our shared thoughts? Is everything that is implicit between Dora and myself, and everything that Dora expresses badly, lost to them? Are they able to reconstruct the obliterated words, rewrite the unfinished sentences? Or has what I still believe to be a perfect dream become a misshapen reality?

Must it be? Project myself out beyond Dora, take my place among the audience, *listen* to Dora play—not just hear her! I could split myself thus all alone, the audience is not indispensable; perhaps, however, its function is to give me the incentive to do so. It is a difficult thing to achieve because I come *before* Dora, the audience comes *after*. When Dora's voice reaches it, a new wave is already forming inside me, covering the first one over. In order to perceive this "before" and "after" at one and the same time, one must live simultaneously in two different time dimensions; split one's mind as Pierre does when he turns a page which he hasn't finished playing; but do it consciously.

Why this division of consciousness? Idle curiosity? The need to know what becomes of Dora's song in that afterlife which is, after all, so brief: the space of a few vibrations? The musical instant is located nowhere; it vanishes before any ear can grasp it completely. For some it will have been the ambiguity of a dissonant chord, for others the impact of a syncopated accent or the furtive trembling of a note. And even if it could perchance be known in its entirety, would it not still be at the mercy of memory's tricks? Is it in order to contemplate the musical instant that I go and glean it out there beyond Dora—not without a certain feeling of expectation which Pierre can never experience when he performs a classical work. Pierre never plays; his deceitful art is equivalent to the actor's: he pretends to be playing when actually he is simply *re*playing. In some respects, Pierre is like a painter working after a model; I am more like a photographer. Dora develops my plates. A bit apprehensively, I bend over her to see how much of what I had glimpsed has been preserved by chance. This subservience to chance and the wonderful surprises that sometimes result from it are my lot.

Saturday

Reading over what I wrote last night, I seem to detect some injustice in it. Had there been no audience, our celebration would have lacked something; the exhibitionistic drive inside us would have been only partly satisfied. Seeing each other is not enough; we must be seen as well. And not by the market! The audience is not a reflection of the market; I don't want it to be. This week spent away from the market has obliterated the market (if this week is real, if it isn't a guile, a variation on my dream, a trick that my dream has played on me the better to imprison me in the awful meshes of its nightly routine).

Somewhere between the real and the imaginary, our bubble-blowing lives tip this way and that at the mercy of the must-it-bes and the must-it-not-bes (as if we were to leave a lasting body of works); yet they never lose their sublime buoyancy. Our easy-going attitude, which is not incompatible with a degree of rigor, whispers yearnings in our ears; thus, Dora's fondness for pretty things (not so pretty tomorrow, perhaps) expresses a love of the present moment which I also detect in the habits of some of those beside me. The market disapproves of them, the audience gains nothing by them, neither does even the group; yet perhaps the artificial moments into which they let themselves be drawn are even more buoyant.

I no longer know the light of day. I wait for nightfall to take Dora out there with the other couples and ride her over and over again until all our strength is gone; and when I release her, when I leave her panting, I will let myself drink in the embraces, the embraces, the embraces all around us. I will lay my head against another dora's side and listen to her beating heart. Low-pitched wood, smooth, high-pitched skin, sound and substance that are one and the same, I will sense your excitement and I will share it.

Have the people on the marketplace, burdened as they are with their responsibilities, ever experienced that ubiquitous lust that enables me (while Dora subsides in my lap) to identify myself with a fellow player and share his enjoyment, as if I were possessing with him his dark or silver dora? Have they ever been told that there are doras whom you can beat, with restraint at first, and then, as the night wears on and the fever rises, with wildest abandon? And what does even the audience, that voyeur, know of our Minervas and their bronze bosoms tipped with voluptuous points, of the invisible nerves that wail when we pinch them, of the monotonous to-and-fro movements of silver slides, soft to the touch, so soft and so well-oiled? What does it know of Dora, of her odor, of the taste of my saliva that lingers in her mouth and flows back into mine with the desire that drives me back to her and forces me to take her again, still passive but ready to vibrate, cool on the outside, already warm within? In her! The same gestures must never be repeated, or new ones invented either, perhaps. In Pierre's world, they make love over and over again in unchanging stopwatch lapses of time. Our time is indefinite: morning is its only limit. A slight loss of contact just before dawn is the only pendulation left to us, a moment of ennui that slips into our solemn frivolity and makes us furtively long for another life.

I have lived.

Played. Pleasure. I know why I play. There is grandeur in experiencing time; there is even more in abolishing it. To replace the noise of the marketplace with Dora's song is to abolish time.

Today, I have loved others. No longer did they intrude upon my pleasure: they helped me to rise above it. Thanks to them, I have come to know joy. Alone, I could never have succeeded.

Everyone played well tonight. Dora did not balk at the impossible. The rules were no longer an obstacle: the whole group floated on a transcendental plane. Yet the god appeared only to me. The audience did not see him go by, but it applauded when Dora, for a moment, glittered in his light.

I love the audience; it was there tonight. I love Pierre; he was there tonight.

Dora's caresses, in Dream's most hidden furrow, like unto. . . .

I am Louis and Dizzy and Miles. I am Brownie. I am beyond Brownie, I am his life-after-life: I play what he himself couldn't play. I am Apollo, I am Dionysius.

Sunday

The week is drawing to a close. Must it be? The air is heavier, the colors run together; Dora has lost some of her polish. As I lay her in her box, docile, ready still for the games I have taught her, she reflects back at me an image of myself tinged with Sunday melancholy.

Tonight we played as we did the night before.

The same phrases came in the same order; the same accents climaxed in the same spots. Everyone played well tonight. But the god didn't come. I realize that *that* god can never return, and that I must give up the idea of carrying the game just a little further.

Around me everything is deserted. Only an old habitué remains. Waiting for what? Cautiously, I lower Dora into her black box. I linger a moment to gaze at her coarsened figure; absently I stroke it with my hand. The habitué doesn't take his eyes off me; his silent pleading weighs on my fatigue. Must it be? Again? Not let Dora grow cold, order her to do *that*? Slowly, I take her in my arms once more; slowly I go toward that man who is looking at me. Yesterday, the moment of ecstasy came for me; now it has come for him. He knows I'm watching him as I put Dora to my lips.

The first notes are "CEGAC–"; she puts the right feeling into it and he responds, "Yeah, baby!" in a quavering voice. Dora continues: "GACEE–CG"; and he, commenting, "Yes, baby, you're right." (I wonder if he knows that he hears all those letters a step lower than I do.) Dora goes on with a long inflection: "E♭–CGF" (the bitch! she knows how to make them wait for the blue note). And the response: "Oh! Baby, baby, do that!" She drives it home: "E♭ EGAE♭," and he sighs, "Yeah!" And suddenly she hits another blue note: "C (A) C–B♭–" and twists it carefully. "Oh! That's right, that's right, baby!" punctuates the old habitué. (The B♭ was a little high but the effect was just that much more lowdown.) He whispers, with his head buried in his arms, "Once more, baby, be right once more," and Dora, in an ageless voice, goes on pouring out her memories.

E finita la commedia. The old habitué is no longer capable of responding to Dora. His ecstasy is definitive, and he has aged a little more. I leave him. Dora is in her box. Tenderly, desperately, I gaze down at her. We have completed an experience together; now the market is calling for us. A friendly hand rests on my shoulder. Slightly veiled with melancholy, Pierre's voice asks, "Will you sell her tomorrow morning? Or else . . . ."

But I smile. "Even Christ wouldn't have pulled that trick on Lazarus twice."

"That isn't what I meant," Pierre insists. "Couldn't you . . ." and he nods toward the case that he carries night and day, in which there lies a corpse. I smile again. My dreams are gone. Dora is dead; I shan't use her body.

"I must be going back to the market," I say.

Pierre thinks it over. I know he agrees. In his eyes an unfamiliar emotion appears: fraternity.

4

Crabwise

My life. This is the story of my life. It's high time it were written. The little memory I've got left is going. Everything gets mixed up in my head. Last names and first names, dates and places. The music is all that remains, the music of my seventy years. Copy it out on these scraps of paper: I only wish I could. The machines they've got today can't bring anything back to life. Player pianos chewing away at music rolls. Ragtime, roughtime.

Sleep. It would be such a relief to get some sleep, it was a hard day and tomorrow will be the same, there'll still be that road in front of us, right now it's winding, hilly, bumpy, at each turn we're thrown against each other, at each jolt the dream that was coming through goes away again, tala, tala, what are all those Indians doing out there, a thought that was about to take shape sinks back into nothingness, raga, raga, why are all those Indians white,

They've lost the secret of high fidelity. Cylinders are the last word in turn-of-the-century technique. And all they cut on them are the fashionable ditties. If I could just go over the lovely choruses of yesteryear, one by one. Put them on this paper, like illuminations. So they wouldn't disappear with me. They were what I lived in. They were what I lived for. As far back as I can remember, in the furthest reaches of my old age, when I used to listen to Billy Taylor. No, David Taylor. No, Cecil Taylor. I can still see him leaning over the piano keyboard. Lost in the belly of the instrument. Scratching the chords with his fingernails. It was pure and it was melodious. Occasionally, he would also touch the keys with his fingers. At the time, I never suspected he was creating a new art. Yet he soon had countless disciples. The most conservative ones turned all their attention to the sound board. They strewed it with small objects: corks, nails, coins. It was what they called a pre-paired piano. But the most daring ones were fascinated by the keyboard with its black and white geometry. So they sat down and figured out what it symbolized. History was on their side. For half a century, playing the piano has consisted mostly of pressing down the keys. That devil Taylor, what a posterity he's had! At the same period there was Archistecp, Tchi-Cagee,

you cast a dull eye out at what little there is to see through the window in the darkness: nothing, really nothing, except that the bus seems to be moving a little faster than before. By day, it's different, there may be something to do until the next stop, and even when there's nothing to do, you make an effort not to look outside. The world is so stingy with surprises, why go looking for them, a surprise is like a good chorus, you mustn't wait for it, you've just got to be there when it happens. Sleep, if only L and A could get to sleep there's bound to be some benevolent devil who'll slip them the word about the mode for the next stop, but here they are wide awake, all worried and up tight, two of the coolest cats around, listening to the dull throb of that engine as though it were going to tell them about a secret vein of ore that could help them shore up their ruins. It must be a cool scene in a bus like ours in countries where tradition determines what you're going to do at the next stop according to the time of day. Alap, alap, murchana, melakarta. Back home the avatar is waiting at the next stop but there's nothing to let you know in advance, it's up to you to draw your own conclusions from the combination of circumstances: time, place and audience. When the bus stops and we climb down in single file,

Iveszenson, Elbert Taylor . . . or rather Albert Ayler. (Better give up on the first names, my memory's playing tricks on me.) Ayler was the hardest of all to follow. An innovator, a voice of protest. Like all the fellows in the ghetto. But he was a rare type. Nobody understood Ayler. His immediate influence was nil, I have to admit that. It's only been felt very recently, as far as I can tell. And yet the ghetto's world-wide protest has died out. Even if they still do protest today, it's gotten awfully folksy. Back in those days people thought Ayler's music was a kind of absolute mockery. They were reading too much into it. Actually, he was already playing in the spirit of the Gay Nineties. A remarkable forerunner: he even respected the sour notes that have become the rule lately. Fifty years behind his time, has anybody done better? And Ornette! It's true that in those days no one really knew how to play the violin. But he put everything he had into it! Those rondos he sawed out with that mischievous bow of his were a foretaste of the closed grooves of *musique concrète*. We discovered the sound object and its acid freshness. How restful that music was, in which everything kept coming back over and over again. Ornette, where are you now? What happened to those high notes you could get out of your trumpet? They were so smooth, so sensitive, so sciatic

not knowing exactly where we are or why we're there, what have we got to guide us, nothing, B signed a contract it has to be honored that's all that's enough. Sleep, it's not time to sleep now, it's time to cope, later we'll see what progress we've made or what disasters the road has caused. If the bus were a seat of tradition, B must have thought of this, there'd be some kind of order, something we could refer to, we'd know, we'd have it made, we'd have security, but back home that's not the scene, what's past is forgotten, you've got to be a road hand to remember. Is there anybody in this rushin' bus of ours who still thinks about that cocktail-concert before lunch, or remembers that sexy F and her velvet voice, she put sex into everything, maybe we thought so more than the audience, we saw her do her grind from behind, from out front you might have been distracted by the mouth even though our mike-trained singers have the knack of opening their mouths only just enough, not like opera singers what a fright that awful funnel. Dear little F, she was B's property but anybody in the bus could make her, even the accompanists got their share, and even fortunately the accompanists' accompanists; that was her time, it was time for songs and time for femininity just like later on it would be time for golden that we forgot the mad modernism of Moffet, alias The Skunk, your drummer. Oh! the world we lived in lacked unity no doubt. Alongside the dreamers and the terrorists, the giants of show business began to loom over the horizon. Louis, Ella, Sinatra. Strong bonds began to form between music and the general public. And the bigger the public grew, the fonder it became of pop songs. Who appreciated the wild ecstasy of Cottrell . . . no, Coltrane? The genuine, original fans like myself. But the masses wanted lyrics that were easy to follow and a tune they could hum. This was the price that had to be paid to get out of the ghetto. In this respect Louis, Ella, Sinatra managed to imitate other, already established singers who had very different conceptions. In those days, teenage audiences showed their enthusiasm by clapping their hands. It's a well-known fact that uninhibited clapping in time to music is caused by a degeneration of psychomotor cells in the adolescent. This phenomenon of juvenile regression to the animal state can still be seen today in the carvin' contests. It was customary to send a delegation of clappers on stage. Sometimes a whole group of them were sent up there rigged out with cumbersome instruments, electric guitars that had a certain charm (unfortunately, they've been supplanted by the banjo). The arms and he-man stuff, time for rape. The songs might not have been very good and the band might not have played them very well, but that's what the people had come for, to listen to those shaky syncopations and watch that sexy F go through her wiggling act. She's left us. Marriage that's what every girl has in mind opportunity knocked and bang. When she starts wiping her kids' behinds she'll forget all the lyrics even her favorites that was her big terror she read them over in the bus between kisses and the tune she always wanted to change a note here a rhythm there to give herself a style a personality all the chicks do that and when she tried to improvise as if a vocalist were an instrumentalist but who started that this morning at rehearsal the brass tried to imitate the vocal style it's true that they imitate each other just the same chorus-improvising is for men and instruments. Just look at that festival concert when our sidemen threw the audience off with their acrobatic improvising at first there was booing but toward the end you knew they'd won we'd never heard them juggle with quotations like that before that's their way of putting the audience on and keeping in touch with it at the same time it's not easy you need unusual powers of persuasion. The big aria in the third act that's what they waited clapper delegate would sing, or pretend to. What he sang didn't count; all that mattered was the pitch of excitement which he could help the crowd to reach. So long as he swung his hips well, who cared whether he sang on key? At the opposite pole, Louis, Ella, Sinatra wanted singing to be musical. They advocated a more elaborate kind of song, occasionally more literary, and tried to give it an artistic rendition. A man named Chayrles, or Raych, I'm not sure which any more, had already foreseen this change of direction. It was irreversible, for the youngsters soon lost all their influence. The pop song acted as a connecting link and promoted the rise of a concert industry that thrived until just before the dark days of Wall Street. The most popular singers and shrewdest band leaders began traveling around the world to the strains of the songs which the public liked best. Even in the most distant countries, it was easy to find a common ground with tunes like *Sweet Shop Suey*, or *Hello, Dinah*, or *I Can't Give You Any Swing, Beloved*, or *Between the Devil and the Deal, Blues Sib*, or *All the Things You Wear*. At least, these conquered hearts that beat in time to the American way of life. However, concerts were not reserved for the big stars alone. If a sticky problem came up, solidarity was the order of the day. When Mr. Granz announced Ella, everyone

to hear Dusa in but what if there is no big aria what then the fish don't bite you have to know how to bait your line because B insists that his soloists keep the audience in mind but they can't really reach the audience unless they forget about it and they know it they pretend to give in and then they go right ahead and do as they please. The difference between B and the sidemen is that the audience is *his* audience he loves it while they hate it especially L one day he'll jump off the stage and start murdering people. The bus only murders chickens there's another one that won't go clucking Ko-ko-Duk any more they say the smartest ones cluck to a three-beat Ko-Koduc-ko-Duck they're brighter than D. B is a great man there's no doubt about that everybody admires his judgment yet at the festival it was the sidemen who were right the time was ripe for it anyway nothing could be done B couldn't have convinced them how can you discuss anything with anyone in that state now they're fine it's all over they've calmed down it looks as if they were dropping off to sleep. Did we sleep a little at the end of the day after the tearoom dance that was real cool there were pretty women high society and it almost looked like we were going to settle down and then that wild session at the festival after dark and everything else that knew that the hall had been full. But if a less experienced manager happened to bill someone from the ghetto, then I would have my say. In those days, active members paid their dues. If they didn't, the hall was empty, and it would have been a defeat for music. So I turned up at the box office for my date with destiny. The same farce was acted out in the record industry. Sure, Sinatra was always a safe bet. But at the same time it wasn't uncommon for a producer to pay a musician like Rollins tens of thousands to disrecord an album that hadn't sold. I, at least, had bought it, and so had a few other nuts like me. That was my claim to fame. And the way I got my kicks. The supremacy of the long-playing record went unchallenged in those days. Everyone derived benefits from this, artist and customer alike. Often a number would cover an entire side. A half-dozen records took care of your whole afternoon. They didn't stint on blowing in those days. There was a tendency to go to excesses, like Mingus, or to be torrential, like Cannon Ball. A degree of moderation appeared with the M.J.Q., who prefigured the cool era, soon to be followed by the great Lester's presidency. Miles, who had dropped out of sight, made a brilliant comeback by associating the crack penmanship of Grandpa and his rowdy grandson to disrecord the Capitol series. He went on to finish his

came later but the tearoom the tearoom what a haven of peace that's what you call real values elegance distinction and those well-bred people and those tame arrangements we brought out of our folders to T's great delight there's only one thing he likes better than reading written parts and that's writing them himself his reams of S.B. & S. are lying all over the seats he could set himself up as a purveyor for needy bands but no that hobby of his is a substitute for ambition maybe he hopes he'll be played anyway is there anybody in this bus who isn't hoping for something. T is an orderly man he has a sense of discipline a quality that's getting pretty scarce between these four wheels we all know he gets very bitter if somebody next to him steps out of line and throws the section off but if the section becomes like a single person and the phrase leaps ahead like a rider glued to his horse then his eyes shine what kind of thrill does he get is it really musical when you come right down to it isn't it just the satisfaction of a job well done true T is also happy but it's not the same kind of happiness when B doles him out a solo eight whole bars what a windfall and what does he do with it he seems to peer at A's music out of the corner of his eye as if it might give him some ideas carbon copy carbon copy still what career alongside Bird, the great man of that golden age. Ah! Parker! Monk! Gillespie and his beret! Minton's . . . that was the end of a world. I sob as I write those names. What do they mean today? Those who bore them are gone now, they belong to the future, it has swallowed them up forever. My memory is those heroes' last refuge! If only it will be faithful to them as long as possible! What a period. . . . They'd just brought out short-playing records, whose chief advantage lay in not gathering dust. This new support changed the listening habits of collectors. Records had been full-blown exhibitions; now they became concise samplings. Soloists never used to be longwinded enough; now space had to be measured out to them. It was hoped that they would learn to appear, shine for a moment and, so to speak, die. They rationed the irrational, they put chance in chancery. Our overall, scattered knowledge of musicians gave way to a knowledge that was limited and precise. The less one knew about him, the better one knew it. I began to learn Parker solos by heart, and soon a man who had never been able to remember anything but the beginning of *Love Supreme* was capable of whistling the whole yellow label Dial series in his bathtub. They say that in Europe many soloists were worshiped for sixteen short bars etched somewhere between a technician take for instance that afternoon at the studio when the boys began to unfold those big paper accordions that B was handing out with a sly smile on his face every page was black there was a moment of panic faces fell hands trembled except for T and two or three cats who can really read the others would do better to work on their sight-reading between stops instead of looking at magazines full of undressed chicks what sex positions what pairs of petite titties what a catastrophe wrong notes all over the place it was complicated complicated B warned the band this time it's not a set of arrangements it's a work of music if you know what that means B rarely makes a mistake it's true he reads the audience like a book and he always knows when the time is ripe he plays it like a chess game but that move wasn't the right one when you think it over calmly you realize that the switch from 78 to 33⅓ didn't justify such a radical change of standards it was just a change of pace from gallop to trot why make our sidemen pay for it and give carte blanche to a white-collar cat who's got it all figured out in his head without ever having blown through a mouthpiece how far out can you get but B isn't far out he knows the public because he loves it he knows the public only likes what it knows conclusion some rich patron was the center and the edge of a single record. This was enough to paint an ideal portrait of a musician, more lifelike than the original. And if an opportunity came to hear him in person, people were indignant when he didn't live up to it. We'd been living in the midst of a diarrhoeic flow of sound frescoes, peopled with arpeggios and various exercises; when it stopped, we didn't immediately realize that the reign of carefully timed miniatures, of a secondhand, artificial reality, would soon lead to poverty and want. And yet this was just a change in habits. A far more dangerous revolution was brewing. It broke out when dancers popped up in front of the bands and claimed the right to monopolize the musicians. The real listeners were banished to dark corners. From then on, there were fewer and fewer concerts. The great names of the day, Fats, Hampton, and Goodman, deserted the concert stage for the dance hall. That's where we went to hear their simplified music "for dancers only," over the noise of conversations and shuffling feet. Of all the old-timers, only Louis was still going strong: Ella, Sinatra had grown too young. It was around this period that I began to lose track of the development of the language. Perhaps because I was getting younger, I failed to understand the workings of the deliberate self-impoverishment

backing him maybe the time will come for experiments like that but that was a complication we weren't ready for anyway at the festival concert B felt he had to let our sidemen have a free hand now they're asleep ah sleep escape from this endless road was it after the recording session that we had that breakdown no it was later before the festival there we were pushing the bus and wondering if we'd get there on time heave ho heave ho the smell of ⊥ so close shoulder to shoulder sweating fuming cursing the fate that made him push our common carrier in a direction that was just the opposite of the one he would have wanted to take ah to go back to that tearoom the cocktail hour his best memories there were chicks back there the music they'd played was easy on the ear the future was scarey what would he have said if he'd known where we were going but he left turned in his badge resigned ⊥ was fed up with this trip there was a cat who liked the easy way good living who else left us T of course and little E with his crazy hopes this morning he thought this was going to be *the* day and then came the letdown B didn't let him play enough so after the festival he refused to get back into the bus he knew perfectly well what was going to happen at the nightclub he didn't want to hear it those cultivated by the newcomers. I couldn't see why it was supposed to be interesting. The playing of old Jones, the great drummer of the day, made me regret his young brothers, whose style was so much more complex and stimulating, especially Elvin's—ah! Elvin—and even Clook Klarke's. That was a name I'd lost sight of since Minton's and one evening he turned up in a band led by a fellow named Bradley. To my great surprise, he'd adopted the style of the day: there was absolutely no difference between his playing and Big Sid's! I have to admit I saw a lot of other similar readjustments. However, in spite of the tyranny of the dancers, there were still interesting vestiges. I can remember bands in which the musicians read music while they played. Such virtuosity would be inconceivable today. The most famous of these groups was subjected by its leader, Ellington, to a process of compression that showed wonderful perseverance. In an eighth of a century, the number of musicians in his band shrank from sixteen to six. I guess he must have gone too far in the way of simplification. One day Ellington just vanished from the scene. They say he took up drafting. All the names that had once been great gradually lost their reputations. These devaluations were to be expected but they caused me much suffering. I witnessed the abdications

tunes you blow at the top of your lungs while the crowd sings along in unison or almost E was an aristocratic cat proud of being alone he had a kind of superior smile cold good manners but he always carried his own horn we should have loved him better maybe he'd have stayed in this tin can on wheels they all hate each other because they know they're all bound together or else it's living in a group all the time that's such a drag they react by forming cliques but that only makes them hate each other worse if only they loved each other inside the cliques but how can people love each other in a bus we're really moving now it must be the big downgrade before you get to no it's another one the instruments are asleep on the roof the bass drum in its box the double bass in its big black sarcophagus if only they never wake up again who wouldn't rather be roadhand for a poor unsuccessful band leader instead of watching over the sleepy ghosts in this dark bus ah sleep not to have to look at D with that toothy smile of his what's he thinking about that slob it's easy to guess he's thinking about that bearded kid at the festival who kicked up such a row in his seat throwing his fists around so much he almost poked out the eyes of the poor chicks sitting next to him they had to of Wilson and Tatum, Carter and Hawkins. They had stanchly defended the rights of the soloist, now denied by the new generation. Indeed, everywhere, the ultramodern polyphonic tendency was coming into its own. The insidious domination of the once scorned clarinet completely changed the coloring of the bands. The Halls, Dodds, Noones, Bechets, Nicholases, and Rappollos were the forerunners of those Lorenzo Tios, George Baquets (the first names are coming back now, the end is near), those Big Eye Nelsons who monopolize the limelight so arrogantly today. Everything was being upended, everything was being degraded. Yet Louis managed to defend his threatened supremacy right up to the last. At the very end of his glorious career, he traded his trumpet for a cornet, and was still vying for top billing with his disciple Oliver, in a group which he had had to stop leading. Life is a bitter thing when your beard begins to grow sparse and you catch yourself slowly running your hand over a face that feels too smooth. . . . When Louis finally had to retire, conquered by adolescence, he left a great gap. I admire him for his courage, yet I still feel that his influence has been harmful. When I see Papa Celestin's cart go by under my windows, I can't help thinking that to some extent this is Louis' work, these insolent parades, turn their backs on him he paid no attention to them what were they doing there anyway he was playing all right he was playing D's part and he was really with it except for maybe a quarter of a second lag like a loudspeaker echoing another one in the distance that takes reflexes D sat up there getting a kick out of this cat copying him anything's cool with him so long as he's noticed he knows how to make himself heard he doesn't stop at anything does he think nobody saw him reverse his sticks at the club bang on his kettles with the heavy end what a disgusting racket a cat who turns his sticks around is like a chick who turns up her skirt obscene obscene it shouldn't be allowed but D will do anything he's an exhibitionist and he's a slave driver too at every stop he adds another piece to his traps does it on purpose he digs watching the poor roadhand bending under the load all the way from the bus to the bandstand and whatever you do don't give him a hand that's all the boy's good for he's paid to carry the instruments it's not for him that they'd build a special stand so a special light could project huge shadows of his waving arms on the backdrop like all runts D digs making like a giant you can tell he's waiting for the moment when the others are going to leave him all alone on stage to do his act always the same one these marching bands with their odd instruments. They make such a fuss over the helicon and the washboard, but in my day there were many technical wonders: Bags's vibraphone and Smith's pipeless organ, straight out of the distant twenty-first century and which the Holy Father had allowed into church. Foolish twentieth century: all the things you let get lost! Even the piano seems to be on the way out; you hardly see it anywhere outside the Storyville whorehouses. I always feel a tug at my heartstrings whenever I remember the subtle sounds of some of those archaic instruments: Oppie's cello, Hairy Charles's flute. . . . How far away it is, that golden flute, no, it was plastic, one of the fine materials we had in those days; it seems to me I can hear it quivering in the spotlight, the way Hippolyte's gnat in the *Idiot* buzzed in a ray of sunlight, and participating, like the gnat, in the chorus of Creation. They tell me that this universal joy is also to be found in the progressive music of Canal Street. The old people maintain that the polyphonic style has finally given the language its full meaning and that we are on the verge of achieving Unity; but in the blessed days of my old age, we spent every moment tracking down that thing that has been allowed to disappear— that destructive madness, how else can I describe it?—that thing

no matter what time it is except this morning for TV it was kicksville to hang the bass drum on his belly at least he'd have something to carry during the parade those marching bands had their good points zoom bam bam and B out in front like a drum major or almost with a groovy striped cap what a handsome man that B is what a man and what a winner he came all the way up from the bottom he's done a lot for the cats in the bus making sure everybody gets a full day of gigs that's his bag and he knows it but what a lot of headaches that's why he doesn't travel with us he has to think his thoughts are what keep us on the go sure in that movie when the hollywood types biographied him you see him sharing the life of the community it looked more democratic but that's just technicolor in real life there has to be a difference another way of living for the audience it's B *and* his band in that little *and* there's the limousine and the private chauffeur none of it's gone to his head though he's still straight D couldn't keep him from having his picture taken with his faithful roadhand it appeared in *Time* with one of those obscure captions man was it obscure "though it's quite impossible jazz ought to be reinvented only every Monday morning" what doubletalk which traumatized us, over-whelmed us, whereas the steady good humor of today's music, whether it's for Carnival or for a disinterment, has gotten so all-pervasive that it's sickening. But then, after all, perhaps music lives the way we do, perhaps it evolves toward childhood and its innocent games. I prefer not to wonder what this city in which I've come to live out my child-hood—where can I go now, where can I go?—has in store for me. I live near Congo Square; a name doubly reminiscent of bar-barity. Around me, oldsters fresh out of their shrouds are talking about the Voodoo religion. They remind me of those "free" musi-cians who were said to be the priests of a musical rite. History is a snake engaged in biting its own tail. And it will all end, if I'm to believe the oracle at Lake Pontchartrain, in the body of a mental patient who has been un-der treatment for decades at the East Louisiana State Hospital, but he'll get well, he'll get well. You always get well. Oh well. On account of my age, I won't see him. I'm young, young. The time has come for me to go to school and forget what life has taught me, and the music that was my life. Farewell music.

luckily it was a great picture hardly retouched at all little things like that make you feel close to somebody and he's tact-ful and discreet after the night-club we had to get back in the bus and go looking for a place to play after hours B went to bed he knows that at that confusing time of night the boss is only in the way that extra stop belongs to his musicians not to him the time for public relations is over it's time to scream time to go round the bend time to shout your hatred and despair for the whole world to hear but the world isn't there nobody hears those shouts except maybe a few eggheads looking for material you can count on them they'll find plenty of it in that incommunicable anguish enough to fill up the pages of their little reviews but it seems that the small hours of the night turn those cloudy thoughts into thoughts of genius because when people wake up they're wide open ready to swallow any-thing the bus moves on sleep tomorrow is almost here will this old crate go to the junk heap will it take us right up to Pnots-padamh palace where the musi-cian prince Angkor Angkor faster forget today dawn dawn sleep.

5

Avatars of a Hero

T hat's him. From one picture to the next, there
is scarcely a resemblance. In the first, the art-
ist portrayed him in his room; in the second, among other musicians,
during a rehearsal perhaps; in the third, he is probably playing in
concert (although nothing indicates that the sources of illumination
are actually stage lights). The three portraits are not contemporary.
In the picture on the left,[1] which ought to be the earliest, the frame
is almost entirely filled by the bed. Every object is the same shade of
gray: the bedspread and bolster, sparsely trimmed with a wisp of
binding, the head of the bed and the wall behind it. The only
decorative element is the pattern on the carpet beneath the feet, and

---

1. Dennis Stock. *Plaisir du Jazz*, p. 96.

this the artist deliberately left in shadow. One senses that the few visible objects constitute a link with the world which is but tenuous indeed. The telephone must be silent; the instrument case seems empty; on the bed lies a reedless clarinet. In his lap lies his tenor, a relic of his vanished empire. His right hand grasps it, still weakly protecting it; his left hand plugs the bell, as if to gag it, that no sound may come out of it. As if to silence it. His stooped figure, which has not yet returned to the foetal position, shows the posture of a beaten man. Arms once capable of raising the tenor to a nearly horizontal position, as in offering, are now drained of strength. The black trousers, the woolen shirt with its vertical stripes and tightly buttoned collar emphasize the sadness of a face grown childlike with fatigue. Only with difficulty do the raised eyes give the lie to the bowed head —and in them there is fear.

In the picture in the middle,[2] the strings of a harp in the foreground run diagonally across the entire righthand side. The harpist's extremely white hand appears on the very edge. Between the strings one sees two violinists in profile; the violist is in three-quarters rear profile. To the left of the harp, one sees only the back of the cello player, the nape of the neck, the short-cropped hair, and the top of the instrument. Beyond them, the setting is banal, the location vague. One side of a double door is standing open, and there are festoons hanging from the ceiling as in a stage set. He himself stands in the background on the left (but the artist has centered all the light around him), wearing a pale suit (against which the triangle of a pocket handkerchief is scarcely noticeable), white shirt, printed tie, and collar girdled by the neck strap on which the alto momentarily hangs, at an angle slightly more oblique than that formed by the harp strings. His hands, held in front of him, are outstretched, with the fingers slightly parted as if in a gesture of blessing. The rounded torso might be that of an oriental god, and so might the face, with its inward serenity (though one also detects a feeling of absence).

The picture on the right[3] shows no setting at all. Man and instrument are shown silhouetted by a faint halo against a black background. The artist has focused the light on the silver (or possibly gold) trimmings of the soprano; but the reflected glow harshly outlines the contours of the face. The eyes are not closed but

---

2. Al Fairweather in Leonard Feather, *The Encyclopedia of Jazz* (New York: Horizon Press, 1955), p. 213.
3. Unpublished. See Jean-Pierre Leloir's private collection.

screwed up, crushed, turned inward like the rest of the face. Strangely enough, the convulsed mask, distorted by physical effort and intense mental concentration, remains pure; the grimace hardly ruffles the regular features. The shape of the left ear remains geometrical: it acts as the sentry of consciousness in the midst of the storm; for the chest, imposingly broad, one can tell, gives tremendous power to the wind driven between the tight lips and through the metal tube whose straightness is hidden by its complicated outer mechanism. The setting would be practically impossible to identify had not the artist granted us a glimpse, to the right of the subject and below him, of the smile of the alter ego, reduced to its essentials: the shining eyes and a row of dazzling teeth.

From picture to picture, the instrument changes: first a tenor, then an alto, finally a soprano. Its decreasing size corresponds to an increase in the energy conveyed by the subject in terms of the different faces and bodies which the artist has attributed to him. Had the purpose been to show the metamorphoses of the bee or gnat, the artist would probably have left it to the entomologist to describe them: by juxtaposing these three portraits, which reflect the process of regeneration of creative energy, he was striving instead to sketch the outlines of a mythology. There does exist between them a temporal relationship. The picture on the left has no future: the subject no longer exists, he is a shell, a shadow; he has exhausted his potentialities, or rather transferred them to the picture in the middle. In this, the earliest of the three, the subject is already ever so slightly removed (as is his position in the space of the picture itself); he is living on his momentum. His future is double: his physical appearance will regress back to a state similar to the previous one and his life force will desert him, but at the same time it will reappear in the picture on the right (the most recent), gushing like a spring torrent.

A tremendous sincerity radiates forth from the picture in the center. The subject depicted here is not making a show of himself. He displays none of those artifices the unavowed purpose of which is to dissemble the monastically austere monotony of the jazz cell. Startling hair cuts, wisecracks, carefully polished gags, "stage presence," postures so spontaneous as to seem contrived, pop tunes magnified out of all proportions, keyboard covers kept obstinately closed, dances in which you almost stumble at each step (while the other musicians stand waiting, aloof, absent), drums that you jump on without damaging them and those you deliberately demolish (before hatred became fashionable, one would tactfully sculpt an accommodating customer's head), a certain way of ignoring the audience, of playing with your back to it, of creating a hostile feeling on stage, and even those stylish concert bows which are so exactly the opposite of the usual relaxed manner—the picture in the center is free of all these things.

At first glance, the picture on the right seems to irradiate a like simplicity; however, a doubt creeps in when the gaze associates the strained pathos of the face with memories of furious twistings of the torso and wild flexings of the legs that call to mind the just-a-shade-too-visible efforts of a medium going into trance (not the gathering of one's strength or the harnessing of the internal bellows demanded by a brass instrument, but the efforts, alien to any technique, which the audience expects of an athlete pitted in a titanic struggle against unknown forces). Why must the man of jazz, as soon as he appears on stage, feel obliged to have something else to show besides himself (if only the contortions of an exasperated body)? After the thousand and one nights in clubs where most of the customers listen distractedly, is he now afraid that the candor of his tales will fail to hold the attention of an audience focused entirely upon him? Whether this corresponds to the personal vocation of one man whose life is a sham and who finds on the stage just one more opportunity for play-acting or whether it is motivated, in another man whose only desire is to be heard (but whose records will be distributed only if he agrees to this exhibition), by the alienness of the concert hall surroundings—each pays this tribute to society, a tribute which leaves traces even in the very texture of a flat color-less image.

At the gates of Hades, innocence returns. Footlights will never tarnish the picture on the left: man in his final hour of distress. The picture in the middle should forever sing the subject's posthumous glory. And yet the artist's composition is such that as the gaze follows its path of cultural conditioning eastward (an Arab might see a completely different symbol here) it discovers, in the harp's trellis, flaws which the future will enlarge. The subject is seen in a moment of happiness; yet his life substance is draining away, and though unaware of it, he is on his way not to the summit but to the bottom of the pit. His outspread wings are frozen; never will they beat again; he is gliding wonderfully and all hope is lost. Even this ecstasy is impure: the profusion of strings cluttering the picture is the concrete embodiment of an error. He believes himself on top of the world and yet his happiness is a betrayal.

True, none can begrudge you this moment of happiness. Though still invisible for many, you were the lighthouse of an uprooted people who did not know whether it had taken root; you were not yet the symbolic leader of a colonized people thirsting for independence. Your name had meaning only for the man of jazz. The myth was starting to form around you, only later would you belong to history: your image could still be marred by sentimental portraits, your art made to merge with the fleeting values of an adolescent subculture (which, once constituted, would chase you from its pantheon taken over by the beatle and the stone); it had already been conceived as a way of provoking or stimulating the spasms of action painting, or of pepping up the musical backgrounds for the orgies and bacchanalia of the prepsychedelic era. Yet none of these things can ever spoil your happiness.

The artist has left your mystery whole. What do we know of you? What do we know of what you played on the night of July 29, 1945? (What did Buddy Bolden play on June 16, 1904?) Had it not been for the issuing, ten years later, of the false starts and bad takes (bad for the others), what would we know of the break in *Night in Tunisia* (the one you couldn't possibly have played *twice*)? You paid a heavy price for being way ahead of your partners, since because of their hesitations, your first inspiration, fiery and natural, was often lost to history. What do we know of your thoughts while you were playing at Christie's, gazing at the lake, alone in one wing (while the other musicians sat in a nearby room), *apart?* What do we know of the source of *Bloomdido*, so entitled, perhaps, in tribute to Blume's day? What do we know of the notes your alto shaped when you played all night long, naked, in a room on Tenth Street? What do we know of the sky, silent forever more, into which so many phrases disappeared, or of the ones that stayed inside you, never noted, never played? What do we know of your "latent schizophrenia" and your "hostile, evasive personality"? What do we know of your drunken fights? What do we know of your monthly pains (you, the most virile of all)? What do we know of your sexual indulgence, except that it would have justified many a phallic figure, such as the plumed javelin (fitted with turkey feathers, like the bigamutous harpsichord of Mars-Solar) brandished by Ulysses in anticipation of the nordic athlete (Ulysses, who also threw the discus—he set more records than Symphony Sid—and stood with raised hand to watch it roll; who sang the nigromance with Sirssy; and who, having lost his name, took a red-hot stake to avenge his brothers devoured by the Cyclops)? What do we know of the black girls, or the white girls, in whose bodies you had to humiliate the enemy race, guessing that one of them would rat on you and that the narcotics squad, who insert probes into artists' rectums, would come running to protect society inside your very body (returning like for like), and that you could safely show them the marks on your black skin (this one was your Cadillac, this one your home)? What do we know of your intermittent good will, of your heartbreaking attempts to readjust, of the promises you made when society, with a touch of cruelty, asked you to become a good right-thinking family man with decent health and a steady bank account, as if all this could have done anything but kill you a little more and a little faster.

Sometimes you surprised people by turning up on time, dressed to kill, and carrying under a dignified arm (on which there was no room left for a last-minute fix) the arrangement briefcase (which actually contained only a bottle of gin). So often you weren't there. What can a man do to be there when he has come to make beauty and the table has been cleared away and the garden is late? Paint a picture right now! How many times did you have to bear the sad amazement of managers, face the anger of owners, and wheedle agents (your judges!) into keeping you on their rolls, at least until the next time you stepped out of line! Shouldn't a man have the legal right not to be present physically when spiritually he is absent? It would be a modest compensation for the incongruous unveiling of beauty in front of three men chatting over a drink and suddenly struck dumb by the musical Phryne, or for a radiant ghost of sound that rose up behind a singer during her number—but she could recognize it. You were the man of these epiphanies (not of those organized phalanxes in which the future is written out so clearly that you fall asleep, sometimes right under the blazing spotlights, in the din of trumpets and drums); and there were days when you knew how to shatter the silence.

Yet you were not completely anonymous. Had your existence created stir enough in the great city for a tiny wave to have sensitized that cop who cornered you for speeding one night? Show me your credentials. Parker, Charles, Christopher, junior—why Christopher? Born in Kansas City—Kansas or Missouri? In 1920—is that quite sure? For a split second, the cop's eyebrow arches upward. False alarm; no criminals by that name. The policeman had hip trouble; or perhaps was simply uncultivated. He didn't know that hundreds of Prousts all over the world were beginning to weave Charlie Yardbird Parker and his little chromatic phrase into their remembrance of things past; that they credited that little phrase with the colors of the bird of paradise, purple, white, pink, red, violet, ultraviolet; associated its forms with those of their most intimate flora, recomposing a reality in which they might imprison just a little of you (which the policeman could not). That little phrase, with its quick ascending upbeat, its measured chromatic outline and its variable terminal flexion, is the perfect expression of Parker tempo, that essence of tempo. It seems to slip into place now and then of its own accord, as if its function were to make sure that the tempo is right. It is also a photographic reduction of the Parker chorus in that it must rocket skyward, like a bucking cliff, before consenting to descend again to the plains, in successive terraces, broken with a thousand ledges. And if it were flattened against a wall, it would be a transparent graph of a career shot through by a blaze of success, followed by a gradual loss of popularity. Arsis, thesis; perhaps it is also (but who can say?) an image of the passing moments in your manic-depressive existence.

You can't do without your little phrase; it's got to be with you all the time. It sings in your head; it's your stereotype, your sister Philomela's legacy. It is the symbol of repetition and the announcement of death, each the equivalent of the other. There comes a time when the growing chimpanzee forgets how to play; there comes a time when man's youth is lost and with it his powers of discovery. The land is bounded now; the time of expansion has ended; it will be inhabited by pale inheritors with whom you ought to learn to live. You could, of course, have repeated yourself over again indefinitely; but your contemporaries were growing old with you (though their time was slower than yours); the single dish would lose a bit more of its flavor for them every day; and newcomers would look elsewhere for their food. Intensely, you embodied the spirit of a period: this is why you could not survive it. Behold: other comets are about to streak across the sky. Follow them and you're lost; don't follow them and you bog down. One day your work alone will rise again—perhaps!—(provided its material support is strong enough). Then, reincarnated, the creator will live forever in his music. But you knew your fate. A phoenix must die ere a phoenix can be born.

And what does it matter, since illness and death come after stagnation and spiritual decline! (One evening, a disciple will open a newspaper in a bus, read the headline and stand up quickly to hide his tears.) Sometimes, unfortunately, they are long in coming. The picture on the left tells of the extreme state of decay in which the sacrifice left the shadow. His soul had abandoned him; only the body was left to suffer.

Eidda Gabbler! Eidda Gabbler! That's a long story, too—the father with all his instruments, the home town and its canals, the river boats, and the set of traps left to the younger brother because it took too long to pack up. Silence over the lifeless years. But for a while, the soul may have lain in two bodies, there may have been two phoenixes in the world. The image on the left is worshiped in more than one memory. When that face wore a smile, gags fairly spurted out, fresh, fresh, from the bell of his tenor. When the features of the flat round face under the flat round hat could hardly be seen through Mili's smoke and his chiaroscuros that were just a bit too slick, what lazily meandering train of thought cast itself into the music that welled up from the depths of the sprawling body which seemed part of the sofa supporting it (a train of thought that had climbed alone, weary of rehashing the manuals and the usuals, to a level on which commentary is possible). And the almost timbreless sound, with its hoarse vibrato, spider web trembling with silver reflections; and the phrasing that had the feminine grace of the turkey's strut; perhaps both were born of a hormonal weakness, or else, through boredom or revolt, of the years of youth seeded with the one admonishment: *play like Bean.* (Bean—every vassal's only thought was to pledge allegiance to that lord of the manor: they tripped over each other to show him the progress they'd made in the art of imitating him. See how much I'm like you! After years of effort, Herschel was so proud of sounding almost like him—almost.) Only Lady Day had said: *play like yourself; play yourself out.*

They admitted I was elegant, lively, sometimes witty; then right away they added: with a thin sound. But after me, others were said to have a thick sound. Neither praise nor criticism could affect the way I felt my own reality; I was as real as the rat I found lying on the shirts in my drawer and looking up at me with its sharp, little eyes. My reality dated from the battle of the Four Tenors, when Bean, by dawn, had lost what essentially had made him Number One; his very style had been challenged. The B-flat tenor had stopped being synonymous with Hawkins. That was when my sun began to rise. Not president yet. But even then (this was in Kansas City, too; those woods produce some of America's finest nightingales) that kid used to come and hear me every night; the kid with the kinky hair, blacker than the others, who stood outside for hours with his ear glued to the wall, drinking in every note of my choruses; that kid was my consecration. His being there wiped away ten years of slaps in the face. Pretty soon they'd stop saying play like Bean; he'd be one of the first to play like Prez. You a fan of mine? Like me, he could play with a cigarette between his fingers. He played pretty badly in those days: how could I imagine he'd grow so enormously and steal my soul away from me—no, it's his soul, too, it's the soul of jazz. Jazz has to have a soul, otherwise how could it survive, how could it assume the vicissitudes of its existence? Thus wrote another youngster who came to manhood in the middle thirties, young Stephen, pale-faced, this one, a helpful boy who was always hanging around musicians, meeting them at the station, carrying instruments for this one, running errands for that one. A bit of a nuisance, maybe, with his far-out questions. Show me your credentials, he'd beg. What? Really? Lester Willis (Willy would have been more brotherly) Young, born August 27, 1909—in New Orleans? Just like the All-Time Greats? He didn't know who I was. (I think it was the other kid, the one with the kinky hair, who let him know.) A lot later, he caught up with history by writing it down for other little Stephens who wanted to know it all. He told about everything we do; he interpreted our behavior and peered into our consciences. There wasn't a groove on a record that he hadn't feverishly explored. What has happened has to be written down, that's in the order of things. But he didn't find our soul; some-one else would have to do that. Only a poet, Nobody in his name, somehow and somewhere, wrote it, wrote it all, wrote it all down. He sang the soul of jazz in his foreign tongue, it's his soul too, he's *us!* and he has the power, the chance and the freedom to create what we have been unable to be.

I fought all alone against Chu and his panting, Hawkins and his volume, Ben and his riffs, Illinois and his harmonics. For a while, I got the best of them. The kid from Kansas City continued me, probably a little farther out than me, it was another image of swing, the most perfect that has ever existed. (If you want to swing, Bud Powell used to say, you gotta go by Bird.) It's been said that Bird put his life into his music. We all do that, a little. And it works the other way around, what we can't put into our lives we put into our horns. His life was fuller, more colorful, that's all. And he was more complete: besides that easy-going relaxation, he had a kind of con-stant tension inside himself, that bursting energy he was disciplined enough to master, that inner fire. His cool jazz was boiling hot. I had been one swing of the pendulum; he was in the center; after that, haven't Chu and Bean and Ben and Illinois all come back in the person of. . . .

With relief, the gaze leaves the picture on the left. Ill-adjusted destiny; regrettable longevity. On the contrary, in his central incarnation, the man was able to sacrifice himself when the time came. Without too many tears. Yet, what brevity! You enter stage left, you have time to shine, just one chorus, and death beckons from stage right. At Monroe's—it was only yesterday—they wanted to hear you sound like Bennie Carter. And that night at Dan Wall's when you came alive! The bones of Bone, your only friend, were fresh in the grave. You were nothing but hunger, hunger to play. Your alto was always in hock and you'd never rest till you'd gotten someone else's strap around your neck; then nothing could stop you. You were going to be one of those Picassos who paint a Picasso in fifteen minutes and thirty years. And you forced yourself to practice constantly, in hotel rooms, at night, in bathrooms. Never again to hear the insulting *Man, you just hold your horn,* never again to have the instrument torn from your hands by a mere Ben Webster. Your turn now to say stand up, not meanly, but simply because the other man has to yield his seat to a better man than he, for music, for the beauty of music. The hunger to play, the insatiable hunger of your early years, the most important years of one's life, the years of possible creation, one day that hunger will be appeased, one day you'll kiss your alto and cradle it, murmuring *there's too much in my head for this horn,* aspiring after an impossible reconversion. One plays better at twenty; one might write better at forty. What can you do now that it's too late and the finale is near? O bitter ending! Other Birds are coming whose themes aren't the same, and the world will turn to them. They appreciate your lyrical spirit, certainly they do, just as you appreciated Johnny Hodges. You won't give them time to show themselves. That day in 1940 when Bennie Carter came to hear you, he was contemplating his own end! Death didn't obsess you then; you didn't find strange pretexts to pay visits to the dead. Repetition, self-repetition. Tired of rethinking the same ideas. The introduction of *West End Blues:* even quoted by you, it has lost its flavor. You can't be Louis Armstrong! Ah! That smile of his! Your only hope left is to disappear. They treat iodine swallowers at Bellevue (hard to hang oneself with an encysted saxophone chord). Psychotherapeutic first aid. That night in Chicago, when not a sound would come out of your alto, that night in Birdland, when Bud, little moon-Bird, ruined your exit; these were lesser omens than that fall you took, one afternoon, at the corner of Barrow Street. A symbolic fall: you flopped down like a horse—not one of those splendid Sixty-fifth Street horses that you liked to talk to in your gentlest voice—but a broken-down, stiff-limbed horse that has been hauling its cart too long and can go no farther (only the legs still move, weakly, absurdly). The words of the Koran ran through your head, Saluda Hakim!—as beautiful as Klactoveedsedstene, as meaningless too. Ah! if only you didn't have to listen to the well-meaning speeches of innocent youths (they would be hadjis some day) who did not understand why you had to die: they thought your little phrase was still alive! What taxi will take you out of this neighborhood? Things moved fast with you:

you were gray at three, like Cygnus the swan, and white at nine, like Dindonnus the peacock; at sixteen you looked thirty-eight, and at thirty-four, the day of your death, fifty-three. Almost as old as that musical genius of another century, also an alcoholic, who vanished one evening in March, like you, in the same burst of thunder. His bust sits on many a middle-class mantelpiece—and you, your image (that picture in the middle where you remain ageless, impavid, inaccessible, out of this world), who looks at it? Nobody.

And now you are nothing more than an article in the Encyclopaedia Britannica, flattering, of course (so was the Reverend David's insipid sermon to the Abyssinians, was it not?), but hastily translated, too short, incomplete: of Leon, the son to whom you could not bequeath your genius (as Saul did to David), no mention is made, nor of the names of the interpreters that another of your sons, whom you never knew, created for you by placing your little phrase in a diva's mouth, at the risk of betraying you twice, for there is a betrayer in every interpreter: Leon Noel interpreted the thoughts of the president, Leonora presidentialized those of Porter and Hart, and the black angel Morel, the angel with the lock (you would have loved him, not because they called him Charlie but because he drew from a violin the same screaming notes as Heifetz) committed endless betrayals; as for Noel and David, sons of Nobody, how could they fail to uncover (as Leon and Morel had not managed to do for his other father) the nakedness of Noah?

The gaze turns away. It can do no more for the subject of the picture in the middle. It has invented him a past; the time has come to put him back in his place, in the picture, to return that statue of gold and paper to its nirvana. Farewell, Birddah! Let us leave the transparent song of the sitar. Perhaps a picture, somewhere, is waiting for the poet, whose page is nearly full. Last words now (the circle is complete); they won't be for you. The names of the gods are beautiful; beautiful the names of the devils, in the reverse world. Slowly the gaze slides toward the picture on the right. Invert the courses of the rivers. Let us stop listening to the song of thy luths, O Western World! Let an older chant permeate our hearts.

The sound of that soprano comes from far away. Beyond Hodges's suavity, behind old Bechet's purplish-blue sustained notes, swollen with blood, trembling like the majestic attributes of the male turkey, there is something Islamic, something Pakistani in the tense timbre, the even sounds that distinguish the subject in this new incarnation. Angry young man? Anger cannot be music, for it feeds on reason. All of that is justice, only justice! We've exhausted ourselves crying out for justice: but art does not descend to the level of life. Art? Is it still? Now that the rafters and buttresses have come crashing down, has not everything held sacred been transmuted into naked violence? Not anger: furor! The undesirable guest of Man, since time immemorial, since animals have reigned upon the earth.

What happens when the lower parts crystallize into a single resonance; when the melodic substance, taking purchase on this crystallization, springs forth, spins, gains height, and crystallizes too, in a wild gyration? What happens when the repetition of a neutral fragment is followed in an unbroken carrousel by other undifferentiated fragments whose length is limited only by the wind of the instrumentalist? What happens when these fragments—variants of, rather than variations on, a single idea which is, in itself, indefinite (sun-rays forever lighting up the same stained glass window)—come one after another in discontinuous continuity? What happens once the gyration is established, once the idea of dynamics has lost its meaning, ceased to exist, once the fortissimo has become permanent and the narrow ambitus of those fragments settled in the highest register where the sound is gradually subjected to a slow process of distortion (on the tenor, this state would inevitably be surpassed by the production of harmonics)? What happens when there is no room left for melodic development, when humor vanishes and quotations are no longer conceivable? What happens when the only form of expression left is the scream?

A genius may write a book and free himself of the evil geniuses that haunt him by unleashing them in its pages; yet, however imperfect, however leaky, it must be a *work*, not just a book. Thus is it possible to rid oneself of a passion for gambling in the turmoil of a work: *The Gambler*. But violence is not a passion, no work can exorcise it; the only way to get rid of it is to indulge it. Playing jazz then becomes a magical act, a kind of incantation without a formula, an attempt to recapture the spinning fixity of the whirling dervish (here, it is not the body but the musical figures that spin). A work would require a dialectical relationship between time and space; the incantation abolishes time, requiring only that it last long enough for the feeling of eternity which is the corollary of incantation to appear; it also strives to abolish space, since everything, in the soloist's nondiscourse, is on the same plane; but space, thus rejected, appears again in terms of the new situation in which the soloist has placed himself with regard to the other musicians, and of the relationships between them (no longer based on an interdependency of values calling for a rigorous metric coordination). The support or accompaniment relationship is replaced by a conflict which is no sooner under way than it becomes petrified; this clash of two skyward-towering, giant turtles will not be resolved. No longer standing behind the soloist but beside him now, the force of the rhythm section, no longer auxiliary but antagonistic, pushes him, pushes him till he screams. In this torture session the drums play the role of torturer (for the drums hate the soprano and it hates them).

The subject does not have the strength to maintain his gyration; left to himself, his motion would immediately flag. Like a mad top, he must be constantly whipped to be kept spinning. Through a dialectics of the afterbeat, expressed overtly or covertly, an organization of the meter in which syncopation is both interruption and appeal, the alter ego provides the indispensable motor energy to drive the sound machine and maintain its density. He also fills, because of his full-bodied sound, another sector of the space only a well-defined part of which the subject wishes to occupy. The static whirling condition in which the subject is satisfied to remain allows his alter ego to exercise his own rhythmic imagination. He can do anything now, freed as he is from the obligation to follow the meanders of a linear thought process. His playing has the authority of complete and utter freedom, it is neither accompaniment nor solo; it is on exactly the same plane as the soloist's screaming, which is also that of his own frenzy. This permanent confrontation between two immovable and complementary forces, which do not transform each other but simply exist by one another, has renewed the basic dualism of jazz and realized one of its most irresistible tendencies: the search for hypnotic lyricism.

The gaze withdraws. How many ordeals had to be surmounted before it was possible to cry out man's naked primeval violence? Travestied by the subject, hidden beneath appeals to love, coated in Christian syrup, it is there nonetheless; one could as easily drape it in white veils, Islamwise, and offer it up to some intolerant god. If the subject happened to die again, would the violence go with him? An unruffled civil servant of the Beyond, seeing him appear alone, would welcome him with kindness. Show me your credentials. So you're Coltrane, John, born September 23, 1926, in Hamlet, North Carolina? What have you done with your alter ego? Left him among the living? Poor Elfe! He's going to get bored. Your time is over; his is ending. The habitable regions have shrunk enormously owing to an unpredictable glacier formation. New men are building the reverse world (you may have been the first Column Man of that Architrane). These indirect heirs of Dada are unwittingly reciting the lesson of the white devil whom they pretend to exorcise. Their contempt for the audience does not prevent them from taking pains to gratify it (the snake circles and elephant bows, both equally indefatigable, are part of their ritual). Their derisive attitude toward everyone and everything does not always include themselves. At times, groggy with violence, one may find them going unexpectedly sentimental over an Ellington romance (is this the fulfillment of the Ellington promise?). They wallow with relish in formlessness and cultivate a sound as barbaric as possible (the supreme sign of sophistication). Bird, perhaps, could have drawn from ugliness some pristine beauty (did he not contemplate an exaggerated interpretation of melodic patterns, a lyrical magnification of certain errors of accentuation, an architecture of the formal flaw?); but these others flaunt their parodic intentions and, in their street fights, they have let Bird's serenity get lost.

The gaze hesitates, dares not look again. Is there nothing more to see? Is everything contained in these three portraits? If the reverse world wins out, will the gaze learn to look differently? But what is the meaning of this reversal of values? Playing jazz was essentially "playing something" (if only the blues). Postulates, deductions, and implications combined to produce, through chemical reaction, a cathartic effect: by rushing into a string of choruses with nothing in the back of your mind, you performed an act of purification. Strangely enough, this whole process of physical externalization (waving mallets, kneading skins, wiggling hinges), which set the surrounding air in motion and peopled it with immaterial characters who organized the drama and took charge of the passions, had only one goal: a return to oneself (which was also an action upon oneself). For internal use only? When the outside man with his uninformed ear crossed the path of the whirlwind, he was splashed, so to speak, by the results of the creator's emotion; thus, he came to know of the drama and its characters. But to achieve catharsis, he would have had to identify himself with the music-man, become his equal. And yet this fortuitous transmission did involve a giving of the self which, though it was not the goal of the creative act, may have been its essential characteristic. (Go further still, make the gift of self complete so that the outside man can fully experience the catharsis. To achieve this, would it not have been necessary to conceive a vaster drama, better organized, and with an architecture born of slow maturation, long meditation? The work of written jazz—which Bird seems to have anticipated and which he did not consider impracticable—could have responded to this need; but it might have implied a temporary abandoning of improvisation which would have deprived the solo musician of his privileges.)

The gaze knows that Bird's art is more complex than its apparent linearity might lead one to believe. With him, the sense of drama is compensated for by an opposite force—one of inertia and immovability—which has grown and asserted itself in the *monocolored, monotempoed* music of Monk (that gardener of a single flower). Let that force free itself and become a pole of violent attraction for all the impulses which the dominant force once held in check, then the drama and its fluctuations will disappear and the only conceivable quest will be for permanent equilibrium, for a kind of happiness which, once attained, must be preserved as it is, secure against accident. The only unity deemed desirable is one based on an unconvertible feeling, "pitch," which harbors no diversity. And praiseworthy indeed is this monotony, desired, achieved and preciously maintained; and perhaps this is where the greatness of the reverse men lies, perhaps they have glimpsed a transcendency of Parker's music in that mad ambition (which, if it had been achieved, would have led jazz to its apotheosis): to stay the instant and make it pregnant with eternity. Illusion? O force that art henceforth sovereign, it is time to name thee: ThaNaTos!—thy guises are many, thou art he who has taught the music-man the voluptuousness of having nothing more to play, who has held up to him the mirage of divine freedom, the long hoped-for vision, which fascinates him, which he thinks he has achieved at last in the abolition, suggested by thee, of pre-existing structures, an abolition which he thinks he has within his grasp. . . . Oh ThaNaTos with thy thousand deceits!

Terrible regression! Everything that seemed destined to evolve, to bloom, to burst, to swarm—stifled. And the best part of Bird, the share of Eros, which prefigured a dynamic expansion—snuffed out. What an ironic situation, historically speaking! The forces of repetition and death blow in the sails of the present, the forces of life and progress fill those of the past! Crucial (more so than Leipzig and Mannheim: what Beethzart will have the wherewithal to collect the sum of such a legacy?). For now, in the name of freedom of improvisation (at the very gates of anarchy), we revive thousand-year-old modes, stiff, starched, motionless kings. A justification for this step backward? One would have to don the cast-off garments of committed art, side with Brecht against Artaud. The reverse men, sitting around their tabula rasa, would tend to do just that. History, ThaNaTos whispers in their ears, has compelled you to be vindicators of violence; the world called forth this militant music. A paltry excuse! All music is struggle, all music is history. The musician has his own historical imperatives, and his struggles are not those that pit peoples against peoples. Enough messages! O Beauty, thou sole sovereign! What alibi—be it even the highly respectable one of social solidarity—would the reverse world dare put forward to excuse the aesthetic failure of a generation?

When the gaze focuses again, the pictures have waned yellow, the subject looks almost the same from one to the other (was this the artist's intention?). The regression has been achieved. But in the depths of the reverse world, someone, by a magical attitude, a conventional sign, informs the community that he, the music-man, the civilized man, the civilized music-man, is performing for the very last time the main play in the animal repertoire, and that his work is going to stop being the *ritualization* of a battle that he cannot bring himself to fight. Then the reverse world starts to dwindle and recede. Eros comes into his own once more. Some-where, somehow, men live—and create a music of Life.

6

Outside the Capsule

by salt and by mercury
by asbestos and by phosphor
by sulphur and by silica
by the Okootoos and by the Allus
by the Voodoos and by the Zulus
by the In Cubi and by the Sub Cubi
by the inexorable figures
by the unconjurable and inexorcisable names
of Ecarerioh and Molahc-Molahc
of Armstroth and Dominavaroth
of Asmodsen and Baileyal
of Amba-Jadal and Leveyathan
of Error Nergal and Murmurossia
by the Choreae of E'Ridan

by the Ellingchtonian Lollards
by the Basielics of the Big Appeal
by the antagonistic figures of Llabnonnac and Ettenro
by the unpronounceable names of Bbewkcihc and Xibekcebredi-
able

and by the unclean shadow of Arpàd the depraved child the
gallinacean child

hitherto follows an exegetical examination also termed analysis

of a phonotype fragment lately unearthed in a post-Christian
crypt (Yelb! Yelredda! Yenracyrrah! Come!)

the object similar in this respect to all other phonotypes previously unearthed and duly described in archeological catalogues

is black of color flat and circular in shape and its surface is graven
with countless barely perceptible anfractuosities

many of which have been destroyed by the centuries but while
damage suffered by the phonotype is most deplorable

its exceptional and well worth considering destiny resides in its
being found outside the capsules

which the Ancients meant for the preservation of their objects of
worship (Snilloc! Enartloc! Elocyzoc! Hurry up!)

from which it may be deduced that it is an object of worship of
the second degree or else

an object belonging to a form of worship (Relya! Rolyat! Get
here!) prior to what is known as the capsule period and already
discarded by then

for it is proven that at that time men attached an absolute moral
value to capsulation

what was *in* being regarded as sacred and what was not *in* as
sinister

such was the way of post-Christian beliefs (Crisscrollinstitt!
Quick!)

notwithstanding which the archeologist whose function it is to make sense out of the insignificant

applied himself to classifying comparing describing examining and cataloguing this object

on whose surface a few fragmentary numbers and letters may still be read (MILES STAR MICROGROOVE BA[S]GROOVE 44 50)

he next entrusted it to the experts of the Foundation for Bioparapsychic Identification

sole possessors of an ancient machine the praying wheel whose artifice is still a source of wonderment today

as it is capable of restituting through gyration and the steady circular abrasion of a wooden stylus the invocations contained in the phonotype

now upon such contact the object produced clearly intelligible sounds in the middle section of its reverse side exclusively

allowing F.B.I. experts to extrapolate the complete and definitive analysis hitherto appended

ANALYSIS BY THE F.B.I.

Preamble

the musical substance condensed in the hollows of this phonotype by a process of inscrutation

closely related to what the Ancients called a synthetic industry

is of especial interest in that it offers no resemblance whatsoever to the musical samples condensed into phonotypes discovered in capsulae

the word groove which appears twice first associated with the Latin prefix bas suggesting depth

then with the Helenic prefix micro suggesting minuteness

is a Saxon term used by the Ancients as a doublettery for furrow

this detail reveals that the phonotype carries music for sowing-time

small seeds buried deep in accordance with the customs of the day

such as mary-jane which nourished industrial man and was sown in rows and broadcast

hence there is little justification in relating however remotely this sowing music as certain so-called experts nevertheless have done either with the Singleton phonotype (*cf.* capsule 585) also known as opus 59 3 and 74 whose substance is bow-hunting music

as expressly stated in the inscription string quar clearly to be read on one of its sides quar being an abbreviation for quarrel a scholarly term for arrow

or with the Berrigan phonotype (*cf.* capsule 858) known as Ebony Con and which carries in its interstices an invocation to Staviski god of the forests (Bellibissie! Elsaraahl! Arrive!)

already celebrated in other invocations known to archeologists as Renard and the Bird and the Fire

all clear examples of hunting music in which the wood rather than the string which it carries is symbolically magnified

while the sowing-music found outside the capsules is dedicated to the god Miles-Selim (A-lou-qha! Suinoleth! Make haste!) no doubt a telluric power

as suggested by the sequence of isometric strophes representing the seasons' periodical return and the regular succession of sounds signifying the fall of life-giving rain

these sounds were produced by an apparatus of archaic type probably a big harpy

which because of its sound volume and above all the superior depth of its register is cast throughout the fragment under analysis in a role of overwhelming preponderance

whence the infallible certitude that this is also true of the inaudible parts of the phonotype under consideration

which big harpy is nevertheless subjected to the obtrusive proximity of other pieces of apparatus difficult to identify pursuing parallel invocations

the first of these being a light and very mobile drone heard only briefly in the audible fragment

and in like manner the last a kind of stable dense flute which appears on the verge of the destroyed section of the phonotype and is therefore doomed to annihilation

between them however is heard an apparatus already known to archeologists as a chopin by reference to a phonotype (*cf.* capsule 855) which made possible its classification

this apparatus has the special feature of emitting several sounds simultaneously and is characteristic in this respect of the cacophonic tendencies of the civilization which brought it forth (Shedim! Shedims! Amdukscias! Adramelewk! Andiam!)

thus we must forgo noting its musical substance shapeless and irregular in any case whose function is perhaps to emphasize the rigor of that produced by the principal apparatus

each sound from the big harpy is reinforced by a paraphernalia of drums and cymbals fairly modern in that it resembles those used by the priests of Ecarerioh in the damnation ceremony

and the brevity and isolation of these sounds arranged like feet in a line of verse

enabled F.B.I. experts after a thorough investigation of this substance and a comparison of each sound with the supreme standard

namely the great bell at the Abbey of Neo Porto (Bac! Lac! Tac! Don't delay!) said in an ancient text to sound a dominant B-flat

to reconstruct the strophic structure of the principal invocation

at the same time avoiding the powerful temptation to assimilate this sowing-music with the symphonic poems of the Ancients

for by a stroke of infernal luck the B-flat rhyme that persistently terminates each strophe is a strong reminder

that other texts of the period make much of an invocation called B-flat blues

whose lines were dodecaphonous in other words composed of twelve sounds as by notable coincidence is the fragment under study

now reference is made to this blues in the famous Shamanic manuscript known as the Collection (Lozit! Nosnhoj! Yajyaj! Sito and Situo and Suessydo! Here!)

torn page number 000 of a book fallen to dust

found in the so-called Chaptal Square Crypt on the site of ancient Paris (Lalos! Rapsaj! Ognajd! Ytnop! Shake it up!)

this text possibly cryptographic in the ultimate sense has so far eluded most minute structuralistic analyses

yet clearly stipulates the existence of three-and-twenty species of B-flats hereafter enumerated in consideration of the fact that in those times distinctions between B-flats were drawn accordingly as they were

(quotation)

1) for tuning purposes
2) long, drawn out
3) vibrant, too vibrant
4) played by Mezz Mezzrow
5) written with the left hand
6) in eight-note triplets at 120 = a quarter note
7) heard correctly

8) spoken of by the critics
9) called A-sharp by ignoramuses
10) high B-flats disguised by transposition to the lower octave (the rarest piece)
11) sounded at 477 vibrations per second
12) recorded at too low a level
13) keys to the B-flat blues
14) doubled in unison by the trombone III and the saxophone IV
15) lasting two and two-thirds beats
16) occurring in the 3rd bar of the 12th chorus of the 55th piece
17) meant to be played at 3:12:55 AM
18) played with the right hand
19) different from the previous ones
20) called B by German scholars
21) called F by Frenglish horn players
22) easily taken for E by ears with absolute pitch gone haywire
23) like all other B-flats

(end of quotation)

whence it appears that the thirteenth article in the Collection (Ekud! Eisab! Yzzid! Snave! Ys! Ys! Right away!) refers specifically to the blues in B-flat

whose pattern known to be strophic is structuralistically thinking the same as that of fragment appended hereafter

and set forth strophe by strophe with explanatory notes written collaboratively by one thousand nine hundred and sixty eight F.B.I. experts

the notation itself is deemed the only correct one in existence being the work of congruously licensed specialists

Strophe 0

so designated because upward of Strophe I which forms a complete and coherent whole

figure an undetermined number of strophes impossible to elucidate owing to the precarious condition of the phonotype

the last of these Strophe 0 incompletely set forth below in fine notation lets one hear the light drone mentioned above

the invocation of the aforesaid unidentified apparatus proceeds no farther than the second hemistich of the penultimate line of verse

henceforth chopin drum and cymbals will be the only accompaniment for the harpy song that follows

```
                                    A   D   G   F
      C   A   D   G   Bb  C   E   F   A   G   F   Bb
      G   B   G   F   A   Bb  B   C   D   Eb  E   Bb
```

Strophe 1

```
      D   C   B   Bb  G   B   G   F   A   G   Bb  A
      F   D   Gb  G   Bb  A   D   C   Db  D   E   F
      G   A   Bb  C   F   G   E   F   G   A   B   Bb
      A   Bb  B   C   Bb  A   Bb  A   G   C   F   Bb
```

in line one of this strophe and the initial hemistich of the following is adumbrated the Great Pattern (Djinnacea! Djinnlevy! Djinn-kirby! Hurry!)

a major ritual formula whose substance corresponds exactly to the full statement of the fifth strophe as shall be seen presently

eighteen feet are thus identical with the perfect model before the strophe diverges

leaving everything to indicate that this first evocation made plainly perceptible by the withdrawal of the light drone could not be prematurely pursued

the rest of the strophe offers no interest until the last seven feet of the final line which constitute a magic heptachordic formula

in keeping with the customs of the time certain sounds enjoying marked predominance are placed at the end of each line forming rhymes

for the first two A which is given eight times rhymes with F heard six times

for the last two B-flat which appears nine times rhymes with itself but in other strophes will be echoed by C or D

the untranscribable invocation of the chopin has nothing in common with that of the harpy and would even appear not to partake of the same time dimension for

its irregular sounds create families of figures that materialize and vanish too early or too late in relation to the strophe pattern as defined above

such is the case with the first ritual formula namely a heptachord based on the alternance of C with F appearing before the end of the penultimate line of Strophe 0 this invocational plurality which requires of the analyst a rigorously dichotomous approach is due to the morbid nature of the industrial age bereft as it was of the sense of globality and dominated by individualism (Htimsymmij! Htimsffuts! Htimspotenip! Don't dawdle!)

Strophe II

G	F	Eb	D	F	Bb	B	C	Db	D	G	F
A	D	Gb	G	A	Bb	D	G	B	C	E	F
A	Bb	B	C	Db	D	E	F	F	Eb	Eb	D
D	B	B	C	A	Bb	G	A	C	F	A	Bb

---

reciprocally with respect to the initial strophe in which the Great Pattern is set forth (Drib! Zerp! Zteg! Sayb! Hop to it!) it is taken up again here on the downward side

from the last five feet of the second line up to and including the fourth foot of the third

this strophe has no wealth of ritual formulae and the perfect model produces only one tetrachord toward the end of the third line

which ends with sound D seven times expressed and rhyming with a quintuple Bb

while the first two lines terminate on F which appears seven times

but here the chopin after a terrible incursion into the top register preceded by a brief feverish period of agitation

puts on fresh finery the more imperiously to implore the telluric god (Retrac! Rekab! Make it snappy!)

and while the harpy voice remains unchanged the chopin flaunts uniformity erratically pursuing its lopsided invocation

and while lopsidedness may not quite be sin it may already be exposing the ground to irregular semina cultivating the mandragore and raising the nether powers with it

---

Strophe III

Ab	G	E	F	Ab	C	E	F	A	G	Bb	A
F	D	Gb	G	Bb	A	Ab	G	B	C	E	F
A!	Bb	B	C	Db	D	G	F	A	Bb	B	C
Gb	F	Gb	F	Gb	F	Gb	F	C	F	C	Bb

This strophe richer in formulae contains a lengthy quotation of the Great Pattern (Onatsirt! Onairam! Move!)

longer even than that in the initial strophe it extends from the end of the first line up to and including the fourth foot of the third

in a grandiose adumbration of the perfect model thereby increasing the intensity of the invocation

in such degree that even before the end of the aforementioned third line there is recurrence of

the five last sounds thus enounced previously associated with a strange and exceptional perturbation to be analyzed later

one of these sounds had been granted abnormally long duration to the detriment of its neighbor

inequality which sought to counterbalance the repetition of the formula rendered here equitable and democratic as the Ancients would have said (Nysrock! Nybrass! Saxarba! Aszhazel! Fly!)

at the beginning of the fourth line follows an incantatory formula of eight feet on two alternating sounds

the lower being F which thus appears ten times in the strophe and is rhymed with A given only five times

while the strophe's final rhyme is Bb with C sounded six times each

gradually the chopin introduces some of those figures of simultaneous sounds which were a secret of the post-Christians

thus this apparatus appears an especially perverse instrument of torture

of which the Gallidemoniac world is deprived owing to a regrettable inability to reproduce its wounding mechanisms

---

Strophe IV

B	Bb	F	Bb	B	C	G	F	Gb	F	C	F
A	D	Gb	G	Bb	A	Ab	G	B	C	E	F
Gb	F	C	Gb	F	C	Gb	F	A	G	F	Bb
G	B	G	F	A	Bb	B	C	D	Eb	E	Bb

---

contrasting in this respect with the previous strophe which offers considerable invocational content

this fourth strophe retains only a single piece of the Great Pattern (Nworbyar! Egdirdleyor! Snap it up!) displaying nevertheless the peculiarity of almost exact coincidence with the second line more remarkable is the fact that the last ten feet of the last line literally reproduce the corresponding sounds in Strophe 0

although there is no disputing the predominant role of Strophe V dwelling-place of the perfect model and geometrical center of the invocation

structuralistic analysis of interrelationships concerning secondary strophes proves that kinships do exist between them

irrespective of the structure of the Grand Pattern thus establishing that post-Christian society (Llewopdub! Rebbub! Sub! Tub! Gob! Come on!)

was polytheistic by nature since no absolute value was placed on references to a single sovereign principle

the function of Strophe IV is to herald the disorder both of rhyme and versification characteristic of the perfect model to come

here for example a subordinate sound such as B is given six times or as often as the rhyme Bb and only slightly more so than C

notwithstanding which sound F culminates again with ten enunciations

while the chopin carries to a climax the creaking of its forks and pulleys

then returns to clearer and more human ritual formulae

which grow more widely spaced and ventilated as soon as the strophe ends

Strophe V											
D	C	B	Bb	G	B	G	F	A	G	Bb	A
F	D	Gb	G	Bb	A	Ab	G	B	C	E	F
A	Bb	B	C	G	C	E	F	F	Eb	F	D
F	Bb	B	C	D	Db	G	F	A	G	B	Bb

this Strophe V constitutes the Great Pattern (Ila! Maalas! Aniahub! Bahihs! Bihas! Jump to it!) the perfect model and universal matrix of all forms past and future

except for the minor kinships mentioned earlier

and its culminating position in the exact center of the invocation of what the partial destruction of the phonotype has left of it is essentially mesomorphic

subsequently it behooves us to enumerate with care the sounds of which it is composed

whatever the difficulties encountered by the analyst as sound G appears here in close competition with sound F eight times given like itself

albeit G is a second class sound and hence never rhymed not even in this strophe wherein it reaches apogee nonetheless

just as B appearing six times here as in the previous strophe is yet not of rank to rhyme

a phenomenon associating here A five times heard with F and D only four times audible with a sextuple B♭

and just as again C having rhyme rank elsewhere but not here appears no less than five times that is more often than D

the other measurable sounds being G♭ and A♭ and E♭ and D♭ and E this latter given twice whereas all the former stand alone

yet complete the structure of the whole for while none of the other strophes employ all the sounds expressed in the fifth

no sound other than these appears in any of them

whence it may be inferred that the Great Pattern (Noside! Sivad! Get the lead out!) is the very image of the universe

and that the disorder whose perverse effects may be perceived here foreshadows the struggle of the Principle of Evil against the then-reigning Principle of Good (Xamaxamaxa! Step on it!) and its imminent victory

for the left side symbolizes Evil and the rhyme on the far right must fall

another sign premonitory of disturbance might be the already observed lagging phenomenon which recurs here between big harpy and chopin

however the clear human formulae appearing at the end of the previous strophe continue to be spaced with calm aeration albeit their outlines gradually change

---

Strophe VI

F	G	A	B♭	G	B	G	F	A	G	B♭	A
F	D	G♭	G	B	A	A♭	G	B	C	E	F
C	A	D	G	B	C	E	F	A	B♭	B	C
D♭	D	E	F	G	A	B♭	A	G	C	F	B♭

---

this strophe situated downward of the Great Pattern (Renrag! Dnalrag! Notrubirag! Digerrag! Come to baby!) still retains a long reminiscent fragment no less than twenty-one of its sounds appear between the fourth foot of the first line and the very end of the second

but essentially the strophe offers striking structural similitudes with Strophe III

owing not merely to the five identical sounds on which the third line ends in both instances

but also because this pentachordic formula as will be remembered was already a repetition

now this phenomenon occurs only here and significantly enough another pentachord appears three feet farther

as is to be seen by comparing the end of the second line and the middle of the following

but even more remarkable is the fact that the first pentachord should have appeared in this same third strophe at the very end of the quotation of the perfect model as does the second pentachord here

and that the latter should have preceded it so closely as to be confounded with it the common sound being precisely the one whose value was curtailed

that a sound appearing as a rhyme should immediately become the pivotal link between two magic formulae defines an incantatory nerve center that must in no wise be underestimated

especially as sound F behaves as a great dominant to use the nomenclature of the Ancients

yet never ceasing its struggle with sound G striving to assert its perturbating force as is confirmed in the course of this strophe wherein it is heard no less than nine different times

whereas A and its rhyme F appear respectively eight and seven times B♭ six times and its rhyme C five

moreover in the fourth line G is the center of a magic formula already heard at the end of the first strophe

a heptachord whose other sounds are precisely the abovementioned rhymes

and whose invocational powers in no wise corroborate those of the Great Pattern (Senyahyor! Senojnivle! Get a move on!)

as though in Strophe VI dwelling place of heresy there were a tendency to substitute one god for another Adad-Dada for Miles-Selim (Ddat and Daht! Dash!)

meanwhile the chopin continues calmly producing its airy spaces permeated with clear human values

until the introduction of a new system of nonrhythmic faintly grimacing and pernicious figures of a kind which only this apparatus proves capable of producing

```
F  Bb  F  Bb  Bb  G  E  F  C  A  C  F
C  A  D  G  A  Bb  B  C  D  G  C  F
C  F  C  F  C  D  G  ?  ?  ?  F  C
F  Bb  B  ?  ?  ?  C  F  A  G  F  Bb
```

this seventh strophe carries on the principle of recalcitration against the Great Pattern (Neb! Naeb! Namdoog! Nosirrah! Nedragaet! Get going!)

which for the first time fails to leave its imprint on any formula except perhaps at the very beginning of the fourth line

in a trichord which is an atoll of sanity pounded by a demented ocean as will be shown

for this strophe is full of many incantatory formulae which follow one another increasingly

the first involving alternation between dominant F and great rhyme Bb occurs at the very beginning of the strophe

the second composed of three repeated sounds of rhyme rank joins the last five feet of the first line with the first two of the second

next appears a pentachordic figure which will have its counterpart in the eighth strophe

then a heptachord characterized by a perfect alternation of the rhyming sounds C and F

from the eleventh foot of line two up to the included fifth foot of the next line

now this heptachord coincides highfidelitywise with the ritual formula set forth by the chopin near the end of Strophe 0

which seemingly confirms the recent insight which holds that the different invocations stemming from superimposed timbres in a single phonotype and emanating from several pieces of apparatus might be linked by some structural module

although such a staggering hypothesis would have to be substantiated by glaring evidence

for these identical formulae may simply have been inspired by Miles-Selim (Sillenod! Yrrehcnod! Ttoillenod! Make good time!)

a sardonic deity quite capable of deranging the harpy player's mind during this seventh strophe

inducing him as may be observed to draw monstrous and totally unidentifiable sounds from his apparatus

such as the series of three ??? in the second hemistich of the
third line and first hemistich of the fourth

which would incline to portend that the harpy player was allowed
to ride roughshod over his harpy break destroy annihilate it

yet the statistical disorder of the previous strophes decreases here
sound G being heard only five times

while the rhymes are F with F nine times cited

and C given ten times with B♭ heard only six

similarly the chopin striving to continue a type of incantation
which appeared at the end of Strophe VI

subjects it to only a few minor transformations at the end of this
seventh strophe

bequeathing it thus modified to

Strophe VIII

F	B♭	F	B	G	C	G	?	?	?	C	F
A	D	G♭	G	A	B♭	B	C	D♭	D	C	F
A	B♭	B	C	D	G	E	F!	—	A	C	B♭
B♭	B	B	C	A	B♭	B	C	F	A	C	B♭

---

in which the predominant sound is C nine times expressed yet not
once called upon to rhyme

but to support and enrich through its penultimate position the
rhymes of F against F sounded six times and B♭ against B♭ seven
times heard

the Great Pattern (Segdoh! Dragib! Yelim! Eitooc! Shake a leg!)
is referred to only at the very end of the second and at the beginning of the third line

following a reference to the pentachordic figure which appeared
in the previous strophe

and to the mad cacophonic trichord which was the chief accident
in it

however Strophe VIII is among the most remarkable not to say
unique

since it contains a long or double foot on F in the second hemistich of line three

which thus constitutes an exception to the isometric conformity of
the strophe

the effect of the resulting hiatus is to dissociate harpy and drum and to cut short the chopin which after showing great turbulence in repetitions of the sound F

coincidentally with the abovementioned long foot which by further coincidence also bears the same name

falls silent for a moment thus adumbrating its forthcoming disappearance

---

Strophe IX

F	Bb	Ab	G	D	C	E	F	G	A	Bb	A
A	Ab	Ab	G	A	Bb	G	D	G	C	E	F
A	Bb	B	C	G	C	E	F	C	A	C	Bb
G	C	G	F	A	Bb	B	C				

---

in this incomplete strophe the last of the preserved fragment exit the chopin toward the end of line three

a probable consequence of the long foot occupying that position in the last strophe

Strophe IX complies with the perfect model at the end of the second line and on the eight first feet of the following line

and in the last line contains a repetition of the beginning of the magic formula set forth in both Strophes IV and 0

the end of the chopin's invocation marks the beginning of that of the dense flute mentioned on the threshold of the present analysis

which unavoidably fails concerning the strophe at hand whose substance remains undecipherable for lack of four feet

though one may conjecture that the last rhyme should be a Bb

a necessary though missing confirmation that the substance heretofore analyzed is indeed the blues in B-flat the jewel of the Collection (Mutattra! Yekalbtra! Sprint!)

Final Note

now the F.B.I. experts having let this phonotype be heard by various animals chosen among the most receptive have recorded the following reactions

indifference among cats but among dogs violent repulsion manifested through desperate howls

loud whinnying and excessive nervousness among horses which with other members of the equine species became sheer panic and flight the screaming monkeys screamed and the gorillas pounded their chests ad libitum with a satisfied air

the chimpanzees snapped their fingers in rhythm at a ratio of one snap to two sounds expressed by the big harpy

the musical substance though strophic and thereby linked with dancing never once perturbed the geometrical dance of the bee

nor the majestic activities of the Accursed Turkey wholly immersed in the construction of his temple (by Bboc and Ssor Ttocs and Ppehs and Llah Llessur Tteltac and Ffolahc! Nnemaa!)

C.I.A. ANALYSIS IDENTIFICATION CARD
(dated 1955)

Object   post-Christian phonotype circular shape black waxy substance

Date of discovery   1827 (Galidemonian calendar)

Place of discovery   post-Christian crypt australic tableland

Circumstances of discovery   nonencapsulated object buried under sediment found at twilight by turkey

State of inscriptions   characters on reverse side phonotype completely illegible but on obverse side following words may be read

MILES   STAR   MICROGROOVE

as well as two slightly deteriorated words

BA   GROOVE

fairly safe conjecture with aid Ecarerioh that missing letter is S immensely facilitating interpretation phonotype subsequently accepted by experts

still legibly to be read numbers 44 and 50 which unlike above-mentioned letters were not drawn by human hand but impregnated into matter by magic process of period

Phonic condition   exposed to gyration of crank-driven detector exclusive property of Center for Infraiconology and Angelology phonotype still sound producing on small portion of obverse side not reverse as according to last century belief now recognized erroneous

Refutation previous interpretations   like faces trees or houses represented on phonotypes same period musical substance condensed by unknown magical practice in phonotype cavities has no objective existence Rrrrazzzzzen classical hypothesis preservation sound apparatus really producing music completely unfounded Mdoupik-vdowvdowvdoow firstly apparatus allegedly capable producing several sounds simultaneously cannot be never could be Ssschhhkadakadahan secondly these vehicular reproductions would have been meaningless Tounnngtbadonbdang however unfavorable Gallidemonian opinion of the Ancients thesis reducing phonotype to ancestor music box attributes them too much futility Psshhcsaarsch thirdly hypothesis hunting or sowing music anachronous since post-Christian civilization proven solely urban knew nothing of agriculture or venery Fdontdragtchickick

Modern interpretation　　C.I.A. experts restore phonotype true function magic figurine made to produce sound by laying on of hands or other psychic process on special virgin wax whose secret lost Zzzzzenvdowvdowvdoow by rendering wax soniferous Ancients obtained concrete projection subject's soul reason why no two phonotypes identical Rrrrassschhhh by inference figurines in capsule are musical representations souls distinguished individuals and figurines extra capsulae souls secondary ones Babonbdangmdoupik which hypothesis confirmed by auscultation this phonotype complex true yet far less abstruse than Young phonotype also called Athenea Hippia which never explained structuralistically will require development new method analysis Kadakadahanposshhh other legitimate interpretation expert animists maintain inscriptions concerning groove in other words subject's soul refer to lowest depths consciousness for what is lowdown is nowise like what is highup Tchickiktounnnngt consequently this phonotype would be only negative figurine soul whose positive figurine alone deemed worthy encapsulation Csaarschfdontdrag superficial analysts previous century neglected key fact Ssschhhzzzzzen contrary to rule of sacred capsules this phonotype unaccompanied by spool brown dull and shiny ribbon having undeniable protective function Vdowvdowvdoowbadonbdang before ceremony soniferisation figurine shaman wrapped neck and arms in Posshhhrrrra ligature paralyzing efforts spellcasters bent on damnation soul Mdoupiktchickik damage suffered by this phonotype proves effectiveness ribbon protection Fdontdragkadakadahan inscription star alludes natural protection astral bodies unfortunately too vague no mention which planet or aldebarranian star small or large magnitude was invoked Tounnnngtcsaarsch post-Christian tradition ascribes astral bodies circular shape in conformity nocturnal satellite since vanished Zzzzzenbadongbdang although as Aristartes said none of soul's properties

belong to body and conversely this shape determined that of phonotypes Ssschhhhposshhh but even more remarkable that musical
figurine hereafter analyzed also has circular form as observed
through minute counting of sounds produced by deep therefore
chief sound source Tchickidvdowvdowvdoow inferior sources once
audible because listed in archeological inventories now imperceptible Rrrrafoontdrag interest practically nil because of inhuman
pitch Csaarschmdoupik C.I.A. experts have transcribed chief
source in scholarly notation known as Germanic with reference
article twenty Collection Kadakadahantounnnngt allusioning that
Germanists masters all musical substance called B-flat B and B-natural H which recent research confirms unequivocally Posshhhhzzzz-
zen considering their pendular regularity sounds produced by this
source certainly convey heart beats subject Badoubdangtchickik
however certain supplementary sounds omitted in last century
transcripts also noted down in small characters Fdontdragssschhhh
these meteorites appear in same disturbed area of cycle at fixed
distance point gamma which is encounter little year and big year
Vdowvdowvdoowcsaarsch must distinguish six flaming sounds
which are A B C F G H and six quenched sounds Tounnnngtrrrra
G neutron sound depolarized characterizes hypochondria point
gamma Mdoupikkadakadahan rarely accepts proximity cold sounds
Zzzzzzentchickik F meson sound of intermediate nature unstable
with propensity meteoritic ambivalence seeks various proximities Pos-
shhhfdontdrag B electron sound overpolarized dynamic and conflictual does not tolerate propinquity non flaming sounds except in
meteoritic zone where its dominance absolute Csaarschbadoubdang
A C H proton sounds totemical components with B have functions
dependency inhibition and identification Ssschhhhtounnnngt circular structure soul demonstrated by eternal return same G neutron
sound every forty-seventh sound Kadakadahanwdowvdowvdoow
number 47 being product of 44 + 50 ÷ 2 formula found on reverse
side phonotype Rrrramdoupik time has effaced last figure Fdont-
dragzzzzzen arrangement inner cycle congruous with following
pattern Tchickikcsaarsch at seven sounds from point gamma is
invariably found an F followed seven sounds later other F Tounnn-
ngtposshhh at thirty-one sounds from point gamma is invariably
found at B twenty-three sounds from first F Badonbdangkadakada-
han these prime numbers 7 7 23 31 47 constitute a series must
consider this phonotype contains sound image soul Ancients would
have qualified serial Mdoupikssschhhh number 7 was probably
number turns around neck shaman gave tape Vdowvdowvdoowrrra

23 is number articles Collection Zzzzzencsaarsch 31 and 47 likely corresponded number of miles ancient linear measure shaman and subject should stand apart for laying on of hands.

Phonic transcript
G B A G A A D G F C A D G B C E F A C F B G H G F A B H C (first appearance of Totem with its components in disorder) D Eb E^F B D (unusual sequence heralded by its supernumerary) C H B G H G F A G B A F D Gb G (point gamma beginning new cycle) B A D C Db D E F G A B C F G E F G A H B A B H C B A (second appearance of Totem whose components are arranged quasi-symmetrically) B A G C F B G F Eb D F B H C Db D G F A D Gb G (point gamma beginning new cycle) A B D G H C E (Ancients gave name of Triplet to this sigilic figure symbolizing humanity) F A B H C (third appearance of Totem in same disorder as first) Db D E F F Eb Eb D D H (function of these doublings to announce pre-adventitiously Totem Tom Tom in order) H C A B (Paranoia Paranoia) G A C F A B Ab G E (rare example cold surroundings neutron sound conveying regression which follows perfect sadism) F Ab C E F A G B A Gb (where last century strangely heard F) D Gb G (point gamma beginning new cycle) B A Ab G B (mistaken for H in tendentious transcriptions) C E F A B H C (fourth disorderly appearance of Totem) Db D G F A B H C (fifth appearance) Gb F Gb F Gb F Gb F (such close Totemic appearances having disturbed its course cycle is recycled by cold and flaming alternation meson sound with opposite sound reestablishing hostility essential to psyche) C F C B H B F B H C G F Gb F C F A D Gb G (point gamma beginning new cycle) B A Ab G H C E (return stereotypical human sigil) F Gb F C Gb F C Gb F (these little triplets last of which is elided are sparks of Great Triplet) A G F B G H G F A B C H (sixth appearance persistent disorder of Totem) D Eb E^F B D (same meteoritical sound heralds conflictual sequence electron sound quenched sound already observed) C H B G H G F A G H A F D Gb G (point gamma beginning new cycle) B A Ab G H C E (Great Triplet in fixation phase) F A B H C (seventh appearance of Totem in quasi-apposition of visible and nonvisible) G C E F F Eb (here meson sound through narcissistic repetition struggles against ignoble proximity in which it wallows) F D F B H C D Db G^F A G^F H B (excessive and impudent hystero-meteoritical disturbances) F G A B G H G F A G B A F D Gb G (point gamma beginning new cycle) B A Ab G H C E (fourth statement of human Triplet) F C A D G

H C E (fifth and last all too human Triplet) F A B H C (second and decisive apposition between Totem in familiar disorder for its eighth appearance and vanquished abolished Triplet) Db D E F G A B A G C F B F B F B^F B (compulsive repetition with meteoritic desinence) G E F C A C F C A (septuplet involving quasi-obsessional false symmetry) DG (point gamma beginning new cycle) A B H C (ninth appearance of Totem in same disorder) D G C F C F C F C (perfectly symmetrical and obsessional septuplet preparing forthcoming disturbance) D G $\left\{ \begin{array}{l} \text{F Eb F} \\ \text{C B C} \end{array} \right.$ (this strange triplet indecipherable last century gives rise to different notations dividing C.I.A. experts into two schools) F C F B H $\left\{ \begin{array}{l} \text{F Eb F} \\ \text{C B C} \end{array} \right.$ (ditto School I advocates truth low sounds for acoustical reasons) C F A G F B F B F (symmetrical sublimatory quintuplet in place of meteoritic disturbance expected at this stage of cycle) H G C G $\left\{ \begin{array}{l} \text{F Eb F} \\ \text{C B C} \end{array} \right.$ (ditto School II maintains high sounds more compatible with cabalistic explanation in preparation) C F A D Gb G (point gamma beginning new cycle) A B H C (tenth appearance of Totem in identical disorder) Db D C F A B H C (eleventh and similar appearance of Totem separated previous one equal number of sounds whereby drive becomes intentionality assumed) D G E (extremely rare cold surroundings neutron sound producing traumatic effect) F —— (unique long sound which breaks cycle ultimate flaming point being reached) A C B B H (components of Totem in last and greatest disorder confirming proximity advent Paranoia Paranoia) H C A B (Advent) H C F A C B (imperfect echo of Totem Tom Tom following advent) F B Ab G Db (masochistic situation neutron sound is final sequel of previous great crisis) C E F G A B A A Ab Ab G (point gamma last incomplete cycle begins here) A B G D G C E F A B H C (twelfth appearance of Totem in reconstituted disorder) G C E F C A C B G C G F A B H C (thirteenth and last appearance after which ruined phonotype becomes silent).

Appraisal

countless phototypes archeological collections studied by C.I.A. iconographers show half naked or even totally undressed women Fdontdragtounnnngt phenomenon obviously inconceivable as objective reality in society in which man had not yet understood necessity submission to Powers of Evil Kadakadahantchickik proves on the contrary that ancient phototype magical representation secret imaginings of subject Passhhhmdoupik similarly thorough examination phonotype heretofore considered shows unconscious effort subject to picture to self Totem Tom Tom B A C H Rrrrabadonbdang perfect state hallucinatory paranoia many times found by C.I.A. experts on phonotypes in capsulae figuring also in surviving period manuscripts Ssschhhvdowvdowvdoow yet would be ill considered omit that subject after several reproductions in disorderic state and first premature hallucination comparable to first rays daybreak destined to greater and more complete glory finally succeeds in voicing taboo name only through inversion Tounnnngtzzzzzen barring inaudible continuation phonotype but this remains conjectural Csaarschkadakadahan subject displaying strong Thanatic and Gallidemonic instincts of repetition Mdoupikfondtdrag now any ancient totemic inversion necessarily adumbrates modern Gallidemonic world Tchickikrrrra since Scriptures say tengier tnetopinmo Dog Drol eht rof Aiulella is exact retrogradation of Alleluia for the Lord God omnipotent reignet Vdowvdowvdowposshhh appears therefore that this phonotype is figurine antechrist martyr Badonbdangssschhhh whose image deliberately profaned was driven from capsule yet Destiny servant of Ecarerioh could not be diverted from bequeathing it to present times Kadakadahanzzzzzzen which figurine thus being destined hottest prices and explosive bidding Tounnnngtmdoupik for nothing in Gallidemonia so precious as beautiful flaming soul Rrrrrraaaassschhhh

PART TWO

THE
SENSE
OF VALUES

Quiz

Seventeen Canons in Enigma Form

1) The world supports Christ. Christ supports Christopher. Whom
does Christopher support?
   a) Addie.
   b) Leon.
   c) A shadow--since Christopher does not exist.

2) Another Christopher, i.e. Columbus, was a great creator. Why?
   a) Because Fletcher Henderson arranged him.
   b) Because he put together a band.
   c) Because he managed to get together three caravels and made
      jazz possible.

3) Sitting on a pile of your favorite records, you let your legs dangle, dreaming of new purchases. And now your feet touch the floor. Why?
   a) You have converted from 78 rpm to 33⅓.
   b) You have grown taller.
   c) The rats in your drawers are jazz fans.

4) Who said: "The arranger composes, the composer discomposes"?
   a) a musician.
   b) the public.
   c) both.

5) Except for Sammy Junior, whose case remains dubious, all the Davises have, at one time or another, been awarded the Beauty Prize. Who won it in 1966?
   a) Kay.
   b) Miles.
   c) Richard.

6) Does a bass-line running from the deepest audible notes to the extreme treble convey:
   a) the bass-player's technical naivete (existentialist sense)?
   b) his manic-depressive pattern (psychoanalytical sense)?
   c) the obsession of a bass-player who lives on the seventh floor of an old house (structuralist sense)?

7) Does a bass-line stabilized in the medium register convey:
   a) the blasé bass-player's loss of technical innocence (he has become an existentialist)?
   b) his new-found mental balance due to therapy (psychoanalysis)?
   c) an improvement in his standard of living—the elevator has entered his life (structuralism)?

8) *Surnames.* With Green, Greenwood (ex-Lawrence of Arabia), Cohen, and Hen Gates, how many three-man combos could you form?
   a) five: 1. vibraphonist + pianist + arranger
             2. vibraphonist + arranger + arranger
             3. vibraphonist + pianist + pianist
             4. arranger + arranger + pianist
             5. pianist + pianist + arranger.
   b) seven: the above, plus
             6. pianist + pianist + pianist

7. arranger + arranger + arranger.
   c) six (combination number 7 being impracticable).

9) Can you give the titles:
   a) of fifty-five songs which have been Number One on the Hit Parade?
   b) Can you only give twelve?
   c) Are you incapable of naming even three?

10) Why are jazz scores generally written in pencil?
   a) Because it's easier to erase than to scratch out.
   b) Because the brand of ink would influence the writer's unconscious while writing.
   c) Because jazz scores are like cheap shoes: they're not made to last.

11) Forty-three years in deep freeze made the Unfinished Symphony an immediate success. What jazz record would have reaped comparable benefits from similar treatment?
   a) an early Ellington.
   b) a late King Oliver.
   c) neither.

12) Who was Gemelli Careri?
   a) A gymel-singer (old-style Renaissance blues).
   b) A sailor who survived the Siren's song.
   c) The discoverer of the cradle-nest turkey, ancestor of the chorus-blower.

13) What other animals go to make up the jazz menagerie?
   a) cat, dog, horse.
   b) grand-duke owl, drawer-rat, Missouri nightingale.
   c) screaming monkey, growing chimpanzee, gorilla drummer, dancing bee.

14) Who described Duke Ellington as an "inspired director of hybrid scripts"?
   a) an unlucky colleague.
   b) a disappointed admirer.
   c) both.

15) Did the work *Balanced Scales = Justice* have the privilege of being
   a) composed by Tom McIntosh?

b) arranged by Tom McIntosh?

c) composed and arranged, or more precisely, arranged and composed by Tom McIntosh?

16) How many splicings does it take to make a living by editing?

a) As many as a pop star requires.

b) As many as the leader of a famous string quartet thinks necessary.

c) As many as a jazz composer would like.

17) Does a truth obliquely expressed cease to be true?

a) yes, unfortunately.

b) no, unfortunately.

c) maybe, fortunately.

FOR KEY AND RATING, see page 138.

A Lecture, Followed by
a Television Panel Filmed
in the Spirit of Cinéma Vérité

I

The development—the development, not the existence—of jazz in the Western world still has many surprises in store for us. A form of music with such diverse potentialities has the power to assail our sensibility from all sides and on every level. But then, of course, we are prepared to cope with this siege: contemporary society has taught us to build defenses against the environment which it creates. More disturbing is the evolution of the most vigorous branch of jazz, commonly called "modern"; composed as it is of a succession of attainments and renouncements, it requires constant reappraisal. Every new choice constitutes a reassessment of a past opinion.

The situation would be less complex were it not for the fact that this deluge of creative activity enables part of jazz to rise above the world of mass consumption in which its lowermost strata are, after all, buried, that weird world in which mass music pullulates like some monstrous plant life, a world that resembles Nazi Germany insofar as it ruthlessly equates success with truth, a world governed by a single unwritten law: *whatever is successful, is good*. Such and such a song is a masterpiece; it has brought in a million dollars. As for its twin, whose title did not happen to catch the public ear, there are doubts as to its very existence. Does a dance record that sells less than 100,000 copies exist at all? Thus the *Billboard* ratings accurately determine the intrinsic value of each marketed product. However, a work of art is not a consumer product; it lives and dies according to internal forces, hangs neglected or revered on a museum wall with no memory of how or why it was born. At the time of its birth, who can evaluate its power and glory? The critics? They would have to be prophets. Our Parthenons and Mona Lisas will be recognizable as such only after our death. Until then, how respectfully or contemptuously should we regard them?

To avoid passing judgment, some people resort to classifying: "This music is not jazz," they decide, simply because it does not make use of their favorite beat, or contains no precise reference to a blues style which they hold sacred. And this refusal to judge is a judgment in itself. Others righteously reject all classifications: "Let's not talk about jazz," they say, "let's just talk about music. Our only criteria should be musical!" Who is it that takes these radical stands, one way or the other? It is us. And we have each taken both at different times.

Each of us has been a classifier. We have liked a certain quality in a certain kind of jazz. If another kind lacks that quality, our reflex may be to exclude it from the world of jazz. "It has no soul," or "there's not enough improvising" (or any one of a hundred other reasons), "ergo, it isn't jazz." We want jazz to be just for us, we need to be protected and reassured. Familiar surroundings are the best shield against fear. We wage a preventive war, destroying the enemy before he can destroy us, before we even know that he is an enemy. Thus, anything that cannot immediately be assimilated to an already familiar and admired model, is destroyed before it can affect our sensibility in any way.

Each of us has also been a rejector of classifications. In all sincerity, we have tried to assess jazz as musicians rather than jazz musicians, as music lovers rather than jazz fans. "What do I care whether it's jazz at all so long as it's good music? For example, what does it matter if the steady beat is dropped when it is amply compensated for by the rich possibilities of the variable beat?" We want jazz to realize all its potentialities, we want it to merge with the full universality of music.

At the same time we are aware of having gone too far. Sensing that we are on uncertain ground, we cast about for a safety rail to guard us against falling into the absurd. For as it moves from steady beat to free beat, from tonality to atonality, as it gives up old techniques and turns to new ones, jazz may gradually lose its distinguishing features. And where will it stop? With Schuller? Stravinsky? Stockhausen? Fairly far, in any case, from what is commonly called jazz.

In this perspective, there is no sturdier safety rail than the traditional appeal to the element of swing. "If the swing feeling is the major ingredient in the essence of jazz, then jazz ends where swing does." This is sound logic; the problem seems to be solved; we have found an apparently foolproof safety rail. Yet one small question is enough to undermine our certainty: are we absolutely sure that we can recognize swing in all its forms?

A half century of jazz has taught us that swing has hundreds of different guises . . . and that it can die.

Swing is many faceted. Frankie Trumbauer did not swing like John Coltrane. And this is not simply a matter of periods. Louis Armstrong does not swing like Roy Eldridge, who in turn does not swing like Dizzy Gillespie. Nor is it a matter of schools. Let us take three different combinations with one common denominator: Monk–Blakey, Monk–Clarke, Monk–Roach. All of them can be said to fall within the framework of a same school, yet they offer three different kinds of swing, three types of forces responding to different impulses. There is not one kind of swing, there are many; "swing," as such, just does not exist.

We must push our investigations further. In order to appraise a musician's swing, a distinction should perhaps be made between quantity and quality, difficult as these are to measure. Milt Jackson may swing *less* than Lionel Hampton (the drive is not so strong) but he swings *better* (his rhythmic sensibility is more developed). Swing may be conventional or vulgar (Roland Kirk, Les McCann); it may be "far out," or wild (Elvin Jones, Charlie Parker). Here is a glimpse of evaluation at its most subjective. We will come back to this problem later.

Swing is a form of magic. It may lose its power at any time. A piece that seemed so swinging yesterday may not seem so at all today. "Why shouldn't it swing any more?" "Why do works of art so seldom retain their beauty?" We are beginning to realize that works of art move in a world as ruthless as the ocean depths: it is kill or be killed, eat or be eaten. What we call swing may, as we believe, be a vehicle of beauty, but beauty itself is no guarantee of immortality. Quite the contrary: a threat hangs over every form of beauty from its very inception. One of its essential aspects may cease to be perceptible; or else beauty may appear in another form, similar to but greater than the first, and eclipse it entirely. Such and such a sax player, whom we once thought capable of swinging all his life, suddenly ceased to swing for us after we first heard Charlie Parker. His music had been alive in our minds and hearts; now it was dead. It had been eaten.

True, it is still alive in other minds and hearts. But what can this matter to us? It lives on the way Stalin and Mussolini live on in old newsreels. The worshiping crowds still raise their arms in salute; they are no more obsolete than the jazz fans who remain oblivious to the Parker holocaust. What is dead for us is truly dead; only our own inconsistency could bring it back to life.

Yet where death is possible, so is birth. However great our dismay when familiar figures decline and disappear, it is far greater when caused by the invariably unexpected appearance of a new one.

The days are apparently gone forever when the appreciation of swing was a shared subjective truth. This was certainly an estimable standard of appreciation. Jazz used to be a simple, well-organized world in which values were seldom contested. In the old days, no jazz musician worthy of the name could fail to notice a really outstanding exponent of swing playing in a band entirely made up of good swingers. Enlightened spectators at a cutting contest would invariably applaud the soloist who outplayed all the others; whether his name was Chu, Bean, or Prez, he was the hero of the day. Those, however, were the days when jazz was still a popular art. We all know how deeply it has been transformed by the forceful personalities that it has produced. As jazz became increasingly diversified, criteria became a matter of schools. Today, however, the individual musician seems to take precedence over the group around him. This has brought a change of perspective; consensus of opinion is a less meaningful notion than it used to be. If a musician is an original creative artist, on what grounds are we to decide that he doesn't swing? And even if we feel that he doesn't, whom can we take as a comparison? What if Elvin Jones's playing were a refutation rather than an extension of Kenny Clarke's and Max Roach's? What if Ornette Coleman's were a refutation of Charlie Parker's?

The multiplicity of swing is an obstacle to evaluation which cannot be overcome by the defunct notion of shared subjective truth. Simply because everyone else agrees with us, we are not necessarily right, even if "everyone else" means the majority of professional musicians. We may grasp Louis Armstrong's, Count Basie's, or Charlie Parker's swing, but a new kind of swing might catch us unprepared.

A new kind of swing means, in one sense, a new kind of freedom and a new kind of order. The relationship between the two may or may not be immediately apparent. This is where an element of uncertainty creeps in. Are we listening to the tentative gropings of a clumsy innovator? Are we listening to a feeble, distorted imitation of an established model? Or does this apparent disorder conceal a deep coherence which may become clear to us at any moment? Perhaps we are dealing with the highest form of beauty in today's jazz. In a case like this, we can only let our musical intuition be our guide. It has been developed through repeated contacts with the objective realities of the past. Now it must serve as our compass.

The music played by a jazz artist is jazz. Fine. This musician whose music swings is a jazz artist; he is playing jazz. Fine. But what about that other man, whose music, in our view, does not swing? Is he a jazz artist playing jazz? And if so, are we in the wrong? This is where we turn to our compass; we shake it this way and that; we discover how fragile it is; but let us avoid referring to the opinion of this or that eminent colleague. He may well be as wrong as we are, for we are entering an age of disruptors.

And so our brake is useless. True, there are all sorts of others available. A European will accept any widening of the scope of jazz so long as it comes from the U.S.A. He feels that Americans have the same right of life or death over jazz that fathers had over their children in ancient societies. Even if he is not understood, the disruptor will be welcomed with open arms provided he is American— and preferably a Black, at that. Conversely, the European jazzman is trapped in a hopeless dilemma: either he is despised as an imitator or, if he does not imitate, accused of disfiguring. However, if this really is the age of disruptors, will the equation "jazz = American music" hold true forever? Why shouldn't a disruptor come from the end of the earth?

A century or two ago, when Western music was still impervious to the "enrichment" of non-European cultures, its capacity for growth was self-contained. The attainment of a new form in the eighteenth century, and of a new style in the nineteenth, enlarged the structures of tonal music without destroying its foundation. At that time, musical art seemed mainly the business of the German-speaking peoples; yet Chopin and Berlioz, though they lacked some of the outstanding qualities of the great German musicians, cannot be accused of either imitating or disfiguring. Should a European jazzman prove capable of making a similar contribution, should his creation, evolved within the framework of jazz, prove to be coherently balanced and organized, however much it might disrupt, stylistically or otherwise, on what grounds could we possibly reject it?

This brake, then, is no better than the first. We live in a world which is dangerous, an adult world from which all brakes must be banished, even at the cost of our own peace of mind.

II

Perhaps we can better come to grips with a work of jazz if we assess it in purely musical terms. Beyond the general outlines that establish it as a work of jazz, there must exist intrinsic criteria which can serve to define its originality. Is it possible to isolate and evaluate these criteria? If so, would this not do away with the need to refer constantly to listening habits—or to a tradition—that weigh so heavily on our opinions? If the basic responsibilities were assumed by our musical intuition, would this not constitute a decisive, liberating step?

We are alone with the music we love. While we listen to it, it exists only in our soul. Do we really love it unless we do so for itself alone, regardless of the rest of jazz?

Our musical intuition tells us that Charlie Parker is still alive. We appreciate in his music certain qualities which we know to be characteristic of jazz, which refer to a familiar language. However, its lasting beauty is not due merely to the fact that those qualities are characteristic of jazz—this would be insufficient—but to the coherence and rigor of the structures which they bring to life. Many other jazz musicians are dead, even if they are still listed among the living, because the jazz characteristics in their music were less tightly knit together and failed to form an indestructible whole. Evaluating Parker in terms of criteria established by his music means, for example, properly appreciating a certain relationship between the tension created by his sound and the construction of his phrasing. This relationship partakes of the essence of jazz; it is all to the credit of jazz; but above all, it is a source of musical beauty which is inseparable from Parker's work and which not even his imitators can take from him.

This analytical approach to musical perception may seem oversubtle. It presupposes a keen ear and a thorough familiarity with jazz. However, it seems better suited to accounting for the achievements and failures of jazz. The mediocrity of a musician like Dave Brubeck should be self-evident: there is no need to do him the unwarranted injustice of excluding him from jazz altogether.

Though these are latent criteria, they do nevertheless have a kind of objective existence; they constitute an area of appreciation on which it is possible to shed light through analysis. Outside that area lie the dark dominions of pure subjectivity. When we move from the musical plane to the poetic, we sense clearly that values are no longer the same. True, there exists a close though indefinable relationship between the creative act and its consequences. Yet these consequences take place in us. Thus, the values peculiar to jazz seem ultimately to refer us back to human values in general, to values of a directly personal nature.

There is no way of predicting from one moment to the next the degree of musical achievement of a work of jazz, for it knits and unknits itself as it moves along. Certain potentialities are realized, others are not; the work attains its objective or it does not. However, we cannot simply refuse to evaluate a work's poetic qualities, its level of aesthetic achievement; otherwise, we should have to regard a Strauss waltz as the equivalent of a Bach chorale. Reluctant as we may be to classify works according to genre (what can be more ridiculous than a bad tragedy?), we must not lose our sense of values. Even in the unsettled universe of improvised jazz, certain basic preliminary choices rigorously determine the negative limits of a work. We cannot predict what it will be, but we can predict what it cannot be. Apish society players cannot possibly attain the emotional intensity of Parker's great paraphrases. At times, the choice of a theme is enough to determine the elevation or triviality of an unborn work. When Monk sits down to play *Smoke Gets in Your Eyes*, he is momentarily cutting himself off from a certain level of beauty which he might have reached had he chosen *Evidence*. This does not mean that his version of Kern's tune will not be interesting. If he is in the right mood he may even extract from it a work of jazz better than a run-of-the-mill version of *Evidence*. However, he is obliged to enter into a relationship with the theme which is such as to give even the most subtle developments a vulgar tinge and continually tends to pull the work downward.

What is vulgar? What is elevated? There is no rule or principle which can decide for us. A work's degree of ambition is no criterion: the world of jazz has its nouveaux riches, too. But neither is lack of ambition a sign of elevation; we tend to regard it rather as an admission of impotence. Something deep inside us seems to respond to a force of attraction or repulsion before we can even form an opinion. Music which we will later condemn as "stupid" or "contemptible" arouses an immediate reaction of physical repugnance. Yet others take pleasure in this same music, which in some cases may be well written—though not necessarily. The best approach to these telling discords is a humorous one. Experience has taught us that on this level of subjectivity, discussion is not desirable. Courtesy inclines us to conceal our nausea and stifle our laughter; intellectual integrity demands that we assume our responsibilities. It is a matter of individual temperament.

There is a tendency today to put a rather loose interpretation on the principle of intellectual steps as defined by Paul Valéry and to rehabilitate facile works insofar as they are supposed to prepare us gradually for the masterpieces. Yet if this is the hidden purpose of such works, why do they flout all the basic values of the art to which they are supposed to provide an introduction? When we are told that this or that rock 'n' roll number is an initiation to the higher forms of jazz, we can only wonder how a plea in favor of mental and emotional deficiency can lead to self-surpassing. Are we dealing with some mystical process by which Tom Jones and Elvis Presley, through successive reincarnations, each stupider and more decadent than the last, finally become Monk and Parker? We see no need to stoop so low. Why bother with these hideous caricatures when the world of jazz has its respectable minor artists, perfectly suited for this intermediary role? One Ella Fitzgerald should spare us a hundred Nancy Sinatras. There are countless works of jazz with enough immediate appeal to provide stepladders for those who have not yet learned to jump. However, we must be careful not to overrate the importance of these pieces: there are so many of them that they would soon blot out the landscape altogether.

Our sense of rigor tells us that there is no such thing as a small masterpiece, barring, possibly, the criterion of dimension. In the long-range view, a perfect achievement in an inferior genre is a trivial one. The work of Tatum, brilliant and even faultless though it may be from a certain standpoint, calls to mind a doctor's comment on a surgeon's brilliant operation: "It shouldn't have been performed at all." An underdeveloped critical sense will degrade a work of jazz; an overdeveloped one will stifle it. If Hank Jones were not such a careful pianist both technically and stylistically, his music might reveal a more vital creative impulse. Which should we prefer: the perfect neutrality of one person or the decorative zest of someone else? The question is immaterial. As an alternative to this kind of jazz, we propose another which, imperfect as it is, attests to the existence of poetic truths of an entirely different order. We deliberately chose Charlie Parker and Thelonious Monk as examples. When our musical intuition speaks out with such strength and clarity on their behalf, how can we imagine that we could be wrong? Our conviction could be shaken only by a contradictor whose musical intuition we consider to be equal or superior to ours. However, is there anyone in the jazz world who disputes the historical preeminence of Charlie Parker? And if so, whom does he rate above him? It hardly seems necessary to argue with those who take the "genius" of Ray Charles literally. Errol Garner also has unmistakable qualities and the Jazz Messengers are said to express a commendable drive. But what of it? After what Parker and Monk have brought to jazz, why dwell on these affable talents? After twenty years' reflection, are we going to repudiate the strange fever that completely transformed jazz toward the end of World War II? Are we going to join in the heavy-handed efforts to set it back on the straight and narrow path of popular music? Are we going to concede that its aspirations toward something greater, something madder, were empty after all? In spite of Coltrane's example, must we give up all hope of convulsive ecstasy? Beyond Miles Davis, is there no further chance for unearthly rapture? Admittedly, jazz may have lost its way; however, the facile, naively systematic search for a paroxysmic expression conducted by musicians incapable of inventing the ways and means of their revolution does at least deserve respect—if we exclude the fakers with their eye on the public—insofar as it rules out any return to a system which now seems definitely obsolete.

III

However, a valid contestation does exist: it is from outside that the world of jazz is mostly bitterly disputed. Indeed, very respectable musicians simply reject Charlie Parker—along with all the rest of jazz. One of the most famous, making fresh use of Eric Satie's expression, equates jazz with "background music," and regards this as its only justification. Such a radical opinion apparently creates a forbidding alternative: either we shut ourselves up in our ivory tower, drape ourselves in righteousness, and maintain that ours is the keener musical intuition (a king does not duel with his subjects), or else we accept the truth of our opponent's assertion and anxiously begin to wonder whether we have not been on the wrong track all our lives. If this were so, the most rigorous thinkers among us would certainly look silly! Fighting eclecticism in all its forms, they would have condemned Brahms, Ravel, and Tchaikovsky in the name of the highest musical values, and at the same time been heaping love and praise on a by-product of industrial society, on "background music"! What a strange aberration!

A bit too strange, perhaps. . . . This alternative stems from our sensibility alone. Let us see whether reason cannot surmount it.

We shall disregard the argument that our famous composer's opinion is a result of ignorance, that he misjudges jazz because he is not really familiar with it. This kind of argument is too banal, too trivial to hold our attention. Let us suppose, on the contrary, that the prosecution has studied the brief, that it is not attacking jazz in its lowest forms but in its highest. Why are its conclusions still diametrically opposed to those of the defense?

Let us borrow an example from Einstein: an observer inside an elevator car and another on the landing looking through the glass door have very different interpretations of the phenomenon which they are watching. Perfectly logical chains of reasoning lead them to opposite conclusions. Let us bring this relativistic outlook to bear on our problem. If we may be allowed to borrow a term from physics, we might say that defense and prosecution have different *systems of coordinates*. Imagine them both listening to a Charlie Parker record. Can we really be sure that both are hearing the same music? In a sense, we cannot. Whenever dissimilar cultural references produce different systems of coordinates, interpretations of the facts cannot be identical, either qualitatively or quantitatively.

Either qualitatively or quantitatively: in our field, this means that differences in systems of coordinates affect the actual perception of the facts. The observer outside the elevator may simply not see certain events that take place inside, as though he were looking through a frosted pane. Jazz has perhaps brought on more cases of organic blindness than any other art. In this connection we might cite a fortuitous experiment carried out with the unintentional help of a clasically-trained musician with a keen ear, capable of reading the most difficult scores. This excellent musician was put in charge of a recording session. Had he been dealing with a piece of "classical" music, it would be inconceivable that any serious errors of execution could have escaped his notice. However, the score before him was a work of written jazz, and errors and omissions accumulated in rapid succession without drawing any reaction from him. This was because he *did not hear* the music that he had been asked to supervise; his system of coordinates was such that he was unable to grasp it organically.

True, our famous composer has never lent himself to a similar experiment. We have no reason to assume that the results would be the same, for his musical perception is known to be very highly developed. Let us grant that he is the exception, that for him the glass door in the elevator is perfectly transparent. It does not necessarily follow that his training, his cultural background, his commitments, his thought patterns—in short, everything that has made him what he is—have prepared him to experience the magic of jazz. We feel, on the contrary, that the phenomena which he is witnessing cannot mean to him what they mean to us. What can swing mean to this pioneer in "irrational rhythmics"? Or the chorus player's circumscribed improvising to a composer who has made such extensive use of aleatoric structures?

In return, a hypothetical condemnation of serial music coming from a jazz artist—but what jazz artist would dare voice it?—would also be primarily motivated by this difference between two systems of coordinates: the man of jazz would be incapable of appreciating the organic coherence of musical phenomena which have nothing in common with those that form the substance of his everyday musical activities.

Of course, well-meaning critics may regard our attempt to introduce a relativistic viewpoint as an unwitting deception, a stratagem aimed at clouding the aesthetic issues which we claim to be studying. "An extension of this curious method of investigation," they might retort, "would lead us to wonder whether there is not artistic value in certain reputedly minor forms of expression such as the pop song. Might not Maurice Chevalier's talent, which some regard as undeniable, transfigure songs like *Valentine* and *Prosper*? After all, Maurice's career goes back prior to the first Original Dixieland record. Who is to say that within a given system of coordinates, Chevalier is not Joyce or Picasso?" We could reply that such a system of coordinates is inconceivable; otherwise it would already have been conceived of. Chevalier's world is immediately accessible; no one has ever been stricken with perceptual blindness before *Prosper* or *Valentine*.

If, on the contrary, our suggestion is valid, it calls forth two immediate consequences. First, we cannot go on rejecting all classifications and at the same time pretend that our value judgments are absolute. One cannot be both inside and outside the elevator. In the second place, the alternative we spoke of no longer exists. It hardly matters who is right, those who claim that jazz is worthy of interest or those who claim that it is not, since they are not referring to the same system of coordinates. Arbitrating the elevator conflict, Einstein points out that "it is impossible to choose between the viewpoints of the two observers," since "each could claim the right to relate all the events to his system of coordinates" and since "both descriptions may be equally coherent." Similarly, from the point of view of an observer whose system of coordinates is neither the jazz artist's nor the serial composer's, the conflict between jazz and serial music would probably resolve itself as an equivalence.

However, who could this observer be? Where would he come from? Could he be a refined musician of Far Eastern culture, a Vietnamese bonze or Tibetan monk? Should we bring forth from the depths of a primitive culture some Alakuluf paddler or Ona medicine man? Another observer might as well come down from Venus, still another from the seventh galaxy: their arbitration would be no more irrelevant. Serial composers and jazz musicians are all in the same boat, and its name is Western Civilization. We are no more universal than the society which nurtures our ambitions, witnesses our failures, and in whose mirror we must contemplate ourselves.

IV

We are faced here with a basic paradox. Our relativistic approach is not operative from one culture to another, as we might have expected, but within a closed world. We are living at a strange conjuncture. A century ago, Western music, in spite of the traditional distinctions between serious, light, and folk music, had a basic unity. Johann Strauss did not betray Schumann, while Liszt, on occasion, could join forces with the Hungarian peasant. Today, things are very different; no intercourse or mutual influence is conceivable between serial music and jukebox tunes. The situation would be clear enough if the evolution of jazz had not upset everything and ruined the historian's peace of mind. For indeed, just what is the nature of this *other* music which claims to be equally representative of our culture and which, like the Western music of the past, has its own internal hierarchies? What is this music which was once folk music and no longer is, which grew up in a ghetto and has such a deep influence on the mass music of the world, which contains, moreover—and in various forms!—its own mass music? What is this music that exists on several levels, with rock 'n' roll at the bottom and the disturbing inventions of Charlie Parker and Thelonious Monk at the top?

Here we have a form of coexistence unique in the history of Western civilization. True, it was prefigured in the Middle Ages when the trouvères and troubadours lived side by side with the

austere church polyphonists. However, the music of the troubadours was only superficially diversified; it involved almost no aesthetic hierarchy. Moreover, the hiatus was only apparent; with the
appearance of a composer like Adam de la Halle, profane music
took over techniques which until then had been considered the
prerogative of sacred music. And when the two streams joined, it
became apparent that their waters were the same.

The antithesis which concerns us here is far more radical. Naive
though it may seem, our image of two systems of coordinates does
convey fairly well the parallel between jazz and serial music. There
is something shocking about this shared sovereignty. The mind balks
at it. And however much we may suffer from the injustices involved
in the negative attitude toward jazz adopted by serial composers,
generally so responsive to the myriad attractions of non-European
traditions, we do ultimately understand it. All things considered,
this attitude seems more realistic than the pious wishing of those
who innocently believe that sooner or later there will be a fusion of
the two kinds of music. Such a coalescing would be miraculous, for
there are no morphological similarities pointing to any such synthesis.

The serial universe is one of discontinuity. It is based on a set of
privative attributes (atonality, asymmetry, athematicism) held together by the unifying principle of the serial concept. Here the
conflict between tension and relaxation, the key to all music, takes
on new meaning. The serial framework suggests ways of renewing
this conflict through the treatment of two components which had
only secondary importance in classical music: rhythm and timbre.
The notion of discontinuity has not simply done away with classical
accentuation and tonal rhetoric, it has also given birth to a new type
of "irrational" rhythm (in which the development of a rhythmic
pattern is not reducible to a single note value) and cast timbre as
such in an active role, tending to incorporate it into the polyphonic
texture (the various timbres are subjected to a variation process and
to a continual osmosis, involving attacks and dynamics, factors
which are a function of both timbre and rhythm).

Jazz musicians responded very differently to the need to renew
the conflict between tension and relaxation, although here, too,
rhythm and timbre play major roles. (This reversal of emphasis is
characteristic of our century and invalidates Olivier Messiaen's
famous proposition: "Let melody remain king.") The chief difference is that while discontinuity sometimes plays an important part
in jazz, jazz in itself does not constitute a universe of discontinuity.
Here, the handling of timbre (the variations of sound production in

a soloist's playing) becomes a factor of variable tension overlaying the "active relaxation" (also variable) achieved by the soloist through swing. Various other aspects of the musical fabric may serve to create tension: the melodic line, the complexion of the individual chord, and its relative position on the scale of harmonic degrees. Another powerful factor of tension is the rhythmic construction of the phrase; syncopated notes, accents, and even the beat itself can reduce or increase tension. Finally, it is the rhythmic "density" which determines—mainly on the interpretive level, but also on the conceptual—the phenomenon of swing and, thereby, that of relaxation. These different elements interact, forming the dialectics of jazz.

Despite their schematic brevity, these descriptions ought to shed light on one important fact: serial structures, as a result of their discontinuity, enjoy utter freedom in both time and space (defining as they do their own limits through the serial principle), whereas jazz structures are linked to preexisting principles. The most advanced jazz contests these principles; but to contest is not to abolish. The syncopated note contests the beat, the asymmetric phrase the four-bar pattern, and dissonance the tonal principle. These contestations help to enrich the language of jazz; the aesthetic benefits which the great jazz artists can derive from them are obvious to anyone living within our system of coordinates, provided, though, that tonality, the four-bar pattern, and a steady beat be taken for granted as constituting the immutable essence of the mechanics of jazz. To do away with them would be to sap the very foundations of jazz, for it is our belief that discontinuity can exist in jazz only against a background of continuity.

V

When we attempt to define how this dialectics is implemented, we naturally look to the most highly sophisticated jazz, to the music we hold to be the most rewarding within the specific confines of jazz. Not Ray Charles, but Monk; not even Armstrong, but Charlie Parker. For obvious reasons, *that* jazz cannot hope, any more than serial music, to enjoy the attention of the general public, who are not equipped to experience swing beyond its most rudimentary form: the dance appeal. It is easy to imagine the average listener's accusations of esotericism; they are the same as those generally aimed at serial music. "It has no form, no melody!" This is invariably the way those who cannot hear how Monk recomposes the material derived from the exploded theme react to *I Should Care*.

However, simply because the best jazz, like serial music, is likely to meet with widespread incomprehension, it does not follow that they are blood relations. Certain characteristics of jazz, as mentioned above, are so foreign to the spirit of serial music that if they were transplanted they would constitute unacceptable limitations.

Yet it is these very characteristics which provide the substance of the dialectics of jazz. The limitations of the jazz musician's language offer a challenge that fires his imagination, and an obstacle that he never completely overcomes. This is what makes creation in jazz possible; it is also what makes it difficult. There are thousands of ways to play the game. Some musicians—the majority—choose to ignore the challenge and avoid the obstacle; others yield to their fascination for the absurd, for the vertigo of the unknown. It is impossible to maintain the level of one's highest accomplishments, and even the greatest musicians sometimes weaken, lapsing back into popular music (from which even the most advanced jazz has never yet completely freed itself), or indulging in empty posturing. Jazz is not perfect; jazz has not reached complete fulfillment. Yet whenever a perilous balance is achieved on those peaks that are so difficult to climb, we know that jazz is worth our while. Only then does it capture an essential facet of contemporary poetics, only then is it an art.

Are the friends of jazz therefore destined to wait for the sky to catch fire, or at the very least for a shooting star to pass? Fortunately, experience has taught us that great jazz artists "find themselves" often enough so that we need not regard beauty in jazz as a statistically improbable contingency. However, we must not fool ourselves; in the best jazz, failure is the rule, success the exception. Paradoxical though it may seem, this is not true on every level. "The lower a jazz musician's aesthetic ambition, the better his chances of successful accomplishment." If there is any truth in this law, it means that there is little risk of failure on the aesthetic level of Louis Jordan or Fats Domino. After all, sociologists teach us that mass culture shuns failure, both personal and social (whereas the contemporary artist lives in the shadow of failure, is actually drawn to it). Of course, in dealing with these lower reaches of our system of values, we have long ago left the field of art for that of *entertainment;* and we can only concur with anyone who described *this* jazz as "background music," reserving for ourselves the bitter satisfaction of pointing out in return that the countless Franz Lehars and Edith Piafs of jazz are merely the counterparts of the puerile Saint-Saëns and shamefaced Saties who make up the bulk of serial composers.

Failure, as against success; art, as against entertainment. These distinctions are clear within our system of coordinates; they may be invisible to an outside observer. Yet it is hard to accept the idea that our serial composer should fail to find any difference between Monk and Bill Doggett. In the jazz that we admire, we feel that he ought to recognize some of his own concerns. Both forms of music are products of the same era and both tend toward the same "convulsive beauty," even though they can achieve it only at opposite poles, even though the word "Dionysiac" has a different meaning in each case. However, their coexistence is not universally accepted. How can a dialogue be started?

Are the barriers separating the two kinds of musicians insuperable? The imperatives of technical specialization would seem to indicate that for the present they are. It is unthinkable that a serial musician playing the piano in a jazz quintet could produce anything but a pale caricature of Monk or Solal. And a jazz arranger's attempt to write a serial score could only result in a shabby pastiche; the two forms of music cannot exchange artists. Can they exchange audiences? Here we must weigh our answer carefully. It is true enough that music lovers who manage to avoid today's eclecticism, generally the sign of a complete lack of discernment, tend to be rather sectarian. They are Democrats or Republicans, Labourites or Tories. However, there is reason to hope that these narrow attitudes are temporary and are brought about by the too rapid development of musical sensibility. Perhaps a public freed from the conventional thinking prevalent in intellectual circles could acquire, through a doubly difficult education, a kind of ambivalent lucidity. We may already be moving in this direction. One is beginning to meet young people who seem capable of really appreciating both jazz and serial music. Is it an illusion, or are they really able to discuss subtle distinctions between the piano music of Pousseur and Stockhausen as intelligently as they compare the best records of Sonny Rollins and John Coltrane? Have they really succeeded in switching back and forth from one system of coordinates to the other? In this age of specialization, one wonders whether such bilingualism is not Utopian.

Can we hope that one of these young people will find the answer to the riddle that no Oedipus has yet solved: what are the meaning and exact role of jazz in our society?

We are not dealing with painting as against sculpture, or theater as against films, but with one musical art as against another. Is this a sign of the tremendous wealth and variety of an expanding culture? Or of the exhaustion of a Western world which Jean Genet sees as "increasingly stricken with death and oriented toward it"? Are we witnessing the last moves of an endgame, or a turning point in a game still rich in unforeseeable developments?

In the last analysis, the philosophical evaluation of jazz hangs on these questions, which cannot be framed in absolute terms for lack of proper perspective. So, once more, we must elude them. However, perhaps we have performed a liberating gesture—or at least tried to do so—by better defining our reasons for loving jazz—and for not loving all of jazz.

> *Silence. At first, the camera remains fixed. The lense is badly focused, the picture blurred. Now muffled voices are heard here and there.*

A VOICE: And.

A VOICE: Or.

A VOICE: Meteor.

A VOICE: Antagonism.

A VOICE: Ambiguity. Ubiquity.

A VOICE: Who is King? Let him come!

ECHO: Doronom! Norodom!

A VOICE: Who is the usurper?

ECHO: Informer! Scribbler!

A VOICE: Who is the vanquisher? Who falls in the list?

ECHO: Bilinguist! Bilinguist!

> *The picture is still fuzzy. The sound, however, is now loud enough so that it is possible to follow the discussion without too much difficulty.*

YOUNG VOICE: All that contempt! Is it really necessary to be contemptuous of so many things?

OLDER VOICE: We mustn't be contemptuous of background music. Backgrounds are very nice.

ELDERLY VOICE: When I was a young man, you were supposed to have a good background.

> *The picture is now in focus. There follows a series of medium or close shots of the participants.*

A MIDDLE-AGED MAN: Everyone lovingly furnishes his own background, after he's gotten rid of his ancestors' paraphernalia.

A PEDANT: There is not enough contempt in all that. How can a comparable terminology be used to speak of cultural music and a perpetual creation of folk origin?

A POET: What doesn't have a folk origin? The *Odyssey?*

PEDANT: Well, there were a few generations between!

A LOGICIAN: One who is outside the elevator listens but does not dance. One who is inside the elevator dances.

A YOUNG BARONESS: Can *you* dance in an elevator?

A JAZZ FAN: Mentally. Mentally, thank my stars.

A SCHOLAR: Thank your swings!

PROFESSOR A: Is it really necessary to set a swing against several swings, so long as the phenomenon retains its generic denomination? A chair as against several chairs . . .

PROFESSOR B: Excuse me, my dear colleague, but I believe I heard swing as against swings. Remember Valéry: beauty as against beauties.

A CO-ED (*glasses and note pad*): But first of all, just what is swing? Let's have some examples, at least!

LOGICIAN: Oscar Peterson.

YOUNG BARONESS: Yes, his swing is awfully elevated! He swings with such nobility!

A YES-MAN: Yes. Yes, yes.

SCHOLAR: Swing is elemental. Like sound.

A G.I.: Ah, sound! The sound of Glenn Miller's band!

A STUBBORN MAN: Glenn Miller's band? It was the best of its kind!

PROFESSOR A: Your basically unassailable assertion is nevertheless predicated on a form of anthropological relativism which does not seem to be professed by our eminent lecturer.

A DOWAGER BARONESS: Sound! Sound! Let's get back to sound!

A BALDING YOUNG MAN: I don't like music that sounds bad. Beethoven . . .

A CONSUMER: Boulez . . . (*He makes a face.*)

PROFESSOR B: Gil Evans . . .

PROFESSOR A: Bill Evans . . .

A LIVER CASE: Miles . . . His sour notes go straight to my liver.

PEDANT: A sour blower is a royal roost sower.

DOWAGER BARONESS: I adore Miles! Oh, those elliptic fits of his!

AN ACTOR: That killer! I get a kick out of his licks! I never get my fill of those trills that thrill!

PEDANT: There's the key: jazz, as has been said before, is music eroticized.

FIRST GIRL: You just can't imagine what Frankie's voice does to me! (*She starts to undress.*)

SECOND GIRL: What about B.C.G.? Ever hear B.C.G.?

FIRST GIRL (*already half naked*): Does he sing?

SECOND GIRL: No, he stings. (*She also starts to undress.*) And he stimulates!

YOUNG BARONESS: And he's so high-born!

OFF-SCREEN VOICES: Stop! That's enough!

SECOND GIRL (*aggressively*): Don't you understand? This is my big day!

OTHER OFF-SCREEN VOICES: Go on! More!

A GOOSE: Me, I dig Herb Alpert! He gives me turkey flesh!

> *There is a lull in the conversation and a bee flies out of a bonnet.*

BEE: Bzz, bz Bzzzz. Bzz, bz Bzzzz.

PROFESSOR B: This discussion is predicated on unsound basses. Let us reconsider our steps.

POET: Let's have your figuring. Give us the key.

PROFESSOR B: Our eminent lecturer gave us to understand that swing was the Great Brake. He forgot to mention another rail that has an even better record.

ALL (*anxiously*): Which one?

PROFESSOR B: Spon-ta-ne-i-ty.

PROFESSOR A: Aaaaah! Every day I'll send you an invitation to hear the thousandth performance of *Everyday*. With Joe Williams. And his sustained falsetto B-flat.

DOWAGER BARONESS: That man lives a whole step above other people.

AN ORDINARY MAN: It's his dervish . . . it whirls too fast.

A BORN ORATOR: At last! I shall seize (*he seizes the lecturer's microphone*) this opportunity. Do you know the one about Oistrakh's Mendelssohn? With its held note on the G-string? Well, he recorded it . . .

JAZZ FAN: Cut that out! Basie recorded *Everyday*. Tell us about *Everyday*. This discussion is about jazz.

A FOOL: Miles cut records, too.

BALDING YOUNG MAN: So did Archie Shepp. Archie Shepp.

YES-MAN: Yes. Yes, yes.

BORN ORATOR (*calming his audience*): I'm coming to that. Imagine Oistrakh (*picture breakdown; the sound goes on alone*) playing his Mendelssohn in cities all over the world. He's got it down pat: every time, he plays the same notes in the same order, including, of course, that hold on the G-string, which happens to be the 666th. I checked. And each time he manages it in one stroke of the bow. But the worst part of it is that he's recorded this Mendelssohn, as I made the mistake of telling you. And in

restaurants all over the world, at dinner time, they play Oistrakh's Mendelssohn, because when it comes to background
music, there's none better (at least this is the opinion of the
restaurant-owner associations). Thus, every day, everywhere, he
holds that note on the G-string during the soup course, like
this, and when the meat is served he goofs a tricky A-sharp
(no, that's not true, Oistrakh never goofs), and it will go on
like that until the end of time. Talk about slave labor! And
what a taste that background has: the steak has the flavor of
underdone A-sharps (no, it's true that Oistrakh always does
everything to a turn) and the peach melba always has the sick-
sweet taste of E-major. I checked (I'm in the restaurant business myself). Suppose you changed the record and put on
Basie's *Everyday* or anything else: it would still be slave labor.
Whether you put on a Miles Davis or an Archie Shepp, it will
make no difference from the diner's point of view. Mendelssohn or Shepp, it's still background music.

> *The picture comes back on. The* BORN ORATOR
> *gives up the microphone.*

MIDDLE-AGED MAN: Spontaneity makes a pretty good background.
  Novelty wears thin. Mellowing comes with age.
LOGICIAN: They ought to invent an inventive record.
PEDANT: That doesn't exist.
FIRST SAILOR (*dressed as in the days of Magellan*): Many things don't
  exist: the Carusi, fabulous tenors with deadly high B-flats!
SECOND SAILOR (*same costume*): Carissimi's German-Hungarian coun-
  terpoint, and Bill Holman's Russo-Californian.
THIRD SAILOR: Carrmancy's legendary Banjo.
FOURTH SAILOR: The all but historical trip to Carson City taken by
  Carey El Rey and his Mute.
FIFTH SAILOR: Carisi, who never existed outside a single chronicle.
SIXTH SAILOR: Körössy, because there are no turkeys in Rumania.
G.I.: What difference does that make! Jazz is American!
A QUAKER: Jazz is universal.
PEDANT: Universalism . . . Cosmopolitanism . . .
THE DEVIL'S ADVOCATE: Angelicism!
A SOLOIST: The Jazz Artist Without a Passport, a play in five
  choruses and verse. (*Puts his tuba to his lips.*)
A POLICEMAN: First show me your credentials. Then you can play.
  Have you got a license?

WANTED

BIG BAND REHEARSER

QUALIFIED MUSICAL DIRECTOR

CAPABLE—MODEST—*NO AMBITION*

If Count Basie style, do not apply.

A MAN OF QUALITY (*with a camelia in his button-hole*): My friend, the Prince . . .

JAZZ FAN (*with growing incredulity*): Lasha? Robinson? Fouad?

A MAN IN A HOOD: Bronze colored, I assume?

AN ESKIMO: What's that about a bonze? Indochina isn't the end of the world!

MAN OF QUALITY (*disdainfully*): Saxophone colored.

JAZZ FAN: If Bird had been out there . . .

POET: The palace gates would have swung wide before him.

YES-MAN: Yes. Yes, yes.

STUBBORN MAN: But Bird was thrown out of Birdland!

LOGICIAN: Jazz is American. Khmerde!

CO-ED: Jazz is black! All the great names scream it at us! Roswell! Gary! David! Paul! Alex! Gato! Barney! Bernard! Jean-Louis! Fran-çois!

CONSUMER: That Negro jazz is so varied!

ACTOR (*dressed as a guide*): His Majesty the King of Jazz! (*He points to a plaster statue of Paul Whiteman on horseback. There is a piece of black crepe around the horse's head.*) Their Majesties the Kings of Swing! (*He points to a group in plastic representing Bennie Goodman and Artie Shaw side by side in a pedal-boat. They have dark brown tans.*) Ladies and gentlemen, I give you the Jazz Singer! A great date in modern history! (*He points to a huge portrait of Al Jolson made up as a minstrel.*)

A SWEDE: He's right. Only Bengt can compare with the Blacks.

A SPANIARD: Only Tete. Tete alone.

A BELGIAN: Nobody but Bobby.

A GERMAN: Albert! What about Albert?

A SOUTH AFRICAN: Besides the Blacks, you have . . .

A BRAZILIAN (*standing up*): Brasil!

A HAITIAN: Assis!

A LAPLANDER: If you don't mind, Matti Ja . . .

ONE OF THE GIRLS: Matti's a pretty name. What's his specialty? The turkey-trot?

ANOTHER GIRL: The peacock strut?

SCHOLAR: Ah! The peacock. A turkey that tries to blow itself up to the size of an ostrich. With its crest-shaped Renard's beak and its music-hall gallery ninths.

A GYPSY: You forgot about Django! And his talking guitar!

A JAPANESE (*bowing ceremoniously*): It is my turn to protest. Toshiko, Toshiko.

DEVIL'S ADVOCATE: Do you listen to Toshiko?

ALL THE WHITES: Yes! Her leg work is lovely!

DEVIL'S ADVOCATE: Do you listen to traditional Japanese music?

ALL THE WHITES: Never!

FOOL: Why do you call it traditional?

LOGICIAN: Because it's exotic.

BEE: Zen, zen Zen.

BORN ORATOR: Tradition! Tradition is what comes from the depths of Time. Hence . . . (*He is silenced.*)

STUBBORN MAN: Jazz tradition first! Let's listen to its guardians!

A RED GUARD: I listen to Lumumba.

A MERCENARY: I listen to Tshombe.

A LIEUTENANT-COLONEL: I listen to Mobutu. I still listen to him.

A YOUNG TRUMPET PLAYER: I still listen to Satchmo. Sometimes.

BALDING YOUNG MAN: When you say you listen, you speak. For whom do you speak?

ORDINARY MAN: I speak for the enlightened spectators at the cuttin' contests, I applaud the soloist who outplays all the others. Whether his name is Archie, Albert, or Abdulla, he is my hero of the day.

A HIPPY: I speak for Eros. Love thy soul brother and sister. It's the acid test.

CO-ED: I speak for ThaNaTos. It's time to put an end to all this.

A MAN WITH GOUGED-OUT EYES: I speak in my own name. I came to give the meaning and the exact . . .

THE WOMAN NEXT TO HIM (*horrified*): You get out of here right now!

PEDANT (*to the* CO-ED): Does a Black mechanic in Detroit tighten bolts any differently from his white fellow-worker?

CO-ED (*in two-shot*): Yeah!

PEDANT: I'll admit that. But does a Black dentist in Washington D.C. treat his patients' canines differently from his white colleague?

CO-ED: Yeah!

PEDANT: I'll grant you that. But does a Black boxer in Cleveland punch his white opponent any differently than he is punched by him?

Relaxing
      Stimulating
           Inspiring
BIRDIFY your canvases! Your paintings will be better investments!
                  Soon to be found exclusively
                  at the Library of Congress

CO-ED: Yeah!

PEDANT: I'll concede you that much. (*Triumphantly.*) On the other hand, a Black mathematician . . .

CO-ED: Yeah! Yeahhhh!

YES-MAN: Yes. Yes, yes.

MAN OF QUALITY: Einstein . . .

ORDINARY MAN: Not again!

SCHOLAR: Some fine physicists could not understand. Their hair was too gray.

MIDDLE-AGED MAN: We didn't hesitate to get rid of their background. We had to make room, didn't we?

CO-ED (*with threatening glasses and note pad*): Exactly!

> *Long-shot. The scene is invaded by a troop of mummers dressed as lizard-headed Martians and armed with tridents.*

THE MUMMERS: Break Kek Kekkek! Break Kek Kekkek! Koax Koax Koax!

G.I.: The Frogs! Drown them! Peace! Peace!

DOWAGER BARONESS: Ulysses! Play *Jump for Joyce* to these Aristofans.

> *The mummers head for the middle-aged man.*

MIDDLE-AGED MAN: Wait a minute! This time they want to throw out *our* background! You're not going to let them do that!

> *The mummers surround him. There is a confused struggle and shouting. Suddenly the shot is empty; the middle-aged man has vanished.*

MAN OF QUALITY (*picking the petals from his camelia*): Sometimes man himself becomes a consumer product.

POET: Hunter today, quarry tomorrow.

FIRST LAWYER: That was the vocation of jazz. Witness the New Orleans funerals.

SECOND LAWYER: Objection! The vocation of jazz was *West Side Story*. Witness *Rhapsody in Blue!*

THIRD LAWYER: Objection! It was dancing! Witness Congo Square and Bennie Goodman's coast-to-coast shows!

FOURTH LAWYER: Objection! It was the work, the written work! Witness Jelly Roll, the Duke . . .

FIFTH LAWYER: Objection! The vocation of jazz was to recreate the call of the gallinacean species. Witness Herb Alpert.

CHORUS OF PROTESTS.

What? Isn't that chicken the leader in *Playboy?*

ORDINARY MAN: He'd be better off as Paul Bley's leader.

YES-MAN: Yes. Yes, yes.

A FAMOUS LAWYER: Objection! The vocation of jazz is to scream. (*His voice becomes very shrill.*) Pure. Dense. Short. Loud! Mad! Blue! In a word, Rock! (*Lowering his voice.*) Witness Ma Rainey. (*Thundering out again.*) Have you also forgotten Ma Rainey? (*He peers around him accusingly.*)

A TEENAGER: Wait! I remember a Jimmy Raney.

AN OLD EXISTENTIALIST: The present has lost touch with the past.

BALDING YOUNG MAN: The present kills the past. After Shepp, can you listen to Monk?

PROFESSOR B: But what if Monk were still Monk?

LOGICIAN: Then he wouldn't be Monk any more.

PROFESSOR A: Monk fought the king; now he reestablishes him.

MAN OF QUALITY: Tutt! Tutt! Tutt! I mean: Hip! Hip! Hip!

DOWAGER BARONESS: After an hour of Heap, what you need is . . .

BALDING YOUNG MAN: Another hour of Shepp!

SCHOLAR: I quote: "Nu înseamna oare să faci dine el un fel de monstru care se distruge singur pe măsură ce înainteară? Nu este în definitiv a te rezuma la această mărturisire; jazzul nu-mi poate place decit ca o productie ieftină, trecatoare, iar dacă totusi îmi place în forma lui actuală o fac stiinde bine că justul meu nu este just?"

QUAKER: Who wrote that? It's prophetic!

ORDINARY MAN: Doesn't sound good.

A FRENCHMAN: C'est l'oeuvre d'un barbu.

AN AMERICAN: Not at all! Must be an egghead's writing!

OLD EXISTENTIALIST (*nostalgically*): Words don't mean what they used to.

DEVIL'S ADVOCATE: He is He. Likes to take on the appearances of uncertainty and error, which are inherent in him anyway.

MAN OF QUALITY: It's tragic but it's a fact: jazz is no longer fashionable!

ACTOR (*dressed as a dandy of the Romantic period*): Fashion isn't everything. There's also modernity.

FOOL: What is modernity?

ACTOR: Everything that is not in fashion but will be later. Or will come back in fashion later.

FOOL: But what is fashion?

CONSUMER: Fashion is what you really like.

ACTOR: Modernity is the deepest meaning of the present.

CONSUMER: Fashion is what you buy.

ACTOR: Modernity is what will sell some day.

NO MORE AFTERBEAT !!!

Thanks to our filters, you'll feel young again! Zutty's cymbals will sound *just like Anthony's!*

Have your old records *restored*

at CARERI'S Art Studio:

"The Turkey Feather"

CONSUMER: Fashion pays.

ACTOR: Modernity is an export value.

LOGICIAN: Isn't there a slight contradiction here?

CONSUMER: That's a tendentious remark! Fashion is an export value, too!

ACTOR: Fashion is exported for profit, whereas modernity bears the burden of a society's international reputation.

CONSUMER: Fiddlesticks! Fashion does a better job of dressing.

ACTOR: Modernity does a better job of undressing!

SCHOLAR (*pointing to the girls*): They're modernists without knowing it.

CONSUMER: Poppycock! The world needs fashion!

YES-MAN: Yes.

ACTOR: History needs modernity.

YES-MAN: Yes, yes.

CONSUMER: Rubbish! Your modernity is a modern invention. It was thought up by some sadist.

MAN OF QUALITY: Very ad lib those two.

A CONCERT MUSICIAN IN TAILS (*cutting him short*): With us, it's the opposite. Since I've become a masochist, I only play modern music.

A CONCERT MANAGER: And since then, you blame your three-quarters-empty halls on the austerity of your programs.

YOUNG BARONESS: If it's serial, nay twelve-tone, nay aleatoric, I'll take it, nay I dig it, nay I want it! (*Melancholically.*) But I don't feel it.

PROFESSOR A: In the eighteenth century, the public felt the music of the eighteenth century and ignored that of the sixteenth century. In the twentieth century, the public feels the music of the eighteenth century and ignores that of the twentieth.

PROFESSOR B: Century.

YES-MAN: Yes. Yes, yes.

A MIDWIFE: Eighteen and twenty, thirty-eight: the public has lost its innocence.

A NURSE MAID: In Centigrade, doesn't this temperature mean rather that serial music is not really representative of our period?

MAN OF QUALITY: If it weren't, how would all those great writers and philosophers who write and philosophize about it unendingly, write and philosophize unendingly about it?

OLD EXISTENTIALIST: When I was a little existentialist, jazz was what we wrote and philosophized about.

PEDANT: When you think back on all the fine things that the little existentialists wrote and philosophized about jazz, eh? eh? eh? you say to yourself: "Just think what the great structuralists of today could write and philosophize about it!"

JAZZ FAN: Our world is fresh and cool. We grind Gesualdo and Gillespie under the same heel.

DOWAGER BARONESS: You're going too far. John Birks is still verdant!

GOOSE: Verdant as Verdurin!

MAN OF QUALITY: That goose thinks she's a Swann!

LIVER CASE: Verdurin's is next door to Macy's isn't it?

FOOL: Does the jazz public have a temperature?

CONCERT MANAGER: Jazz lovers suffer from the fact that they are not representative.

QUAKER: They'll have to live it down.

JAZZ FAN: At dawn! And it's just too bad if dusk is more beautiful!

DOWAGER BARONESS: We ought to investigate further. The fusion of continents . . .

YOUNG BARONESS: The superposition of cultures . . .

MAN OF QUALITY: How coxal! My dear, what you just said was unutterably coxal!

STUBBORN MAN: This stuff about being representative is meaningless. When Bach passed Debussy on a Leipzig street corner, he didn't ask himself whether he was more or less representative.

OLD EXISTENTIALIST: Maybe. But when Louis Armstrong meets Ornette Coleman on Broadway, what does he ask him?

QUAKER (*imitating Louis*): What about the race of the saywint up me ambushure?

JAZZ FAN: Shh . . . If we start getting technical, I'm splitting.

FIRST GENTLEMAN (*entering*): After you.

SECOND GENTLEMAN (*stepping aside*): After you, Mr. Chorus.

FIRST GENTLEMAN: Thank you, Mr. Chorus.

YOUNG BARONESS (*going to meet them, disappointed*): My Prince will come. He will. (*With poetic enthusiasm.*) He will! Some day.

MAN OF QUALITY: We must draw the badger.

ACTOR (*dressed as a peddler*): A cadger?

FOOL: I thought I heard "a gadget."

An Incoherent Newspaper
For Incoherent worlds

THINGS AND NEW THING

The only paper in which you never find what you're looking for.
The only paper that renders the outward disorder in terms
of an even greater inward disorder.

CONSUMER (*respectfully*): Those commercials! You have to hit the bull's eye!

A TURKEY HUNTER (*shouldering his gun*): Pull it! (*He fires.*) A rare bird! (*A volley.*) A phoenix cock!

ORDINARY MAN: A pigeon! A sitting duck!

TURKEY HUNTER: Mahagonny! I got it!

STUBBORN MAN: This stuff about being representative is meaningless. As soon as you let relativism in the door, it's obvious that everything becomes representative. Who is to say that within a certain system of coordinates Joyce or Picasso is not Chevalier?

PROSPER: Yop la boom! I'm H.C.E.

ACTOR (*wearing a toga*): *The Knight and the Professor*, a Kansas City foible based on hysterical data. (*He bows.*)

MAN OF QUALITY: Couldn't you recite some excerpts from Wittgenstein, instead?

YOUNG BARONESS: Or a jazzy page from a gangster novel?

YES-MAN (*enthusiastically*): Yes, yes! Yes, yes, yes!

A CHILD: Sartre says that gangster novels are preferable to Wittgenstein.

OLD EXISTENTIALIST: Of course! A good pop song is better than a bad opera.

DOWAGER BARONESS: Of course! A good Strauss waltz is better than a bad Bach chorale.

CONCERT MANAGER: Of course! Of course! A good Miller is better than a bad Ellington.

STUBBORN MAN: Glenn's band? It was the best of its kind. It sure was! The best!

MAN OF QUALITY: A good riff is better that a bad row! Of course!

QUAKER: A good Monk is better than a bad Bishop. Of course! Of course!

LOGICIAN: And similarly, a good Bishop is better than a bad Monk. Of course! Of course! Of course!

MAN WITH GOUGED-OUT EYES: Incidentally, Bishop was once a demon. He said so.

PROFESSOR A: Beauty as against beauties, my dear colleague. Don't forget Valéry.

PROFESSOR B: Did he say that?

PROFESSOR A: In any case, everyone has his own and he hangs on to it. For life.

ORDINARY MAN: You know artists, once they got a good gimmick, they squeeze it for all it's worth.

DEVIL'S ADVOCATE: Not my client. He always varies his gimmicks. With simplicity.

MAN WITH GOUGED-OUT EYES: Someday another Tarski will come along and solve all his paradoxes.

MAN OF QUALITY: You old Hip o' the News, you!

FOURTEEN DAYS IN CAMBODIA $10,000

The Orchestra of the Royal Residence

If the Prince does not play, the Agency makes no refunds, either.

BORN ORATOR (*taking his time*): Bird is dead. Prez is gone. Trane has left us. All the world is at a loss to think what Monk will do.

LOGICIAN: He's going to change tempo.

OLD EXISTENTIALIST: Do you think he'd dare? At his age?

CONCERT MUSICIAN: I don't give a hang about his tempo. If I like Monk, knowing nothing at all about jazz, it's because he's got the whatsit of serial music.

DOWAGER BARONESS: The Duke hasn't got the whatsit. No, he certainly hasn't.

YOUNG BARONESS: But Cecil has the whatsit. He petrified Pousseur.

PEDANT: And what's more, it's a whatsit that doesn't distanciate.

POLICEMAN: The whatsit isn't everything. You have to have order too.

FOOL: How much is fifty-five divided by two?

SCHOLAR: Twenty-seven, you fool.

FOOL: And how much is two times twenty-seven?

SCHOLAR: Fifty-four, you fool.

DEVIL'S ADVOCATE: The powers of mathematics rule the world.

JAZZ FAN (*disgusted*): I'm splitting. (*He limps away.*)

MAN OF QUALITY: Poor boy! The way he sways his hips is a sign of hypomania.

OLD EXISTENTIALIST: There's too much order in all this and not enough human values.

PROFESSOR A: Russell says of the serial composers: "We could make what they do more human."

PROFESSOR B: The devil with synthesis! I prefer compensation.

SCHOLAR: In short, the balancing of opposites? As in psychiatric pharmaceutics?

AN UNDERNOURISHED INTELLECTUAL: Did I get the right dose this morning? My swing isn't up to par.

ONE OF THE GIRLS: I'm up to forty-eight rows a week.

CONCERT MUSICIAN (*in admiration*): With their transpositions and inversions?

GIRL: No, naked. Like me.

PEDANT: Then that only makes one.

GIRL: Oh God! They're so bitter as it is!

A DISRUPTOR: A gift from the others! (*From the background, he flings toward the camera a few of the most proliferating species, which threaten to overwhelm the whole frame, and even the frame of reference, if they weren't stamped on in perfect tempo.*) Philistines! (*They throw him out.*)

LOGICIAN: This is illogical! We were just told we've entered an age of disruptors, and now you throw him out!

BORN ORATOR: But first of all, *who* told us that?

CO-ED (*looking at her note pad*): It was in the lecture. I took it down.

DOWAGER BARONESS (*to the camera*): So you're the one who said we had to classify.

YOUNG BARONESS (*to the camera*): You said we *shouldn't* classify.

ORDINARY MAN: You said sumpin' about pop music that I didn't like.

A REPUBLICAN (*tempers are rising*): You said I was a Democrat.

A DEMOCRAT: You said I was a Republican.

YES-MAN: Yes? Yes, yes?

CONSUMER: You said the world was like Nazi Germany.

G.I.: You said that we lived in a dangerous world.

AN ANARCHIST: Where are those fellows who are incapable of inventing the ways and means of their revolution? (*He hurls a big black ball which rolls slowly across the screen.*)

MONK'S VOICE (*off-screen*): The Mad Bomber! Fire!

> *The camera pans with the bomb, which finally knocks over a lone ten-pin and vanishes.*

MILES DAVIS' VOICE (*off screen*): Exactly what does "beyond Miles Davis" mean?

RED GUARD: You said that the world of jazz had its nouveaux riches.

ONE OF THE SAILORS: You said we were all in the same boat.

FOOL: You said that Parker was still alive. Didn't he die in '55?

LOGICIAN: Therefore this is '54.

FOOL: Ah! Now I've got it!

A GIANT OF JAZZ: I didn't get it when you said they shouldn't have operated on Tatum.

MAN OF QUALITY (*to the* GIANT): You must be outside the elevator.

GIANT: Say that again!

MAN OF QUALITY: Sorry. I meant, outside the capsule. (*Sotto voce.*) This fellow's algic!

QUAKER (*to the camera*): You said I'd never learn how to jump.

CO-ED (*to the camera*): You said the conflict would resolve itself as an equivalence.

TUBA SOLOIST: You said we were full of unacceptable limitations.

ACTOR (*dressed as an explorer*): You said that someone from the end of the earth . . .

CONCERT MANAGER: Pretty good act you've got there. *Who* are you?

> *The camera slowly pans through one hundred and eighty degrees, slowly enough to give glimpses of all the people who have taken part in*

the debate, standing frozen like so many wax dummies.*

POLICEMAN'S VOICE (*off screen*): Show me your credentials. Have you got a license?

At the end of this pan, the camera comes to a stop on a close-up of the motionless lecturer. He is wearing a mask. His lips are parted; it is impossible to tell whether he is smiling.

CONSUMER'S VOICE (*off screen, with a suggestion of tears*): All is consummated.

Very gradually, the camera moves in toward the lecturer. The soundtrack has gone dead; gradually the picture goes fuzzy. In this blank silence, the black massive camera keeps moving toward the mask.

Quiz Rating

With reference to the *Musical Offering* and out of respect for the reader, we will not give the answers to the proposed canons. *Quaerendo Invenietis*. Nevertheless, score one point for each answer a), two for each answer b), and three for each answer c). If your score is:

51 points   Reading *The Worlds of Jazz* is a luxury for you. The author hopes to be capable of understanding your criticisms.

47–50   You may skip directly to the second section of Part Three, Chapter 7.

42–46   You may continue reading.

37–41   You are requested to read more slowly.

33–36   The author suggests that you go back to Part One, Chapter 3.

29–32	You had best lay the book aside for a while. You will improve your score next year.
25–28	You are advised to read a number of books considered less difficult[1] before tackling this one.
21–24	You're coming close to the Quad. Your case looks pretty hopeless.
17–20	Maybe you ought to listen to a jazz record.
0 points	You have not read the book in order. Bravo! It was not written in order.

---

1. Besides the Bible, Homer, Shakespeare, Pepys, Bossuet, Molière, Racine, Diderot, Beethoven, Hugo, Ibsen, Nietzsche, Mallarmé, Valéry, and Freud, the author especially recommends Samuel Beckett (*Waiting for Godot*), Jorge Luis Borges (*The Babylonian Lottery* and *The Garden of Forking Paths*), Georges Feydeau (*Le Dindon*), Jean Genet (*Letters to Roger Blin*), James Joyce (*Finnegans Wake*), Thomas Mann (*Doctor Faustus*), Marcel Proust (*Remembrance of Things Past*), André Pieyre de Mandiargues (*Le Musée Noir*), Raymond Queneau (*Zazie Dans le Métro*), Alain Robbe-Grillet (*La Maison de Rendez-Vous*), and Zanonymous (*The Return of Magellan*).

PART THREE

THE
MAN WHO
WRITES JAZZ

1

Lecture in Jazz Aesthetics
Delivered by Professor Tie
at the University of A.

The annual literary awards, so typical of modern society, have produced a rather strange corollary in the world of jazz: the yearly poll. The ethical function of such votes is obvious and their usefulness to the public undeniable. For lack of a Nobel, Goncourt, or Pulitzer prize, some way had to be found of making the classifications indispensable for our peace of mind and of offering the deserving jazz artist some hope of reward for a brilliant career. However, an examination of the structures of this social phenomenon, insofar as it concerns at least one branch of jazz activities, leads to interesting conclusions. We find we must reconsider our vocabulary and revise some of the concepts implicit in it.

In the beginning, the polls were democratic. Anyone could wield a bit of power; he did not even have to be a regular reader of this or that magazine. A stroke of a pen helped to decide for a whole year whether the Charlie Mingus fans had the edge on their bitter rivals the Ray Brown fans, or vice versa. Thus, the referendums allowed the voice of the people to make itself heard in all sovereignty. Then, the magazines that usually conduct these polls, while continuing to consult the body of their readers as a whole, decided to ask musicians and critics to take part in a separate and simultaneous ballot. This amounted to creating a "higher court," designed, some felt, to compensate for the vagaries of universal suffrage. It also gave new weight to an institution which not even its founders could still pretend to take seriously. Indeed, as long as the polls had been addressed only to the general public, they could be regarded as a means of taking the pulse of public opinion and as a sampling useful for those who seek to shape it. After all, what the magazine editors somewhat cynically expected of their gullible readers was a mirror image of the world of jazz as it had been described to them in previous issues. And this, in fact, was what they got. Of course, classifications of this kind are constantly evolving, so that there was always some minor detail in need of correction ("Wes Montgomery deserves that number two spot, but Barry Galbraith ought to be a little higher than nineteenth; let's run a couple of articles on him so that our readers will do him justice next year"). However, this mirror relationship between the opinions of canvasser and "canvassee" did reflect an orderly, unified state of affairs which was destroyed by the introduction of a new kind of poll. Truth now had two faces. And the personal prestige of the experts invited to participate, combined with the prestige attached to a function which was in itself a prestige, lent far more weight to the experts' truth in the eyes of those who were not experts than their own truth could possibly have. It was all right for *them* to be unwitting sociological guinea pigs, but it would be unthinkable to cast the distinguished members of this electoral college in a similar role. When a body of critics as large as the National Academy of Arts and Sciences—and representing ten different countries besides—agrees to set forth its preferences in an international poll, to the accompaniment of all the necessary publicity, only a subversive mind could regard the results as anything but a true honor roll of jazz, a fine example for fans and musicians alike.

Yet once the authority of the electoral college is established, certain anomalies become even more apparent. When the results of a public referendum reveal signs of confusion, usually involving the distinctions between genres (i.e., the abusive promotion of a pop singer to the rank of jazz singer), this has only a statistical significance; however, a similar confusion, if only one of terminology, in a poll reserved for experts, may reveal that those whose role is precisely to enlighten the public, harbor basic misconceptions regarding some of the major problems of contemporary jazz. Remarkably enough, experts capable of holding perfectly lucid views on the men who play jazz are suddenly struck blind when they turn their attention to those who write it. Asked to choose the three best trumpet players of the year, everyone will vote intelligently; leaving it to professional musicians to decide whether Joe Wilder, Ernie Royal, or Benny Bailey is the best section leader, they quite rightly choose Miles Davis, Dizzy Gillespie, or Louis Armstrong as original personalities, soloists, and improvisers. If they prefer Jimmy Giuffre to Buddy De Franco, they are consciously choosing the stylist over the technician. This capacity for judgment vanishes as soon as it comes to written jazz. Who is the most skilled orchestra technician: Gary McFarland, Oliver Nelson, or Manny Albam? Only a professional musician will answer without hesitation. Critics seem to regard writing jazz as an occult science. We might resign ourselves to this state of affairs. But as soon as we tackle the actual functions of the men who write jazz, an even wider rift appears, affecting the public as a whole. Instead of capturing their fascinating variety, the pollsters try to reduce them to a single, artificial category. Just what is meant by "arranger-composer"?

The way the question is put is, in itself, a source of confusion, which the answers can only aggravate. Reading down a list which includes the names of Ellington, Evans, Lewis, Mingus, Strayhorn, Jones, and Russell, we suddenly come upon that of Monk. This is a significant anomaly. For despite the instrumental nature of his themes and his keen ear for color, Thelonious Monk is not a "composer" any more than he is an "arranger." Having him compete in the same category as Gil Evans, comparing the thirty-two bars of *Criss-Cross* with an arrangement by Jimmy Mundy, and this arrangement with George Russell's *All About Rosie,* for example, is like holding a race between a bird, a fish, and a horse. Who would have thought that forty of the world's most famous experts would associate themselves with such an aberrant conception, that an Englishman and a German would be the only ones to find anything strange about the question put to them—were it not for the fact that this mistake is so common?

Consequently, Monk's case may be regarded as a typical example which may be used to lay bare the mechanism of this confusion. The dual and ambiguous term "arranger-composer" may be taken in various ways. If we see it as a reference to *written* music, we may prefer to stress either the word "arranger"—and vote for Gil Evans, Quincy Jones, or Billy Strayhorn—or else the word "composer"—and let our choice go to John Lewis or George Russell. However, since Thelonious Monk is undeniably one of the greatest theme makers in the history of jazz, anyone who instinctively associates the words "melody" or "theme" with the word "composer" will be tempted to put him at the top of his list. If the electoral college had been larger, the list of possible names would have included Neal Hefti, Ernie Wilkins, or even Gunther Schuller on the one hand, and Miles Davis, John Coltrane, and Milt Jackson on the other. Even more hybrid than the first, this list would have revealed more clearly the contradictions inherent in a terminology which is simply not appropriate; but the presence of Monk's name alone should be enough for anyone willing to see them.

And yet it has already been pointed out that the notion of written jazz encompasses at the same time three essentially different states. A man who writes jazz may be a theme maker, an arranger, or a composer. Working out a theme of twelve, thirty-two, or forty-eight bars; making an arrangement for a small or large orchestra; composing a finished work or a work in progress—these represent three distinct types of activity. The confusion arises from the fact that a single jazz artist often engages in all three at one time or another. John Lewis composed *The Comedy*, arranged *'Round About Midnight* for Gillespie's band, and conceived the theme of *Django*. Sometimes one man may turn his hand to all three at once: Duke Ellington, working on the theme of *Ko-Ko*, may already have anticipated its orchestral and formal developments; if so, he was theme maker, arranger, and composer all at the same time. When Dizzy Gillespie wrote the interludes for *Night in Tunisia*, he was anticipating the future developments of his theme, stepping out of the theme maker's role and, at the same time, encroaching on the arranger's and curtailing his freedom. Similarly, the introduction and coda of a theme like *'Round About Midnight* establish a framework which prefigures the arrangement to be woven around it. However, insofar as Horace Silver conceived the melody of *Doodlin'*, or Errol Garner that of *Play Piano Play*, solely in terms of their immediate substance, they did not communicate in any way with the world of arranging, let alone that of composition, which they do not even glimpse. The theme maker may very well know nothing of the most elementary techniques involved in these two disciplines; even if he knew them, they would be useless to him. Charlie Parker, Thelonious Monk, and Milt Jackson have conceived some of the most beautiful themes in jazz; but when it came to writing the arrangements, they turned to Gil Evans, Hall Overton, or Quincy Jones. Conversely, a great arranger (or, for that matter, a great soloist) need not be a theme maker at all. And it is quite conceivable that a composer of genius, skilled in developing his own melodic ideas, should prove incapable of providing an improviser or an arranger with the simple well-balanced skeleton that he requires. Moreover, it is doubtful whether such an artist would take pleasure in devising themes destined to be appropriated and reworked by others.

True, usage has been called the father of language, and the loose application of a term may eventually be justified, but only so long as it does not give rise to two contradictory acceptations, only one of which deserves to be regarded as rational. In a case like this, we should perhaps refer back to the tradition which lies at the origin of the word and ask ourselves whether the concept of musical creation associated with Bach or Beethoven can rightly be called *composition*. If so, then no amount of usage can ever justify applying this same term to the work of Irving Berlin or Fats Waller. This is not an aesthetic judgment, it is simple logic: these two forms of mental activity cannot be reduced to a common denominator. So long as the notion of works in jazz existed only on the performing level, there was no harm in accepting a solecism which was too widespread to be really offensive, i.e., in calling a theme maker a composer. Today, however, a more rigorous terminology is necessary. Composer, arranger, and theme maker are three careers which may be carried on simultaneously, but it does not follow that they can be looked upon as identical.

What is a composer? Is he someone whose creative faculties are concentrated entirely on inventing melodies? Is he someone skilled at handling tone color but incapable of conceiving and organizing a complex whole? It is only slightly ironical to suggest that composition proper begins where the theme ends, after the thirty-second bar. Composition consists, first, in placing the theme—or in the absence of a theme, the germinal element of the work—in a formal perspective defined in terms of musical space and time, then in developing these premises along the lines implicit within them. Superficially, an arranger differs from a composer in that he generally works with ideas that are not his own; however, the composer, too, has the possibility, though not the "right," to borrow material from others (we would scarcely call Bach's great organ chorales "arrangements"). On a higher level, however, there is a real opposition between these two types of artists who both write jazz, for their conceptual approach is not the same. The true composer is active, his is a "masculine" principle. He has an original vision which it is up to him to impose upon his musicians, allowing them to enhance but not distort it. The true arranger, on the other hand, conforms to a passive, "feminine" principle; not only is he dependent upon others for his basic material, but his talents are primarily meant to serve others. The composer expects to obtain a response from his musicians, the arranger brings them whatever they require, which is why his world is necessarily restricted. And yet the arranger sometimes succeeds in breaking out of this passive role; there is nothing which actually prevents his assuming the composer's role, to a certain extent. As for the theme maker, he has no such latitude: he is neither active nor passive, he has no dealings of any kind with the forces involved in the work of the arranger or composer. His art is static. Whatever the intrinsic worth of themes like *Godchild* or *Jordu*, Gil Evans, developing borrowed material into a work like *Miles Ahead*, comes much closer to qualifying as a "composer" than Jordan or Wallington ever have done. The theme maker's main function is to provide a springboard; the sequence of choruses comes later, unpredictable, outside the realm of his volition. Gershwin never foresaw Charlie Parker's inspired paraphrases on *Embraceable You*.

There is no more paradoxical figure than the theme maker. More often than not he is an outsider; almost invariably, his theme is used in his absence. Yet, as it happens, he has sometimes exerted an influence on creative jazz which neither soloists nor arrangers, despite their full-fledged "citizenship," have been able to neutralize completely. If writing jazz consists in inventing the only features of that music which, by their very nature, are capable of being written down, then it can be said that the theme makers were the first men to write jazz; yet in some instances, they knew nothing of the techniques of writing music. Thus they helped construct the world of jazz without actually belonging to it. When Armstrong recorded *Big Butter-and-Egg Man*, when Parker recorded *Ko-Ko* (*Cherokee*), there were only five or six musicians in the studio. And yet a seventh man had a share in cutting those famous platters, but from a distance and without even knowing it. Suppose one Mr. Venable for the first and one Mr. Noble for the second had never written those themes; the developments which Armstrong and Parker built upon them, the works they derived from them, the seminal effect that these works had on the younger jazzmen who heard them—none of these would ever have existed, and the world of jazz would not be quite the same. Now, it is very possible that neither Ray Noble nor Venable was ever really familiar with jazz; neither of them, in any case, can be called a jazz artist. Was Gershwin a jazz musician? Were Vernon Duke, Jerome Kern, and all the other authors of popular ballads?

True, the most beautiful jazz themes were written by genuine jazz artists, from Fats Waller to Monk, from Ellington to Miles Davis; but their efforts in this direction were sporadic and their successful achievements few. In order for a rich and varied repertoire to be built, it was necessary to draw constantly on the output of Tin Pan Alley. This concern with broadening the repertoire went hand in hand with a need, more keenly felt by some musicians than others, to communicate with an audience whose sensibility was jarred by the language of jazz. For many years, jazz musicians looked on their music as a popular art form. In the days when the concert hall was still closed to it, jazz may have had to cling to the dance hall in order to survive; consequently, the risk involved in mingling its repertoire with the hit tunes of the day could be regarded as a lesser evil. The sales figures of records like Armstrong's *Dinah* and Hawkins's *Body and Soul* prove that jazz was able to survive and jazz musicians to continue to express themselves during the thirties by countlessly reworking popular songs with which they deceptively identified their art whenever this was what the public seemed to want. Moreover, this popularity made it possible for other recordings, based on real jazz themes (Goodman and Henderson's *New King Porter Stomp*, Basie's *Sent for You Yesterday*), to sell better than a record firm could have hoped for under other circumstances. Thus, whether they were jazzmen or song writers, and whether or not they were present at the actual performances, theme makers did contribute discreetly, but effectively, to the artistic and commercial success of works which might seem to owe them nothing more than their titles.

Aside from this kind of sponsorship, the theme maker exerted another influence on the repertoire, one which is more difficult to evaluate. Of course, the jazz repertoire, as we are using the term here, is not made up of works, but merely of raw materials. However, a work necessarily contains the raw materials that went into it. Composed as it was of one quarter blues and "instrumental" themes written especially for jazz, and of three quarters ballads and dance tunes suitable for jazz treatment, the repertoire could not but develop a motley aspect which in turn could not fail to be reflected in the work of jazz artists, thus affecting the musical substance of jazz. If we go back further, we find the situation even more confused. Jelly Roll Morton used to say, "Any kind of music can be played in jazz." And we have to admit that this sweeping statement is not entirely inaccurate. Early jazz did have an extraordinary capacity for absorbing outside material. It was melophagous, capable of devouring any thematic element that was structurally related to its own system. The backwash was inevitable. True, jazz did benefit to a certain extent from the diversity of the lavish contributions provided by the huge reservoir of American "commercial" music; and even today, composed jazz, having eliminated the facileness of popular music, may still reflect the smile of a pretty ballad. However, the residues of a repertoire noted for its sentimentality may still be found in the styles of many jazz artists, including some of the greatest, whose music would undoubtedly have remained purer had they never come in contact with it. It is significant, for example that insofar as we can judge from records, no jazz soloist, no matter how famous, has ever managed to do away with the sugary sentimentality inherent in one of the tunes most often pressed into service by jazz artists: *Stardust*. No matter how hard they try to eliminate that distasteful "poetic" atmosphere, no matter how many liberties they take with the theme, altering the changes, diluting the melodic line until it is unrecognizable, there is always something left over, some essential part of *Stardust* which resists their genius for transmutation. In the long run, one wonders whether it is not the jazz artist who gives in, letting himself be permeated against his will by the sentimentality that oozes endlessly forth from tunes of that ilk, to the point of corrupting the best part of an artist's soul: his violence. It would even seem that this thematic material had its most dulcifying effect not on the most primitive musicians, but on the most sophisticated ones, on those who professed a need for melodic and harmonic subtleties which they did not find in the blues, on musicians like Benny Carter, Art Tatum, Errol Garner, and even Duke Ellington. Their works (and those of many others) make us realize to what extent a man's musical conceptions may be debased through constant contact with a repertoire which he is incapable of dominating completely. Thus, in the last analysis, the ambiguous figure of the theme maker may have harmed jazz more than he has helped it.

However, the repertoire has provided a common, albeit a somewhat marshy ground on which jazz artists of all kinds have been able to meet. The question "what do we play now?" which precedes each episode of a jam session is echoed by the question "what tune shall I arrange for you?" on which the arranger-soloist relationship is based. Just as within a band, a trumpet or a saxophone player does not so much expect an arranger to be inventive as to write agreeably for trumpet or saxophone, so too the soloist, though he may seem anxious to be backed up by a well-voiced and stylistically original arrangement, is even more anxious that it should be based on a theme which he is fond of and which he knows will provide him with a good basis for improvising. In this type of collaboration, the soloist's best safeguard is to see eye to eye with his arranger. Most often, the arranger was once a soloist himself, and his basic instincts and conception of jazz are still very much the same. Far from wishing to challenge a supremacy which has the added advantage of limiting his own responsibilities, he is quite prepared to write the arrangement which he is known to be capable of writing on *Willow Weep for Me* or *Perdido;* after all, he would have asked his band's arranger to develop these same themes for him when he was a soloist himself.

On the rare occasions when arrangers were tempted to invert the roles, to take the initiative away from the soloist and demand that he fit his improvising into a preexisting work, they foreshadowed the coming of the jazz composer. The composer's function is not to manufacture jazz tunes, that elementary raw material which is grist for the mill of both soloist and arranger, nor to develop them through orchestration and variation, but to create a type of jazz work involving new and substantial relationships between written and improvised music. Many regard composers with an unsympathetic eye, as interlopers out to upset a world of jazz with which they are perfectly satisfied. A composer voices new demands and unexpected principles which must be disproven in block or accepted with all their devastating consequences. His specialty is that latest acquisition of jazz, that frail, precious thing called *musical thinking;* he may not have been an instrumentalist himself, which would have helped establish a reassuring family relationship with the men who are going to play his music. Improvisers know they are up against someone who will no longer allow their imaginations to run wild, who will place strict limits on their creative freedom. However, they may also sense that this demiurgic figure has the power to make gold once again of something which was gradually turning to lead in their hands.

From the very outset, the composer's status in the world of jazz is quite unprecedented and this is why he has rights which no other jazz artist has ever had before. Whereas the traditional arranger was, in a sense, a further development of the soloist and the theme maker, the composer subjugates the one and ignores the other. He could not conceivably collaborate with those distant cousins of his, the theme maker and the arranger. The themes he writes are not meant to add to that pile of ever-available building blocks which constituted the repertoire; they are cast in the body of his work and nothing can separate them out. His ideas can be used only as he intended, only as he allows. And though the result of his labors may be indeterminate, unfinished, or even dependent on improvisation, it nevertheless constitutes a *work*, a circumscribed whole.

The problem is not to decide whether the jazz composer can coexist with the theme maker and the arranger. This coexistence will come about; in fact, it already has. The important thing is to realize how much the sudden appearance of a troublemaker in a world which is a bit overorganized can elevate the meaning of creation in jazz. Anyone who understands the meaning of the term *composition* can no longer put up with workaday mediocrity, with the thousands of choruses that are played just to fill time. An unprecedented effort will be required of jazz composers if they are to conquer the prerogatives which they claim for themselves. The fact that they have already begun to make that effort deserves due credit and respect. It is true that certain solos by Armstrong, Parker, or Monk represent the greatest beauty which improvising can produce; it is also true that jazz composers have, at best, only glimpsed the higher plane of beauty which might be attained by works resulting from a slow and painful process of gestation in the minds of their creators; and it is equally true that on this higher plane, there will be a hundred lamentable failures for every real achievement. The jazz composer's grandeur lies in his staking his life in what is almost invariably a losing game—one which has never been won to date. However, perhaps he is sustained by those threads that history is wont to weave together, by those dilemmas that are thrown up to men as so many challenges. Then when the time is ripe, the composer might bring the promise of a new jazz; his failure would probably mark the death of jazz as a whole.

22

Lecture in Jazz History
Delivered by Professor Deadbeat
at the University of B.

Now I expect you're all wondering why I read you *in extenso* my esteemed colleague Professor Tie's lecture—and I was happy to see you giving it your undivided attention, even though a few of you did show signs of restlessness toward the end, and I understand this attitude, though I can't share it, don't you know, there's nothing more confusing than a lecture in aesthetics which begins like a lecture in history but isn't really one—no references, don't you know, no references—and there's nothing more obscure than a lecture in aesthetics like the one I just read you which begins with a pseudohistorical introduction and then goes on to become a genuine lecture in aesthetics, do you follow me, in other words, the exact opposite, because after all, what is an aesthetician, this is a difficult question to answer, it's a bit beyond our scope, and I'm afraid aestheticians themselves would be hard put to give a definition of their activities which would satisfy positivists like ourselves, but I'm going to suggest one just the same, I would say an aesthetician is someone who tries to rearrange history in order to give it an original interpretation, it's the idea of originality that counts here, don't you know, an aesthetician is an artist.

So that's why I read you that lecture, despite the fact that some of you may have been bored or annoyed by it, and I'm really very sorry about that, oh yes, please, I really am, and the reason I took the trouble to bring it today was to point out all the errors of method which you should learn to avoid, now they may not be errors in aesthetics, I wouldn't know about that, if my distinguished colleague saw fit to adopt this approach, it's probably quite legitimate and it's not up to us to evaluate it, don't you know, but as historians we cannot use it, that's the important point, no historian worth his salt could accept this way of working.

I expect you all noticed that my eminent confrere often speaks of "works" as though everybody in jazz took this notion for granted and understood what it meant; now this may be acceptable from the standpoint of aesthetics, I wouldn't know about that, I've never been able to take such an elevated view of things, but I can assure you that as far as the historian is concerned, this idea of "works" is simply an abuse of language, and I'm not asking you to take my word for it but that of Mr. André Hodeir, who tends to be on the aestheticians' side of the fence, anyway he's certainly no historian, I'm sure we all agree about that, he's the kind of writer who renders unto Winding what rightfully belongs to Zwerin and who could easily take Argonne Thornton for a sadist and Jimmy Foreman of Philadelphia for a propfeiffer of philosophy, so anyway let's see what Mr. Hodeir has to say on the subject in an article he wrote for a musical encyclopedia recently published in France:

> True, Mozart may have written this or that orchestral score under outside pressure, in haste and without committing himself to it completely; nevertheless, everything about the work is a product of his volition, down to the last semiquaver. On the other hand, the jazz work, or what we have come to call by this name, is more often than not a moment of music rescued from oblivion by magnetic tape; had it been captured only slightly earlier or later it would not have been the same. A jazz musician's career is made up of thousands of just such moments; they live and die between midnight and dawn in the smoke-filled clubs of New York, London, or Chicago. If historians could

have heard those lost moments, their image of the musician would be quite different. If we knew only two of Beethoven's symphonies, three of his quartets, and five of his sonatas, we would probably have a clear notion of his greatness, but not of his creative range. Thus, our image of Charlie Parker or of Lester Young is fragmentary, indeed, deceptive. The records they left behind, the occasions, rare or frequent, on which each of us may have had a chance to hear them in person, are mere random samplings of a body of works which is not necessarily homogeneous. The most famous "masterworks of jazz" are merely the "masterworks of recorded jazz."

And Mr. Hodeir concludes, quite correctly, I feel, that the notion of "works" in jazz is nothing more than "a necessary point of reference." Of course, this didn't stop Mr. Hodeir, in his earlier books, from building a lovely house of cards on this totally unreal foundation, and again I quote, bibliography is a hobby of mine, don't you know, and anyway we're among historians, I quote from *Jazz: Its Evolution and Essence*, page 46, I'm translating directly from the French, just listen to this or, as Armstrong used to say, "Hear me talkin' to ya": ". . . It was during the classical period that most of the *works* that made jazz great were recorded," now would Mr. Hodeir agree with that today, since on page 40 he wrote that "classicism implies durability above all," yes it would be interesting to know, as the *works* in question date from the period 1937–1941, even though a few lines back we read that before André Hodeir "those who were concerned with defining classicism in jazz ascribed it to the New Orleans era," and more recently he speaks of "Parkerian" and even, I believe, "post-Parkerian classicism," it's an obsession with the man! Where was I? Oh, yes, so now the author—or rather the one-time author—of *Jazz: Its Evolution and Essence* wants nothing more to do with this idea of "jazz works," so let's see what he has to say in a more recent book, *Toward Jazz*, Part Four of which is precisely entitled "On Works," and what are we to make of the subtitle of Chapter Fourteen: "The Recorded Works of Milt Jackson"? does this imply that there might be other works that haven't been recorded? but this would contradict what Mr. Hodeir himself says on page 145: "Obviously, only recorded improvisations or compositions may be regarded as part of jazz history," now here's another instance of that unbearable habit composers and aestheticians have of posing as historians! they really are impossible people! you'd think they had an inferiority complex! but to get back to Chapter Fourteen of *Toward Jazz,* I could comment at length, but I suggest you read it, you'll be astonished as I was to find the most banal three-part outline: 1) the works in general, 2) some works in particular, 3) a work by itself, now please gentlemen, don't any of you take it into your heads to use an outline like that for your term papers, I don't think you'd get very good grades, do you follow me, it's a wonder to me that an author who claims to be so obsessed with problems of form could precisely stoop to that, but I understand he's working on a book with a very strange, mazelike construction, so we'll have to wait till we read it, anything can happen after such a long silence, because the excerpts I read you are old stuff, don't you know, old stuff indeed, and perhaps by now Mr. Hodeir has forgotten all those antedeluvian ideas, but it doesn't really matter as long as he admits that the notion of works has no meaning, no practical meaning, that is, and impractical speculation is just what we don't want, we'll leave that to the aestheticians, don't you know, and to my esteemed colleague, Mr. Tie.

We historians are after facts, don't you know, hard verifiable facts, and Mr. Hodeir does mention a very basic fact when, with commendable intellectual honesty, he apparently goes against his own convictions and writes that jazz is made up of moments, now this is the crux of the matter, don't you know, momentsss, the crux is this plural, jazz is a spur-of-the-moment art, you never can pin it down except by sheer accident, when there happens to be a microphone around, don't you know, and of course microphones are very dear to historians, because if it weren't for them we couldn't study the jazz of the past, we wouldn't know any more about the early bop combos than we do about the New Orleans marching bands of Storyville days, but after all we mustn't let ourselves be hypnotized by that mountain of records that we dig into from all sides with all the means of investigation at our disposal, we mustn't forget that it's only a sample, and here I'm quoting Mr. Hodeir, don't you know, it's just a random sampling, think how much bigger that mountain would be if all the music played since the beginning of jazz had been recorded, do you follow me, and the chances are that the best moments of jazz are not in the little mountain of recorded moments but in the big mountain of lost moments, is this quite clear, but above all I wish to make the point that all those momentsss of jazz which Mr. Tie regards as works simply because they happen to be recorded, are not works at all, any more than the lost moments are, because however creative he may be, the jazz artist has an altogether different approach from that of the artist who looks with cool concentration at his work, don't you know, things are different in improvised jazz, you plunge right in and try to do the best you can, don't you know, and depending on how good your best is, why that moment of jazz may be good or bad, rotten or highly inspired, you can't have any second thoughts on the matter, and I think we may safely say that where there are no second thoughts there can be no works, do you follow me, jazz is then to the work of art as the practice of magic is to science or, to borrow a term from my famous confrere, Mr. Lévi-Strauss, we are in the tinkering stage, and of course he doesn't mean this pejoratively and neither do I, quite the contrary, quite the contrary.

Of course things are very different, don't you know, obviously very different when it comes to the men who write jazz, the arrangers and composers, composers as defined by my learned colleague Mr. Tie, whose terminological arguments are quite sound, don't you know, we have to admit that Fats Waller and Sebastian Bach did not follow the same profession, on the other hand, have there ever been any Sebastian Bachs in jazz, that's another question, but where was I, I'm afraid I've gotten off the subject, oh yes, as to the composer's activities as defined by Mr. Tie (and even by ASCAP) we have to admit that anyone who writes music contemplates what he writes, and this brings us back to the classical notion of works, for a work is a preconceived thing, don't you know, or at least its general outlines are preconceived and this is why we wonder whether there is any room in a spur-of-the-moment art for a form of expression so alien to it, unless one is to be allowed to turn everything inside out in the process, don't you know, the way improvisers will twist a Cole Porter piece around to suit them so that it loses part of its identity and becomes a moment of jazz, but at the same time stops being a work, in the words of my distinguished confrere it becomes nothing more than a raw material, do you follow me, whereas the authentic, thoroughly preconceptual work which Mr. Tie has in mind would demand the most respectful treatment, it would have nothing in common with the songs that improvisers often take for their themes.

I wish to point out that we are familiar with this idea of a composed work, don't you know, since it first appeared in 1935, in Edward Kennedy Ellington's *Reminiscing in Tempo,* so you see it's not a recent discovery, it's been around for some time, it's as common as apple pie, and on the other side of the fence, those of you who've studied the history of modern music know that the most fashionable Paris composers of the early twenties imagined that they could domesticate jazz, it was a kind of early version of the Third Stream, except that in those days they didn't insist on hiring jazz musicians to perform their music, they preferred to play it safe with classical musicians, but of course this is a little off the subject, let's stick to jazz, and in jazz Ellington was the first, *Reminiscing in Tempo*, 1935, a work which was way ahead of its time since in those days the absurd idea of putting jazz in the concert hall was not yet ripe and people went to listen to jazz wherever it was played, far from those huge halls in which the poor horn blower can't even hear the double bass, while it sounds like a church bell in the first balcony where Mrs. Cluckman sits in state peering through her lorgnette at General Henpecked's wife, who is anxiously wondering when to applaud, because you have to applaud, don't you know, you have to applaud everything, fortunately it's a different matter with records, otherwise the beginning of Monk's chorus (you know: C, C, F, C, F, C, F, C) would have been drowned out by the applause that followed Milt Jackson's solo, and which he would have deserved, by the way, what's that? he wouldn't have deserved it? No, the pure horn blower, the man who makes those momentsss wouldn't be at ease on the concert stage. You can still blow *Reminiscing in Tempo,* but it's not really a blower's music any more, it's a work, and as I was saying an avant-garde work, as advanced as they come: three decades or so later most jazz musicians still don't feel any real need for that kind of conception, don't you know, even though some feel that the idea is secretly making headway, that it's got an explosive power that sooner or later will revolutionize jazz structures and force musicians to adopt a new creative outlook, at least that's what these people hope, don't you know, but it's also what other musicians fear, because if such a revolution does come along, there are bound to be casualties, and the first to go will be the theme maker, since he won't be needed to supply the repertoire any more, and the arranger, since he won't be able to keep on drawing on an out-dated repertoire for his themes, but all this is just guessing, and guessing isn't what we're here for, don't you know, it isn't what we're here for at all and my only reason for taking time out to do a little guessing was to remind you that nobody can set the clock ahead, is that quite clear, to go into this any further we would have to pretend to be time travelers looking back with our historians' eyes at a past which is still the future for us today, a future which isn't ours to dispose of, and that would be science fiction, don't you know, and science fiction is a matter for poets.

Anyway, is it even likely that composed works will ever play a major part in jazz, are there any serious reasons to back up such an hypothesis, people who think there are claim to base their arguments on an historical constant, they take the example of Europe, where all the currents of folk music finally came together in one great sophisticated art form, and they think that this should happen again here and now, and maybe it will, but nothing is less certain, don't you know, because the historical context is not the same at all, we know that in the Middle Ages church music was already very sophisticated and had complex rules, and that for dramaturgical reasons the aristocratic society of the Italian Renaissance had developed highly refined techniques in the madrigal, which later led to the opera, so the ground was thoroughly broken, don't you know, whereas jazz has been rightly regarded as a reaction against ten centuries of organized music and preconceived works, and anyway what do we want with determination in a time of mobiles, a time when the serial composers themselves are trying to introduce indetermination in their works and when chance, aleatoric forms and all that, don't you know, are appearing in the most sophisticated contemporary music, not to speak of those who reject elaboration of any kind and who regard the very idea of works as a thing of the past to be buried once and for all, so we have the right to wonder whether those who are trying to steer jazz toward determinate forms are not going against history, do you follow me, and whether they aren't bound to fail, not only economically, as seems more than likely, don't you know, more than likely, but also artistically.

However, let's take a look at the kind of work which Mr. Tie holds up for our admiration, let's examine as objectively as possible the actual results of a system in which the composer controls the improviser, or, in the exact words of my colleague, "assigns strict freedom to his creative limits," no, I'm sorry, that's wrong, "assigns strict limits to his creative freedom," it's easy to see why this sort of speculation is so attractive from the composer's point of view, since his work is necessarily conveyed to his performers in code, and no code is adaptable enough to convey a thought process with absolute fidelity, even if it includes quarter tones and irrational note values, because quintuplets on a sheet of paper are ideal objects, they cannot be exactly the same as the quintuplets that an improviser blows on his horn, for he moves in a space-time continuum which is more loosely articulated, its coordinates are less rigid, do you follow me, let's take the transcriptions of Charlie Parker's great slow tempo improvisations made by that Scandinavian fellow, Suominu . . . Suominen . . . don't you know, what could seem wilder, don't you know, than those cascades of thirty-second and even sixty-fourth notes, frozen on paper, yet in spite of their photographic accuracy, those transcriptions show us only part of what we can hear, the relief of the tone is missing, the dynamic variations are only barely indicated, which shows you the limitations of a written score, is this quite clear, can you sense the need composers feel to transcend these limitations, they want their works to benefit by a scope of possibilities which is still beyond their range, this is why they have to call in the improviser, don't you know, so now let's see how they might collaborate.

Method One: We let the soloist do exactly as he likes, and to make sure that nothing will interfere with him, we prepare several neutral passages, either between two orchestral sections, for example, or in the extended part of a number, where he'll be alone and can do anything he pleases, is that clear, there's nothing very new about it, I'm sure you have all recognized the *cadenza ad libitum* of the classical concerto, it's a recipe best suited for the piano, and if you're lucky enough to get Mr. Bill Evans on a good day, the results may be interesting, but I don't see how the unity of the work, since we're supposed to be talking about works, is strengthened at all.

Method Two: In order to make it easier to assimilate the guest soloist, we place him in familiar surroundings (who said the chorus was dead?), we allot him two times thirty-two bars or eight times twelve bars, plus a few four-fours with the orchestra, we give him plenty of support, a strong accompaniment, all this is very commendable, but now we're caught in a dilemma: either the structure of the work will be so rudimentary as to annihilate the very notion of "work," or the general shape of the work itself and that of its improvised part will have nothing in common, and here again unity will suffer.

Method Three: Having realized the danger of simplification on the one hand and of causing a rift between soloist and orchestra on the other, we decide to place the soloist in a uniformly complex structural context, which means giving up the four-bar pattern and the simple harmonic sequences generally used to support the improviser, don't you know, now this solution is theoretically correct, but in practice the going will prove too difficult for the soloist, he'll be forced to simplify his playing in inverse ratio to the complexity of the structures, which will emasculate the contribution that was expected of him.

These are all the reasonable methods, don't you know, now we come to the unreasonable ones.

Method Four: We take a complex, fully composed continuity and over it we lay a solo in the "free jazz" spirit, with all the corrosive anarchic violence that the word implies, do you follow me, now I'm not against mixed marriages, but this one seems to be based on a principle of mutual repulsion and I wish someone would tell me how it could possibly succeed, unless a divorce is taken for granted from the very start and the intruder put in quarantine, but then this takes us right back to Method One.

Method Five: Taking the opposite approach, the diametrically opposite approach, we get around all these difficulties by giving the soloist a complete part to play instead of a simple pattern to embroider on, this way he won't have any paternal responsibility to worry about, all he has to do is take the rap for someone else's paternity as naturally as he can, is this quite clear, do you see where this kind of bastardization can lead, let me quote a passage from a work where this kind of pseudoimprovising is carried to absurd though perfectly logical extremes: just a minute . . . ah . . . ah . . . I've got it! "ba – lee – ah – da – bee – ah – da – too – bee – ah – da – lee – ah – da – bee – ah" pardon my falsetto, but the quotation is accurate as far as syllables and notes are concerned, and it's completely prefabricated, don't you know, completely prefabricated.

Method Six: Or rather an experimental hypothesis which combines the relative or absolute freedom of the soloist with a system of indeterminate structures, one of those variable itineraries so dear to exponents of the open work, which are designed to be followed by both the soloist and the orchestra, don't you know, and I'd like to emphasize in passing that this approach would be better adapted to jazz than it is to serialous music, first because it would be served by suitably trained performers instead of by those so-called improvisers whose academic training has left them completely unprepared for improvising, and secondly because the concert-going public is invariably frustrated by an aleatoric work, even if it is repeated, whereas nightclub audiences are generally made up of habitués who would undeniably benefit from this system, since they would be offered a perpetually evolving work which they could get to know without having to hear every version, is this quite clear, and if the historian may be allowed to philosophize for a moment, I would like to add that this type of work would externalize a need for unity that has been latent in jazz ever since the first written arrangement "with hot chorus," for the individual sections would be subjected to the same rules of fluctuation as the work as a whole.

No, I would have nothing against a work like that, provided it were feasible and existed anywhere except in my own mind, don't you know, actually I was simply trying to rouse your curiosity, stimulate your imaginations, and of course I could have carried the matter further, but it's not our business to speculate on other people's speculations, so we'll draw the line here, my eminent colleague wasn't thinking along these lines anyway, he had in mind another kind of work, one which reminds *me* of a famous literary description, do you follow me:

> then the subdued brasses are heard once again with the previous choral hymn and comes into the foreground. The brass does not start from the beginning as it did the first time, but as though its melody had already been there for a while; and it continues, solemnly, to that climax from which it wisely refrained the first time, in order that the surging feeling, the Ah–h effect, might be the greater; now it gloriously bestrides its theme, mounting unchecked, with weighty support from the passing notes on the tuba

we all know this passage, don't we, we all sense the irony of that description and we can hardly refuse to accept the hero's conclusion, even if he did sell his soul to the devil: "almost all, no, all the methods and conventions of art today are good for parody only," but now I ask you, doesn't this same potent idea come to mind as we read certain descriptions of the works of that Nordic composer, Jarvinu . . . Jarvinen . . . aren't they identical and behind the disguise of the panting cymbal, chee-ka-daa chee-ka-daa, don't we find the same unwittingly parodic music with its declassified chords, decadent cadences and chromatic diatonicism?

And is this not, after all, a subdued form of revolt aimed at rather than against the propertied classes, a compromise which they can accept, a polite protest and, at the same time, a discreet bid to take over the succession of an officially recognized music which we have to admit is getting rather old hat and will have to be replaced pretty soon, don't you know, but please note this carefully: when that succession is declared vacant, you can be absolutely sure that all our horn blowers will be left out in the cold, because in the eyes of the powers that be they offer no serious guarantees of seriousness, don't you know, they'll be ignored and snubbed, the way all the lusty outlaws who've livened up the history of art have always been snubbed and ignored, and I'm talking about beatniks like Villon, Rimbaud, and Van Gogh, those ancestors of our modern knights of the double bass or trombone, who are more at home with the bass clef than with the treble clef, my sympathy goes to those fellows, because no matter how much they insult us, we always co-opt them in the end, don't you know, they may spend their lives on the streets, indeed, behind prison bars, but as soon as they're dead we start dissecting them in class and they can't do a thing about it, everything they ever did is taken in tow by a disciple of the great Bensohn, old man Deadheat with his falsetto voice, and by his dear colleague Mr. Tie, is this all quite clear, and here I want to dedicate a sympathetic word to horn blowers everywhere, because blowing is playing, I can never repeat that often enough, and *who* keeps jazz alive if not the blowers and *who* is the first to suffer from this blind idealism which claims to separate conception and execution, the blower again, because he is unlucky enough to embody and implement the flaw in a system for which he is not responsible, now this is awfully unfair, don't you know, because it's an established fact that the blower does his job very satisfactorily so long as it is within his means, as Mr. Lee Konitz puts it, "the simplest and most common sounding music is going to be the most successful music," Basie, The Four Brothers, that's where the truth lies, do you follow me, on the other hand it's also an established fact that a blower is inhibited when he suddenly comes face to face with a part that poses many problems, first there are the instrumental problems (have you ever noticed how difficult that kind of music is?) and once these are overcome, there's the phrasing, the accentuation which is unnatural for him, don't you know, and then there's the problem of putting the parts together, and when all that is settled, if it ever is, he still has to assimilate the musical meaning of the work, now, I maintain that the reason why *all* the recording sessions ever directed by an independent composer, to speak only of those, and don't expect me to mention any titles, there are far too many as it is, don't you know, the reason why *all* those recordings went wrong at this very point of the proceedings, is that the man in the driver's seat was trying to go faster than his horses could run, and as a result the first definite impression you get from the music is that the men who play it have not understood what it was all about, probably because they were too busy with the technical problems I just mentioned, don't you know, but then if the performers couldn't get at the meaning, then how can the listener, unless he happens to be a musical genius, don't you know, but then what kind of music is it that demands more genius from its listeners than from its performers!

This reminds me of something my revered master Gerry Bensohn used to say in connection with the relations between artist and public, I'd like to quote one of those caustic remarks that he was wont to throw out, right in the middle of a conversation, this was in private, of course, but he has been dead for so many years that I, his disciple, have a right to propagate his ideas in the classroom, for they certainly deserve it, one day he said to me: "Are you sure that jazz is an art? To all intents and purposes it would seem to be a game, and whether or not you're any good at it, the important thing is to play, because a person who plays a game gets more fun out of it than a person who watches," and Bensohn referred to the various written forms of jazz, still in their infancy then as moderately complicated variants (something like contract bridge as against auction bridge) that in no wise altered the basic rule, which is this: everything must be sacrificed to execution in order that execution be as fervent as possible, and this implies, don't you know, that the man who writes jazz must humbly subordinate himself to the man who plays it and not the other way around, do you follow this idea of Bensohn's, it's perfectly logical and it sheds light on our problem: if jazz were an art, it would be perfectly acceptable for a force outside the performer to push him past the traditional limits of his scope of action, for art is an extension of what already exists, but if jazz is a game, an outside force can only warp its basic principles, and once the game is disrupted to that extent, then perhaps Mr. Tie would be well-founded in speaking of roles being reversed, of initiatives changing hands, of improvisation being ruthlessly integrated into a preconceived master score, all things which our late teacher Gerry Bensohn would have regarded as so much poppycock!

I wonder if any part of a system as unrealistic as this one is worth saving, there's the freedom, of course, but even if we look at it from the completely unbiased viewpoint of the pure historian, we can only regard this "controlled freedom" that is granted to the soloist caught in a system for which he is not responsible and which he may not even understand, this "controlled freedom" can only be regarded as highly suspect, I hope you all agree about that, moreover, there is another aspect of this system that I'd like to comment upon if there's still time, yes, we have five minutes left, and that is the thematic aspect, I mean those themes that a composer thinks up, themes that have nothing in common with, are in fact fundamentally different from the ones thought up by "theme makers" as my friend and colleague calls them (and I think he is being delightfully naive when he claims, now I'm quoting from memory, but this is the gist of it, don't you know, that nothing can separate a theme from the work in which it is *cast*, I believe that was the word he used, yes, that's right, *cast*, well now let's set our clocks ahead a couple of decades as we did before, do you follow me, and let's imagine that a melody from a work of jazz has become as popular as the second theme from the Unfinished Symphony, you know: *re la re do re mi re do re mi la si do re la,* et cetera, now, seriously, is there any reason to think that the movies, TV, not to mention all the other highjackers in show business won't have managed to lift it out of context and give it a less esoteric celebrity?) but that was in parentheses, the real question is this: what's behind all this fuss about written jazz and composed works, what are all these theoreticians trying to do, they claim to draw definitive conclusions from a picture book history of jazz, you know, "from the bawdy houses of Storyville to the auditoriums of UNESCO," they say that eventually you have to give concert goers concert music, don't you know! yet, when you come right down to it, all this amounts to is picking up the old clothes of thematicism cast off long ago by the established concert composers such as Boulez, Berio, and Stockhausen and at a time when our avant-garde (I'm talking about our old friends, the blowers) has gone so far as to reject their precursor, Ornette Coleman, as too deeply rooted in the past on account of his themes, don't you know, on account of his thematic conception, you see, that is suspect too, and it should make us a bit leery of this endeavor to use coercion on the improviser, this attempt to pollute the very essence of jazz, this conspiracy in the name of the notion of works to overthrow those momentsss, don't you know, all those lovely momentsss.

If I had more time (but we've got to make way for the next class) I might indulge in play myself, don't you know, man was born to play, *homo ludens*, I'd play the well-meaning gospel preacher delivering a sermon on the following theme (the clergy are still thematicists): "Thou shalt earn thy bread by the sweat of thy brow," in other words, work is work and play is play, do you follow me, this would provide a fine opportunity for dramatic conflict, it might almost be the subject of a play: stage right, the blower, a member in good standing of Local 802, he works six nights a week and earns $0.28 for every thirty-two-bar chorus—stage left, the composer with no commissions, you can imagine what he's like even if you've never met one and I hope for your sake you never do, he's the film maker without a camera, the scientist without a laboratory, the general without an army, he doesn't earn a cent and yet devotes himself day and night to a perfectly gratuitous act, a game: writing music, don't you know, because after all the other man's work is a kind of game, true, it's a game which he plays under duress and gets paid for playing but actually it isn't all that different from the game as it's played in its purest form, I mean after hours, whereas the second man's game is more like work, these unpaid efforts are real enough, they certainly take their toll on him, Gerry Bensohn used to say that writing music is an unnatural act that should only be performed to order, and we have to admit that most composers feel the same way, but there are always a few exquisite masochists! For instance, I mentioned the Unfinished Symphony, that's an excellent example of what I'm talking about, because suppose the manuscript had never been found, the composer's work would have been all for nothing (even from his own selfish point of view, don't you know . . .) and in this case we are not only dealing with a real *work*, but also with a *piece of work*, witness the development (sometimes called *working section*) which it contains and which is not, by the way, the best part of the work, but this is no time to quibble over the strengths and weaknesses of Franz Schubert, rather let's see how we'd answer that preacher of mine: "Pretty poor work," we'd say, "what is that working section compared with the splendor of the Universe?" "But that humble labor is commensurate with man," he would answer, and we could go on and on like that, but I must go, I must disappear!

A very curious notion, this is the last point I want to make, yes, very curious and very dangerous, this notion of jazz works defended by Mr. Tie, oh, he doesn't come right out and defend it, we know how these things are done, you pretend to be giving a lecture in history, you begin by talking about polls, don't you know, and the various types of referendums, but what is it all leading up to? Well, anyway, all these ramifications have given me a chance to tell you, somewhat more rigorously, I hope, what one jazz historian thinks about the dangers, I insist on that, don't you know, the *dangers* of this subversive idea which I've just discussed, and in this connection, one moment more, I urge you to read a pamphlet I published recently, it's quite short, really, it's about the Brotherhood of Arrangers which I see is on your program this year, and in the back you'll find a paper by a student like yourselves which I recommend very highly, it's a remarkable piece of work and as a matter of fact, we'll talk about it next week, thank you, thank you very much.

(*Applause*)

3

The Brotherhood of Arrangers

A recent thesis by a brilliant Princeton student has attracted public attention to a phenomenon which was previously known only to musicians and a few jazz experts. And while this scholarly, accurate paper brings forth no further revelations on a subject which enlightened people would like to know better, it does contain a pertinent refutation of a subversive hypothesis to which certain ill-meaning persons lend hypocritical support. Now that this paper has been published, it is time to shed as much light as we can on that strange institution known as the Brotherhood of Arrangers.

One day jazz history will tell us if, as rumor has it, the Society was secretly founded during World War II. We do know so far that it asserted its power only between the Korean and Vietnamese wars. Yet a secret society it remains; even today no one knows the name of its Grand Master. Faint ripples on a normally inscrutable surface suggested that the Brotherhood had been deeply shaken by the death of Frank Costello, and it was assumed that he had been the Grand Master; but there is no actual evidence of this. In any case, knowing who the last Grand Master was would hardly help us to identify the present one.

This neomasonic phenomenon in twentieth-century America is a sociological avatar which has not yet been analyzed with all the scientific care it deserves. Prior to our Princeton student, only jazz historians had paid it any serious attention. Barry Ulanov regards it as "a monstrous distortion of the trade union idea," while Leonard Feather considers it "an empty victory in the name of racial integration, expressed as it is through the cowardly device of anonymity." Both are quite right, of course. One may say that this particular aspect of the segregation problem was, in theory, solved in the mid-thirties when Benny Goodman hired Fletcher Henderson. However, such partnerships have not always been free of constraint, despite the undeniable achievements of Miles Davis and Gil Evans, Count Basie and Neal Hefti; moreover, white band leaders (Stan Kenton, Woody Hermann, Gerry Mulligan) have followed Goodman's example only occasionally. As for Ulanov's severe condemnation, it seems amply justified by the confusion which the Brotherhood seems to have deliberately maintained, first letting its followers consider it as a kind of underground union, then asserting its authority on the aesthetic as well as the professional plane.

Through a few strictly confidential revelations it has been possible to put together an account of certain stages in the Brotherhood's development. In the beginning, its avowed objective seems to have been nothing more than the recognition of the arranger's rights as an artist, as the *choreographer who stages the ballet rather than simply the costume designer*. Indeed, for many years an arranger's commercial value was practically nil, unless he was also a band leader or a soloist. Around 1950, European critics hailed the "new sound" created by the arrangers of the Miles Davis–Capitol group, but since the recording company had not deemed it necessary to name the arrangers on the labels, those same critics innocently attributed Gerry Mulligan's work to John Lewis and Gil Evans's to Mulligan. As recently as 1961, *Down Beat* observed that in a world in which the show came first, Hampton's wild gesticulations were infinitely more important to the public than the high standards of Quincy Jones's writing; and every evening Frank Foster's second-rate tenor solos were greeted with ovations that he never got for his remarkable arrangements (in fact the public was not even told that he had written them). It is impossible to deny that the Brotherhood's underground activities brought results in this domain; today, many jazz lovers will buy a record on the strength of the arranger's name, when, as is often the case now, it has a prominent place on the cover.

In advising its members to take a firm stand in their dealings with record producers and band leaders, the Brotherhood appeared to confine itself to professional problems. However, the success of this policy was such that it was soon in a position to extend its rule to an entirely different area. It is now fairly certain that the first goal of the Brotherhood's aesthetic dictatorship was to bring about an insidious purge of the jazz repertoire. When arrangers became firmly convinced that it was to their advantage, that it was even their duty, perhaps, to follow the advice handed down from above, the Brotherhood gradually began to limit the activities of its members to standards, "pop" or "instrumental." It became necessary to obtain special permission to arrange a new theme, and such a departure from custom was nearly always refused by the Grand Master. The result was to curtail the proliferation of new themes and, indirectly, to bring about revivals of old ones, previously considered to be out of date. Thus it was not long before a pool of "approved" or "recognized" themes was created. There was nothing revolutionary about this situation; it reflected a natural tendency of long standing in the world of jazz. The Brotherhood simply turned a general, rather disorganized trend into an unwritten law. What had merely been a side effect of day-to-day routine and lack of imagination came to be regarded as a real obligation.

The ritual quality of the themes on the Brotherhood's list had one consequence which, sudden though it was, came as no surprise to sophisticated observers: the pattern of the arrangement itself was laid down once and for all. Henceforth, any arrangement of a "recognized" theme had to consist of a four- or eight-bar introduction, followed by the exposition of the theme, several improvised choruses (the arranger was still free to decide how many), and a final *tutti* section involving a steady rise of tension and volume. Here again, we must concede that the Brotherhood's dictates were not at odds with custom in any way, and this new law—which first revealed the Brotherhood's higher motives—seems to have aroused very little protest. The measures that followed dealt with matters of style and bore out the hopes—or fears—of clear-sighted observers. For example, it was recommended never to "hide" the melody but to set it forth as clearly as possible, making a discerning use of doubling at the octave. Thus, all the Brotherhood's activities were aimed at forging a foolproof brake that would prevent jazz from slipping out of the realm of popularity into that of sophisticated music.

These laws, laid down in view of an unspecified but easily guessable objective, suggested many historical comparisons. Some were reminded of the firm traditions of the sixteenth-century Meistersingers, who worshiped the notion of established order; others of the Council of Trent in 1563 and its condemnation of Josquin-style polyphony; still others of the more recent Zhdanov phenomenon and of the notion of "progressive music," whose main goal also was to keep art within the grasp of the people. In a sense, these parallels were justified; all clearly suggested that the Brotherhood was waging war against the dangers of creation and the risks of a polymorphous conception of jazz, offering in their stead a set of rational rules, and tempting rebels with a brand new uniform as a reward for honorable surrender. However, from a more specific angle, these comparisons are false, for they take no account of the fact that the Brotherhood was a secret society and that its activities took the form of hidden coercion, wielded outside the control of any political or religious authority.

By the early sixties, the situation was described by Nat Hentoff in the following terms (and they are in no wise exaggerated):

> I doubt if there has been a thoroughly new Woody Hermann arrangement in the past ten years. Count Basie will not accept a score that deviates too challengingly from the groove in which he has become so comfortable. The Maynard Ferguson band appears to be trying to draw attention away from the clichés of its arrangements by playing at an almost incessant triple forte. . . . Most of Kenton's arrangements are all too safe. . . . It is a reflection of the general conservatism that Duke Ellington, after more than forty years, still heads the most individual and imaginative of all regular big jazz bands.

And, quoting Marshall Brown, Hentoff laconically summed up a state of affairs which the timed reappearance of big bands had made even more apparent: "We are living in the era of the interchangeable arranger."

During the years that followed, a number of signs showed that the Brotherhood was torn by bitter internal struggles. One of the most serious of these pitted the so-called radicals, who fought for a pure jazz approach to writing, against certain right-wingers bent on preserving the tried and true charms of the "commercial" arrangement. This was regarded as a revival of the old quarrel between "hot" and "straight" jazz. Taking a firm but reasonable stand, the Brotherhood worked out a compromise that satisfied both parties. Later, it came to be regarded as an intolerable privilege for an arranger to lead a regular band, since this placed other arrangers in a position of obvious inferiority. Band leaders were asked to choose between the two activities. All complied with the new ruling, since in those days the Brotherhood's decisions were never challenged. Actually, some band leaders secretly went on writing arrangements which were signed by others; but since most of them were bent on reaping the moral benefits of their toil, and since on the other hand it was necessary to pay the price of the strawman's silence, this practice gradually died out. In its infinite wisdom, the Brotherhood had no doubt foreseen that such would be the case.

The Brotherhood's last significant act already belongs to a relatively distant past. It was the most radical of all; in fact it was so extreme that it flabbergasted everyone. According to reliable observers it nearly caused a schism in the Brotherhood. When it became known that the Brotherhood absolutely forbade any arranger to compose so much as a twelve-bar blues theme, consternation drove some to commit acts of despair. Two famous arrangers, who had been writing thirty-two-bar themes with bridges in their spare time, finding themselves deprived of a pleasant and not altogether unprofitable pastime, are said to have quarreled with the Brotherhood and left it. One of them even took up band leading again, but he never managed to arrange a rehearsal: musicians and studios were always canceled at the last minute by a phone call. As for the other, an hour before an important recording session, his copyist informed him that scores and parts had vanished. One wonders whether such an irresponsible rebellion was really justified. A little reflection shows that the Brotherhood's decision, brutal as it may have been, was inevitable. It was absolutely necessary to guard the arranger against the constant temptation to compose, be it so much as another *I've Got Rhythm* routine. To compose is to change the order of the universe. Having thus exterminated in its bosom that dangerous parasite, composition, the Brotherhood had to embark on the next logical step, which was to wage war on composers, especially those whose work tended, in one way or another, to flout established forms. Duke Ellington, John Lewis, André Hodeir, Matti Jarvinen, George Russell, and Carla Bley were singled out as chief leaders of the enemy hordes whose interests went counter to those of arrangers and who had to be broken. (Gunther Schuller and the

"Third Stream" composers were not attacked directly; perhaps the Brotherhood regarded them as a peripheral phenomenon.) With splendid insight the Brotherhood sensed that one day the jazz composer might grow to monstrous proportions and relegate the arranger to the pop field. To fight against such a peril, no measure could be drastic enough.

Recently, if we are to believe our most reliable sources of information, the Brotherhood seems to have imposed upon its members a discipline which would be quite unbearable were it not for the contingencies of this new Cold War. One spectacular ruling, expected any day now, is said to call for complete anonymity, as it was practiced by the cathedral builders and image carvers of the Middle Ages. When a band leader commissions A to do an arrangement, it will actually be written by B or C—or by B *and* C—and D will attend rehearsals. No name at all will be made public, not even that of a fifth man who would have had nothing to do with the score. By thus voluntarily discarding one of its earliest achievements, i.e., the recognition of the arranger's right as an individual, the Brotherhood might seem to have gone back to where it started. Actually, however, this is another step forward, possibly the most important of all; it is ultimately aimed at implanting in the public mind the revolutionary notion of a single all-powerful body of arrangers as the source of all orchestral jazz, a huge, anonymous legion with a monopoly on all orchestral music for dancing, shows, or just plain listening, a completely impersonal music whose unimpeachable unity is utterly at odds with the impure "individualism" of the composer and his thirst for change.

As the days, months, and years go by, however, and as this momentous decision, expected by all, has not yet been taken, the thought occurs that the only possible explanation for this delay is a tragic one. The Brotherhood is obviously going through a crisis of exceptional gravity. Torn apart under the strain of its own ruthless discipline, wrecked, perhaps, by obscure individual rebellions, the Brotherhood, according to certain reports, may have ceased to function; the Grand Master, it is said, no longer has any hold over the members. According to even more panicky rumors, the last Grand Master was never replaced. Has the Brotherhood become a huge ghost ship aimlessly wandering the ocean? If such is the case, anarchy, once rampant in this field, will soon raise its head again. The time may not be far off when the individual will have to solve his own problems once more. Skeptics are then bound to appear, casting doubts on those certitudes which the Brotherhood so clearly demonstrated; others will insinuate not only that the Brotherhood has ceased to exist, but that it never did exist and never will. It is easy enough to answer these doubting Thomases, these heresiarchs in disguise, with the arguments used by the religious against the destructive fury of atheism: "If God didn't create all this, who did?" And indeed, if the Brotherhood had never existed, how could the events described here, events which are, in their way, undeniably real, possibly have taken place?

Adams and Leverrier, two nineteenth-century astronomers, became famous by demonstrating the existence of a planet which no telescope had yet been able to detect. "If Neptune did not exist," they claimed, "the orbits of the known planets would be slightly different." It was tempting to provide a negative proof of the existence of the Brotherhood of Arrangers by describing the world of jazz as it would have been on the obviously absurd assumption that the Brotherhood did not exist. Our Princeton student has devoted the best pages of his thesis to this very demonstration. We can do no better than to reproduce them here.

Excerpts from a thesis on the Brotherhood of Arrangers by Mr. Kibitz, student of humanities at Princeton University

The chief characteristic of the jazz arranger is that he is not indispensable. It is quite possible to do without him. Afflicted with a status which entitles him to exist only occasionally and obliges him to let his very output depend on the wishes of others, the arranger is the most defenseless and vulnerable of all jazz makers. This doubtful privilege constituted such an acute challenge that a Spartan attitude was his only possible response. The Brotherhood with its strict regulations was a direct consequence of the constant threat that hung over the arranger after a certain point in jazz history. Without the Brotherhood, how could he have survived the unpredictable ebb and flow of fashion that governs the world of jazz and can easily deprive him, for years at a time, of the means to express himself or even practice his profession?

It is quite possible to do without him; to eliminate him, you merely have to reduce your band to five or six pieces, a recipe that owes its success to economic factors. The jazz of the thirties thrived on the absurd idea that a fifteen-piece band, which necessarily costs more than a combo, was for this very reason more "commercial." In those days, the arranger was king: the Brotherhood would have served no useful purpose. When the small orchestra came into its own with the rise of bop, arrangers saw the handwriting on the wall. Ensemble passages, considerably reduced in both space and time, could once again be conceived by one of the musicians and played by heart, as in the New Orleans and Chicago eras. The author of one of these head arrangements can scarcely be called an arranger; this lofty title (lofty in its very lowliness, like the title of "beggar" assumed by the rebel Flemish peasants) is properly reserved for those who actually write music. One even wonders whether the word arrangement is applicable at all when Miles Davis and Milt Jackson play a two-part exposition (with different voicings, it is true) of the theme of *Bag's Groove*. Or when Parker plays *Parker's Mood*, or Monk, *Misterioso*. And yet these are three of the most remarkable jazz records ever made. It is doubtful that they have ever been surpassed or even equaled by written music. No arranger was involved, and jazz achieved its highest form of beauty. Is this not a way of saying that the jazz arranger is a parasite?

The founders of the Brotherhood certainly realized the dangers of this syllogism; they could not fail to see how it could be foiled. Instead of bowing down to the dictates of fashion, camouflaged or not beneath artistic or financial considerations, they resolved to fight to maintain the supremacy of big bands, the source of all genuine instrumental color. Their attitude was based on several historical constants. Already, in the early days of jazz, a conflict had arisen between pure improvisation and the first attempts at written jazz. In those days, jazz was intended almost exclusively for dancing, and dancers preferred the mellow tones of a big band to the seemingly uncontrolled savagery of spontaneous polyphony. However, the style of the early arrangements was so foreign to jazz, and they were so badly played, that in the long run techniques of both composition and execution were forced to change, adhering more closely to the improvisational styles, admittedly more authentic. In the meantime, the improvisers had become soloists, inventing clear melodic phrases which were easy to manipulate for any musician experienced in swing. The arrangers took advantage of this. As they grew more accustomed to writing for big bands, they were able to reincorporate the basic components of the jazz vocabulary, simplifying them rhythmically but endowing them, by way of compensation, with the immediately perceptible opulence provided by harmonic structures, simple though they might be, and by the combination of a sufficiently large number of instruments, crude though it might be. This development, however, was possible only insofar as prevailing circumstances were favorable. The concept of a *reading band* had to exist first. It was the "old arrangements," even if they were jazz in name only, that gave birth to the big jazz band through the intermediary of Fletcher Henderson, whose biographers stress the fact that he wanted to be the "Paul Whiteman of the Race Records," of Jean Goldkette, Casa Loma, and the young Ellington; they were the sickly deformed archetypes which preceded—and made possible—the orchestral conceptions popularized by Jimmy Lunceford, Bennie Goodman, and Count Basie. The musicians responsible for this evolution never lost sight of what seems to be the essential ingredient of American music, from *Rhapsody in Blue* to Leonard Bernstein's musical comedies, from Hollywood film music to Frank Sinatra's accompaniments, i.e., a rich orchestral palette. Don Redman, Gene Gifford, Fletcher Henderson, Sy Oliver, Bennie Carter, not to mention the greatest colorist of all, Duke Ellington, were primarily concerned with coloration. The band leaders who employed them, when they were not their own employers, finally realized that the success of any jazz formation was predicated essentially on the audience's hearing a new sound (or, at the very least, a sound slightly different from that of other bands). Instrumentalists were incapable of producing this magic sound all by themselves, so it was up to arrangers. Thus, Jimmy Lunceford's band (which got off to such a bad start), Glenn Miller's, and later on Billy May's owed most of their success to the so-called inimitable flavor of their arrangements. The basic idea behind the Brotherhood seems to have been this: if that success was based on a fundamental truth, this truth, momentarily hidden though it might be by contingent factors, could not fail to play a role in any lasting success to come. With this in mind, it is easier to understand the Brotherhood's policy. In order that the reading band, and consequently the arranger, might recover their lost dignity, it was necessary to steer the imaginative powers of those who wrote jazz away from erring paths: tone color had to be their sole concern.

Thus, the essential rule is to soothe and caress the ear. However, it is also necessary to hold the listener's attention, and to this end the color scheme has to be fitted into a pleasantly shaped design. It is not advisable for this design—the melody—to be an original one; on the contrary, it is much better to offer the listener a theme which he already knows; this spares him an extra effort and induces him to participate directly in the music. He has been conditioned by the radio and by records, he has learned to recognize his classics. Get the listener to beat time with his foot and you've won half the battle; get him to hum along with the tune and he'll be eating out of your hand. An arranger mad enough to treat a new theme, necessarily unknown to his listeners, is obviously running a tremendous risk. True, there are a few highly skilled theme makers who know how to create the illusion that their melodic material stems from a common fund of jazz themes past and present and that the novelty which they have to offer is simply a new presentation of a familiar vocabulary. However, had the thematic repertoire been allowed to develop, it might have led to a revolution in style. Who knows? Eventually some theme writer might have invented a new type of theme, like Parker, Gillespie, or Monk. We can be sure that the Brotherhood had appraised this danger when it decided to ban all new themes. This ban must be regarded as proof of its existence. For had the Brotherhood not been there to act as a guiding, unifying factor, there would surely have been first one arranger, then ten, then a hundred eager for fresh air, who would have refused to write a thousandth version of *April in Paris* or any other tune already treated a few days earlier by a fellow arranger who was treating it himself for the third or fourth time. And if the Brotherhood had not backed up this ban with an even stricter ban on composing, if it had not set up a rigorous system of control to enforce it, planting agents in ASCAP and BMI to find out who was writing under this or that pseudonym, then the most imaginative arrangers would surely have yielded to the evil temptation of devising not just twelve or thirty-two bar themes—some managed to do this anyway—but *works*, in the fullest sense of the term, which would inevitably have tainted jazz, inbuing it with that which it had hitherto managed to withstand: the spirit of Form.

Collin de Plancy's *Dictionnaire Infernal* states that a devil named Béchet was to be exorcised on Fridays. We have every reason to believe that the Brotherhood's self-appointed task was to exorcise the devil Form, whose name is so formidable that, not knowing what day to exorcise him on, you simply avoid writing or even saying it. (If you are very brave, you may cloak it in adjectives and speak of extended forms or traditional forms; but generally you prefer to avoid it with a circumlocution.) The devil is always there, of one substance with music of any kind; but since we do not name him, we can pretend to be unaware of his presence. This cautious, strictly ecclesiastical approach seems to have been compulsory for members of the Brotherhood. We do not know the exact content of its directives since no one has actually ever seen a written instrument from the hierarchy; yet though they were probably given verbally and in private, they must have been worded carefully indeed, at least when they dealt with important subjects. That sensational decree that determined once and for all the pattern of an arrangement certainly did not mention the infamous name. Yet it was definitely dealing with a problem of Form, even though many arrangers were unaware of the fact. No more effective magic circle could be drawn around the spirit of Form. And it was none too soon: there were already signs, in the work of a few undisciplined arrangers, that the slight formal innovations and timid attempts at asymmetry observed years before in the Capitol sessions were gradually bearing fruit. And it is well known what becomes of those apparently imperceptible evolutions if they are not stopped in time. Without the Brotherhood, the arrangement's traditional frameworks would eventually have burst apart; as it is, they still hold fast together.

A few arrangers have made subtle attempts to get around the law. In 1957 the most brilliant of them all, the master of tone color in jazz, Gil Evans, turned out an album called *Miles Ahead* which contained artfully disguised yet recognizably formal intentions. It consisted of ten pieces based on an odd assortment of themes by different writers and grouped together in a long suite. Above and beyond the immediate appeal of a highly accomplished orchestral technique, an effort was made to achieve ultimate unity through the organized succession of the component pieces and the transitions between them. Written to be performed with only one pause between the fifth and sixth pieces, this suite successfully blends themes which would seem to be wholly incompatible. More exactly, they seem to grow out of each other: the coda of one piece contains the premises of the introduction that follows. Sometimes the dividing line can no longer be distinguished: it is hard to say exactly where *The Duke* begins and *Maid of Cadiz* leaves off. At other times, an exposition seems to spring from an element heard in the preceding piece (where it was consequently alien to the theme); thus, the theme *Miles Ahead*, one of the most original in the album, nevertheless begins with a melodic figure that is at the core of the introduction and coda of *My Ship*. This desire to integrate material from various sources is most apparent in *Lament* and *The Meaning of the Blues*. These two pieces are so intimately linked that the second seems to be part of the first, a commentary on it and nothing more. This masterly achievement seemed to prove that Gil Evans had discovered how to "compose with other people's ideas," like certain great composers of the past, or like Jorge Luis Borges. Some regard this as the arranger's ultimate goal. Yet in his subsequent works, these formal considerations disappeared. The album that appeared the following year, *Porgy and Bess*, also written for Miles Davis, was nothing but an unstructured group of pieces stuck end to end and seems far more fragmentary to the ear than *Miles Ahead*, even though the material was drawn from a single source. Henceforth,

Gil Evans's sole concern was instrumental color. Yet who could possibly complain? By thus reducing the musical phenomenon to the pleasure of the ear, he gives music back its true meaning. "Music is the art of combining sounds in a way that is pleasing to the ear." This dictionary definition is to be taken literally. Two famous jazz musicians who have carried on this epic struggle with varying degrees of success, the one using academic techniques, the other seeking to broaden the scope of his personal experiments, concur in their estimation of music's ultimate end. The first once said, "I wanted to write because it sounded right, I don't need to know all the reasons why," and the second, "If the music sounds good, it's good music." These two musicians, who express the basic truth of American music in almost the same terms, nevertheless belong to opposing aesthetic trends: the first is Dave Brubeck, the second Duke Ellington. Both, however, lead their own groups and regard themselves as composers; in this respect, perhaps Gil Evans's reversion is more symptomatic of the fact that occult forces are at work. An arranger encroaches on a domain held to be outside his province: his venture is partly successful . . . yet it ends with an unexpected retreat that can be explained only by the existence of the Brotherhood.

Letter from David La Rosette, arranger, to Mr. Kibitz, student at Princeton University

Dear Sir,

I have read your thesis on the situation of the jazz arranger, and I beg that you will allow me to state a few remarks which have since come to my mind. My sending them to you is only right, since it was you who set in motion the train of thought leading up to them. Had you not written on this subject, my vision of my art today would be less broad and less clear.

You, sir, are a sociologist; and your scientific learning seems to be associated with a taste for aesthetics and some surface knowledge of matters musical. Allow me to speak as a musician and jazz artist, even if my notions of history are too vague for me to back up my personal opinions with such lively and telling comparisons as yours.

And yet to begin with, I ought to have a historian's authority to rely upon, for I wish to speak first of a situation that existed long ago. You yourself readily claim to be such an authority when you describe the genesis of jazz arrangements. I wonder, however, whether your erudition goes hand in hand with a thorough technical knowledge of the subject. There is a danger of distorting the facts if one interprets them in the light of inadequate technical knowledge. Allow me, sir, to set my own conjectures against yours, for though I am no scholar, but just another practitioner ignorant of his predecessors' accomplishments, mine may be just as valid. For all I know, they may even be more valid, inasmuch as common sense tells me that it is easier for a surgeon to imagine the details of an operation he did not witness than for a chemist or a mathematician, no matter how familiar the latter may be with the history of surgery. And since we are both in the same situation, let me, in turn, set forth a few hypotheses which seem to me better justified than yours.

First, however, I wish you to know that my heart swelled with pride when I read that such a distinguished authority as yourself, sir, regards the title which I share with my colleagues, that of arranger, as possessed of a certain beauty. As you know, the word has an obnoxious ring to the ears of classical musicians, who are only too quick to pun that we are "disarrangers," as if our only function were to upset the Olympian order of Mozart's symphonies, delivering them to the barbarous paraphernalia of beer-hall orchestras and their impatient audiences; as if Bach had not arranged the music of Vivaldi, and Beethoven the music of Beethoven; as if Palestrina, who composed a mass on a folk song, and Brahms, who borrowed themes from Handel or Haydn, had not long ago established the arranger's respectability—and please, sir, what else do we do?

Unfortunately, my gratitude immediately gave way to resentment: what in the world can have incited you to hint, in the very same paragraph, that Miles's and Bag's exposition of *Bag's Groove* is not an arrangement, or at least, if I read correctly, may not be an arrangement? What a mistake! True, it is explained by the strange hypothesis which you later set forth, when you suggest that the ancestor of the written jazz arrangement is not the "head" arrangement but the old-time, so-called "commercial dance arrangement." The fact that this type of arrangement was popular among dancers —but which ones, sir, those of Harlem?—after the First World War may seem primordial to a sociologically oriented mind; but to a musician like myself, there can be no doubt that the jazz arrangement, originally mental, *was born of a need to create a framework for improvisation,* and that it only moved into the written stage *when a new necessity made itself felt, that of enlarging the orchestra.*

This same need to establish frameworks for improvising explains the unison arrangements of early bop; it also explains the special importance and distinctive mood of the thematic exposition in *Bag's*

Groove which, though it differs greatly, I am sure you will agree, from the mood of the choruses that follow, leaves its mark on the performance as a whole and predominates again in the final reexposition. A musician who establishes such frameworks, if only by thus differentiating his theme statements from the intervening choruses, is acting as an arranger and has the right to a title which you, sir, can hardly refuse to grant him when you have rehabilitated it with such relevance and such dialectical skill.

It seems to me that the expositional style of King Oliver's Creole Band, in certain arranged passages, already revealed a determination to establish frameworks. And I am sure that ensemble writing of the same type goes back long before the Lincoln Gardens era to a time when there was obviously no such intention to be found in society dance music. Not only did society arrangements have no "hot" improvisations to accommodate, but they actually constituted the very substance of that kind of music, if we discount an occasional performer's variant. I do not deny that the simultaneous existence of a *written* form of dance music, dull as it was, had some influence on jazz. Likely enough, many a veteran learned to read music not by playing Wagner, but the early arrangements. In fact, had dance music, and the earlier quadrilles and marches, not played this connective role, one wonders whether jazz musicians would ever have discovered in the works of the classical masters the writing techniques which they needed. For every Bix Beiderbecke who would have done so, how many Jelly Roll Mortons would not? And how would the necessary transition from the "head" to the written tradition have come about then? I must confess that I have no idea. But now I have lent enough support to your arguments; I have done so only out of conscientiousness and not, believe me, because I am intimidated by them.

As soon as young jazz musicians sensed that the true future of jazz lay in the concept of frameworks—thus sentencing to an early death the art of ensemble improvising—the limitation placed on the number of parts in New Orleans jazz by the collective character of the theme statements and final variations suddenly became as unnecessary as the medieval ramparts after the invention of artillery. The trend, it is true, was toward more instrumental color, but it was also toward greater volume and homogeneity. Please note that this development came about gradually. If, as you claim, the society orchestra had been the archetype of the big jazz band, would it have taken so long for the latter to expand its instrumental range? In 1929, if I am not mistaken, Duke Ellington's band still comprised only three trumpets, one trombone, and a puny three-piece saxophone section. How many players were there at that same period in Paul Whiteman's orchestra, which descended directly from the society dance orchestras and the early arrangements?

I well realize that by then Whiteman's band, which we still associate with Gershwin's *Rhapsody in Blue* and "George White's Scandals," was not so much a dance band as a stage band. Consequently, he paid more attention to appearances; experience had taught that shrewd businessman that a large number of performers was even more pleasing to the eye than to the ear. I am also aware that it was the pop orchestras, as we would call them today, that made the jump from dance hall to concert stage before the jazz bands did. In so doing, however, they merely blazed a trail which jazz would have followed in any case. Perhaps it was an inevitable development. In its earliest stage—perhaps we are entitled to find here an antique vestige of the sacredness of art—this music seemed to call for movement as its sole justification. In the next stage, movement is no longer directly experienced by the listener, it has to be shown to him. The listener then no longer dances; he sits back and *looks* more than he listens. The eyes of a person in search of entertainment are so avid that they leave his ears completely crippled; we all know those people who will always prefer a bad television show to a good radio program, just as they will cross town to sit with people whom they regard as boring rather than remain alone with themselves. This shift from an active to a passive role may be regarded as a step down; personally, I also feel that from a musical standpoint the second stage is a step backward from the first. The arranger is no longer driven by the intoxicating incentive of movement, he no longer calls forth the pure, bacchanalian soaring of the dancers, roused for an instant by the motion implicit in the rhythmic figures he has drawn on paper. Now his time is taken up with secondary considerations which are nevertheless essential to the quality of the show which the listener-spectator expects of the band employing him. He has to think about the saxophone "solos" which the members of that section will learn by heart and play standing with their eyes glued on the public. The idea of adding a trombone to this or that ensemble passage may be musically very fine, but it has to be rejected for the sake of balanced staging. The show comes first! This is the basic principle behind all the laws governing the world of the musical show, which is also, in a sense, the world of jazz, ever since the two were drawn together by irresistible forces of attraction.

Beyond this zone of transition, we begin to catch fleeting glimpses of a completely different mode of being whenever we forge suddenly ahead—only to beat a hasty retreat. Somewhere in the near future there must certainly lie a third stage, if jazz is not to stagnate and slowly degenerate. I think of it not as a Promised Land, but as a mountaintop difficult to conquer and even more difficult to hold; but once it is attained, our scope of vision will be enlarged and the horizons that hem us in will roll back as if by magic. Music will at last be stripped of extraneous elements; having broken once and for all with dancing and shows it will speak only its own language; it will no longer have spectators but only listeners, since there will be nothing at all to watch . . . and those who listen with undivided attention will at last be face to face with themselves.

I cannot sincerely claim, sir, that I am eager for this development to come about. I can scarcely ignore the fact that if the world of jazz evolves in this direction, the arranger's status will be precarious indeed. You say that we are not indispensable; this is only partly true. A large-scale musical show, insofar as it employs jazz, needs the structural framework that an arranger provides, the multitude of separate elements that could never mesh together without his painstaking craftsmanship. The arrangement can subsist on each of the three levels which I have attempted to describe, but not, perhaps, to the extent of thriving equally on all of them. In spite of the unparalleled success of the big bands of the past, I am still convinced that the arrangement as such was not structurally bound up with dance music; still, it managed to adjust to it fairly well—and our livelihood was assured. The musician in me has everything to gain from a radical change; the arranger can only look forward to it with a touch of anxiety.

Well do I imagine, sir, that you may be growing impatient with this queer humility of mine; you probably still have in mind my braggadocio at the beginning of this letter. Unfortunately it is part of the arranger's lot never to know whether he should speak out loudly or make himself as inconspicuous as possible. This is a result of his ill-defined position in the world of jazz; like the surveyor-hero of *The Castle* he can never really put down roots. You are evidently aware of the threat hanging over us. In a way, it is only too true that an arranger who is that and nothing more, writes "special effects" music; crude if it is popular music, subtle at times if he is thinking like a true jazz arranger; but it is still nothing but "special effects" music. How could it be otherwise? Nine times out of ten the tunes we arrange are current hits, one-time hits, or would-be hits that accidentally fail. The only way to arrange these tunes is to dress them up with outward effects. Pop arrangers or jazz arrangers, our technique, our immutable approach to musical time, may very well imply that our true allegiance is to the variety stage and to the shows we decorate. If the show disappears, if the colors fade away, abandoning the stage to the naked ceremony of the concert, what will become of the arrangement?

Don't look so surprised: the visual presentation of a concert is more closely related to the musical program than you may think. If the leader stops talking to the audience between numbers, and if the man in charge of the spotlights is no longer instructed to create a special mood for certain ballads, the listener's receptiveness will change accordingly. Suddenly forced to concentrate on the music alone, he will discover the weaknesses and failings which were hidden by the trimmings, which a lighting effect or the gesticulations of a soloist at the mike had kept him from hearing. The listener is now as different from what he once was as you yourself, who respect music enough to listen to your records in silence, are different from that friend of yours who regards records simply as the interchangeable ingredients of his daily background music. Thus, we may assume that concert halls will be peopled by a new race of listeners, for whom the decorative music implicit in the arrangement concept will be too frivolous fare. A concert—collective audition rather than show in disguise—calls forth autonomous works; these, in turn, require a degree of distanciation. As a logical corollary, the lion's share of the program is devoted to original compositions; arrangements tend to be eliminated. It is easy to see this as an ominous foretaste of the concerts which our children will one day attend.

As you may observe, sir, I am now caught up in the contradiction which I spoke of earlier, and I can readily imagine that your irritation is growing by leaps and bounds. Is it really up to me to appear to condemn a form of creation—the arrangement—which a moment ago I thanked you for having exalted by your apt description? The ambiguity of my attitude is due to the ambiguity of the subject. I see it as a building with two fronts, one facing toward entertainment music, the other toward pure music, and both being the main front of the building. For while the function of an authentic arranger may consist in dressing up a nice tune so that it will sound even nicer to a public whose main requirement of music is that it chase away boredom, equally authentic, though less common, is the arranger who reflects on a tune, considers it from a distance, circumvents and transcends it, sometimes finding implications in it which its author could never have conceived of. Historically speaking, the latter may owe his existence to the former, though some may claim that, on the contrary, the real source of his art lies in the creative freedom of improvisation—and it is true that while the former type is first cousin to the so-called commercial arranger, the latter belongs to a species which today (I mentioned some remote precursors a moment ago) exists only in jazz. When we compare these two types of arrangers, whose respective ambitions can hardly be compared, though they may collaborate within the same band or even be combined in a single man—an odd example of this is Duke Ellington, who made an authentic work out of *Moonglow*, a tune which he did not write, while generally applying the decorative arrangement techniques to his own themes—we find that the arrangement actually represents an intermediary stage in the development of jazz, halfway between improvisation and composition, embracing the dance hall, the musical show, and the concert, that it has lost the coarse vitality of the folk music from which it derived but has still not discovered the glamor of sophisticated music, that it nevertheless retains at times something of the primitive spirit of the one and foreshadows, though rarely it is true, the poetic feeling of the other. Yes, an intermediary stage and in this sense, analogous, though not identical, with the representational stage from which our music is now emerging.

The word "intermediary," which I used here without malice aforethought, was the word I had been holding in reserve to qualify the arranger's role in the world of jazz. After all, it is up to him to translate the band leader's intentions, to make them intelligible to the musicians. This is an almost impossible task if arranger and band leader are not one and the same person. True, a band leader may be satisfied with someone else's arrangement; so much so, at times, that he will insist on regarding it as nothing more than the arrangement which he expected, which he himself had vaguely imagined. In very rare instances, to make his goal even clearer, he may go so far as to sketch out the foundations of the structure he would like to see built. However, the arranger takes over and a completely different structure appears: pieces like *Boplicity* or *Miles Ahead* begin the way Miles Davis intended, but develop along lines unforeseen by him. And this example is taken from the higher planes of jazz; on a lower level, the notion of collaboration disappears altogether and the arranger simply does his best not to lose a customer.

Our function, then, places us in the difficult situation of intermediary—or more exactly, at the intersection of opposing forces. These forces are the band leaders' wishes, the musicians' aspirations, and the properties of our chosen material. The work we create is original yet composite (by an odd twist of language, the word *composite* cannot be applied to a composition, but only to an arrangement); it cannot belong to us entirely. A composer often meets with incomprehension, be it benevolent or disdainful; however, he can at least be sure that none will say to him, "You had no right to compose that work." But we, who sometimes find it necessary to disrupt and reshape a melodic figure unwillingly relinquished by its author, cannot expect him to show any sympathy for this distorted version of his original, even if he is an arranger himself. Mingus's arrangement of *The Golden Striker* met with the disapproval of John Lewis; Lewis, in turn was criticized by traditionalists for his free treatment of a famous theme by Purcell; judging André Hodeir's arrangement of *Swing Spring*, Miles Davis exclaimed, "It was never meant to be like that . . . it was meant to be just like an exercise almost"; and one wonders what Hodeir thinks of Pete Rugolo's reworking of his *Parisienne*.

From *intermediary* to *subordinate* there is only a narrow margin. An arranger rarely makes the essential decisions. The theme he treats is not of his choosing, because the band leader with whom he works is keen on audience appeal or yields to pressure from his soloists; whichever the case, the scope of his possibilities is not widened appreciably. There was a time when you picked *Tea for Two* if you had an eye on your public, *Honeysuckle Rose* if jazz had the priority; later the choice was, at best, between *Lullaby of Birdland* and *Jordu*. The musical advantages are undeniable but small. The main tendency is for arrangers to draw on the same repertoire as the improvisor, since the latter is purported to find it more difficult to adapt himself to a new repertoire. And I can assure you, sir, that this is an obstacle to the development of new jazz themes.

Some arrangers feel tempted to rebel against the tyranny of the repertoire. If they are young, at the beginning of their careers, they are likely to find within themselves the violence indispensable to revolutionary action. These men are theme makers before they become arrangers and remain so first and foremost. The result is a whole crop of unusual sounding, startlingly constructed themes. However, a theme maker/arranger soon realizes that he also has to assume the responsibility of leading a band or combo. Alone, he would have no hope of forcing upon band leaders the new conceptions whose necessity is obvious to him, but is not yet apparent to anyone else. Gillespie, Parker, Monk, and Mulligan were all theme makers and, as I understand the word, arrangers; it was not surprising that they should become band leaders. Moreover, in their case the creative impulse may have come from farther afield; as soloists their desire to renew jazz rhetoric may have paved the way for the theme maker in them. Charlie Parker's own evolution seems to have followed this pattern. If we are to believe Professor Deadheat and his disciples, an arranger is not capable of giving birth to a style; at best, he can only capture the poetic essence of a great soloist's improvisations and by using the techniques at his disposal, develop it just a bit further. I am not sure that this is always so. The Ellington phenomenon might be explained by a process of opposite nature that began with the discovery of an arranging style; this in turn called for the invention of new themes and ultimately influenced the playing of the soloists who found themselves obliged to yield to the greater will-power of a greater artist. But then it is true that Ellington's work is so rich as to lend itself to various interpretations. I would tend to prefer the version which pictures the Duke in his youth as an author-arranger, identical in this respect with Gillespie or Monk. The laboratory that he managed to put together—his band—was undoubtedly the key to his unparalleled career. Had he not invented along the way an entirely original type of band writing, had he been content to treat his own themes in a workaday spirit, without favoring them in any way, as it behooves a professional respectful of tradition (as he usually was), he might have put that incomparable instrument to wiser use and thereby avoided such dangerous experiments as the one that resulted in *Ko-Ko*. For it is perilous indeed to write variations on themes composed of material which lacks that neutrality typical of most jazz themes and which contains a potential capacity for expansion; such material may start living a life of its own and cause a convulsion which may, in the long run, have even more serious effects than a stylistic revolution.

You will grant me, sir, that the other arranger, whose sole temptation is to draw on the standard repertoire, need have little fear of such a mishap, even if he secretly hopes for a new development to which he will not have contributed but which he will not be loath to follow. Please note that this man is not necessarily a second-rate artist, although mediocrity is more frequent in the family to which he belongs than in the other. He simply cannot release his potential of imagination and sensibility without an outside stimulus. It is said that Alain Resnais, the maker of *Hiroshima, Mon Amour*, is one of those artists who are incapable of conceiving a subject; he is nonetheless one of the most subtle poets of the screen. And the great Racine was not above modeling his plays after the ancients. Getting back to our little world, we find at least one great arranger, Gil Evans, whose work can scarcely be said to have revolutionized jazz themes. Like Resnais, Evans waits for someone else to set before him the material with which to build his work. This does not mean that he is ready to accept any theme at all; on the contrary, Evans knows that his artistic integrity can be maintained only by severe selection, by the elimination of all subjects which he does not recognize, even in the act of borrowing them, as already his.

The attitude of this type of arranger may be the result of a difficult decision; in fact, it may not lack grandeur. Rather than plunge into the task of creating a new repertoire, which would mean partly breaking with the world of jazz and forming a group (for you won't be played and you'll have to find musicians to play with you), an arranger who does not happen to be a gifted performer and who shrinks from the social responsibilities of a band leader, may quite legitimately feel under obligation to the musicians whose collaboration is essential to him and choose to adjust himself to the world of jazz and its customs. While Monk is condemned to a loneliness that is softened only by a small entourage, Ernie Wilkins is held to a rather strict etiquette. His music cannot move beyond certain limits to which he has deliberately restricted it once and for all.

Not unlike an architect in this respect, such an arranger works only on commission; like an architect, he is always free to refuse any offer which might not suit him. According to his temperament and the requirements of his style of living, he will make the most of this freedom or relinquish it altogether. Some of our colleagues— Neal Hefti is said to be one of these—take pride in accepting every offer worthy of their standing, thus bringing to jazz the spirit of the "commercial" arranger; they flatter themselves they can do anything and do it well. Hefti has no qualms about it; to him, an arrangement for Count Basie is no more important than an arrangement for some fashionable pop singer. This is a position which a professional can understand. I do not claim to know all my confreres and I do not have the means to investigate the matter, yet I feel I am reflecting the almost unanimous opinion of our profession.

Here, sir, is where I see one of the main causes of those effects which you prefer to explain very differently. Consider: a profession which lives on the commissions of others can only evolve very cautiously. The ethics and aesthetics of our profession are determined, as Molière put it, by "the golden rule" which is "to please." Our clients are like those of architects: they do not expect experiments from us; these are relatively costly and therefore practically impossible. Even the shapes of buildings ultimately change, you will argue; but in the first place this is true only from one generation to the next, and in the second place, the architect can resort to a drawing or even a model to convince his client, expedients for which we have as yet found no satisfactory equivalent. Playing an arrangement on the piano for a band leader blinded by his preconceptions is tantamount to suicide. And remember that if, having miraculously overcome these obstacles, we find that our new-style arrangements do not please, every door will be closed to us, sometimes forever; and in that case our first experiment will have been our last.

I am about to conclude, sir, and hope that you will excuse the presumptuous length of this letter. You will appreciate that until the previous paragraph, I have avoided any hint of that Brotherhood to which you attribute, rather recklessly, I fear, such heavy responsibilities. My description of the arranger's world, incomplete though it no doubt is, should suffice to point out the origin of all its ills—or, if you prefer, of all the joys it is likely to provide. And my last word, kind sir, may come as a surprise to you: yes, the Brotherhood exists! It exists because every jazz arranger—and myself among them—carries an image of it in his heart, because he has created it within himself and for himself.

4

Dischord of the Atriades

All things considered, the Aldebarran brothers' odd undertaking was aimed at nothing less than a transformation of the ethics and aesthetics of the jazz concert and consequently, perhaps, of jazz itself. At least such is the opinion expressed by an eminent historian, Sir Stephen D. Lawless, in the second volume of his monumental *History of Jazz in Manhattan under the 35th and 36th Presidencies*.

The Aldebarran brothers were of foreign parentage; from their early youth, they had displayed remarkable gifts for the social sciences. The elder, Fenimore Winthrop, had graduated from Yale with the highest honors, while his brother, the younger by a few minutes, had gone through Harvard with equal success. At the age of twenty-eight, the younger brother, whose complicated given name has never been recorded with certainty (Lawless is inclined to favor "Bartholomew Cleophus Gideon," and although he is unsure of the third part of this name, sometimes refers to him as "B.C.G."), and who had gone through medical school as well, adopted the sobriquet of "Doc." His lectures were attended by a very select audience; it was even whispered that his demeanor, his stylish, somewhat aggressive attire and his Assyrian beard won him many female admirers, some very attractive, whose regular attendance and sustained attention did not seem entirely justified by the subjects which absorbed him at that period (he had devoted an entire series to the works of Sibelius). As for Fenimore Winthrop, he said he preferred the quiet atmosphere of the library. His friends hinted that he was secretly preparing a sensational book on fourteenth-century Avignon painting, which had never been properly studied in the light of psychoanalysis; and though his physical resemblance to his brother was so scrupulously exact that it often created mis-understandings—for they did not move in the same circles and did not have a single friend in common—his monastic life was above reproach in every way.

How did the Aldebarran brothers, when they were already in their thirties, both suddenly acquire a passion for jazz? Nobody knows exactly. It seems that two very separate paths, which could never have been expected to meet, led them both on the same evening to the Composer, where they sat at neighboring tables. Bernard Peiffer was playing the piano in his tempestuous style. Fenimore Winthrop was intrigued by the music he heard; as for Doc, he was frankly captivated. The next day they ran into each other crossing Fifth Avenue. Doc was carrying an impressive pile of freshly purchased books, which included *The Literature of Jazz* by R. G. Reisner; *From Jehovah to Jazz* by Helen H. Kauffmann; *How They Become Name Bands* by Paul Specht; *Strictly Ding Dong and Other Swing Stories* by Richard English; *Mood Indigo* by the English author Preston; *Il Jazz della Origini ad Oggi* by the Italian Caraceni; *Das Neue Jazzbuch* in the 1929 edition by the German Baresel; *L'Estética del Jazz* by the Argentinian Ortiz Oderigo; *U Brzejów Jazzu* by the Pole Tyrmand; *Discographie de Jimmy Lunceford* by the Belgian Demeuldre; *Jazzens Väg, en Bok om Blues och Stomps, Deras Upphovsmän och Utövare* by the Swede Helander; *The Book of Clarifying Lies and Unutterable Truths* by the Mozarab Nahum Cordovero, plus a few Japanese reviews. Fenimore Winthrop had just come out of a record store across the way with an armload of albums. One thing which the two brothers had in common was a certain stinginess, and it was decided that Fenimore Winthrop would lend Doc his records, while Doc in return would let Fenimore Winthrop read his books. A month later, Doc had come to the conclusion that the records his brother had picked out were not worth much, while Fenimore Winthrop suspected that Doc had made disastrous mistakes in his choice of books. In the meantime, however, Doc had made the most of his personal charm, Fenimore Winthrop of his reputation, and both had managed to penetrate deeply enough into jazz circles so that they no longer had to buy books or records but could easily borrow them.

One night, walking up Park Avenue after a jam session at Teddy Charles's, they had a long conversation in which they took stock of their most recent findings. At the corner of Thirtieth Street, they discovered a common passion for reform; two blocks farther they realized that jazz had no repertoire; in front of the Seagram building, huge indistinct phantom with its bronze trimmings gleaming silver in the moonlight, they decided to give it one. Sir Stephen D. Lawless does not adequately stress the fact that for these cultivated men improvisational jazz could never be anything more than a happy accident. There can be no doubt that they took the word *repertoire* in the narrow academic sense. What interested them was not the mass of themes drawn on by jazz bands large and small, but very specifically the arrangements and original compositions which were written for them—preferably at a period remote enough to be regarded as historical—and which were no longer played. They had attended a concert of Jazz at the Philharmonic and had both felt that there was something essentially gratuitous about the unending string of choruses played by Roy Eldridge and Oscar Peterson, unrelated as they were to any classifiable work and based only on perfectly interchangeable themes. Doc had gotten hold of a complete collection of *The Record Changer;* Fenimore Winthrop had spent nights at the home of an old collector listening to the complete works of Fletcher Henderson and the McKinney Cotton Pickers. By the time they reached Grand Central Station, they had agreed that the jazz of the twenties and thirties contained treasures which deserved to be rescued from oblivion, that neither the existence in certain record libraries of venerable but inaudible pressings nor even the sporadic attempts of record companies to reissue them with a hi-fi veneer were enough to satisfy such an urgent need.

Fenimore Winthrop postponed work on his post-Freudian interpretation of the *Pietà* of Avignon; having once realized that the many jazz masterpieces of the past could provide a foundation for this latent repertoire, he began to dream of assembling it and revealing it to the world. The more practical Doc immediately began to consider ways and means of putting this lofty project into practice.

Some of his fervent lady admirers, whom he visited occasionally in their Village apartments, had introduced him to jazz musicians. Confident in his experience as an orator, he brazenly gathered them together and talked to them. To begin with, he pointed out that he was acting in the best interests of jazz, for jazz could never achieve recognition in the better circles until its classics, properly catalogued and studied by experts, could be performed in concert. The public would regard a Town Hall performance of *Davenport Blues* as meaningless unless one and all could be convinced that they were hearing a faithful rendition of the real thing, just as the divine Bix had conceived it. Interpreting jazz should be a fairly simple matter if you consider the fact that Mozart is played on the basis of an archetype which, though it does, of course, exist, being handed down from one generation to the next, can never be checked for accuracy. A violinist playing the Handel sonata, said Doc, solves the problems of the ornamentation by simply leaving out three fourths of it. Records, on the other hand, provide a wonderful means of perpetuating tradition; anyone can know exactly how Fletcher Henderson's saxophone section accented syncopated notes in 1927. As he summed up his arguments, Doc became particularly persuasive. When he cried out that he was appealing to the jazz artist's sense of culture and to cultured jazz artists, a murmur ran through the audience that told him he had struck a sympathetic chord. And indeed, more than thirty musicians volunteered to join the First Group for Historical Experimentation which was founded that very evening. Fenimore Winthrop, who had some legal knowledge, drew up the by-laws which were enthusiastically adopted.

In order to divide up the work according to individual abilities, the Aldebarrans immediately engineered the election of a committee, which in turn set up various subcommittees. The first of these was assigned to draw up a catalogue of the principal band recordings of the twenties and thirties. After several weeks' work, and after listening to a thousand records or so, it came up with a list of fifty-three titles which were submitted to another subcommittee made up of the musicians in the Group who had the best ear. These went to work on the least worn records and were soon able to produce a few skillfully reconstituted scores. In the meantime, a third subcommittee set about unearthing original scores. Through some of Doc's connections, one was found on which the second subcommittee happened to have worked already. It was thus established that this subcommittee had done a remarkably good job. Fenimore Winthrop, who had been unanimously elected president

of the Group (Doc, respectful of the time-honored law of primo-
geniture, had backed him for the post), complimented the commit-
tees on their success during a triumphant general meeting of the
Group. A fourth subcommission was set up with the task of
forming an orchestra. While pursuing its musicological work, the
Group was at last entering into the phase of musical activity.

Rumors spread quickly; long before the band's first rehearsal, all
of Broadway knew what was afoot. There was talk of it at the Alvin
Hotel, in the Village clubs, in the lobby of Nola's Studios, and at
amateur nights in Harlem. When the orchestra got together for the
first time, a few interested spectators managed to sneak in. One sax
player in his sixties, who had played with Luis Russell, even brought
his horn. Fenimore Winthrop and his brother showed these unwel-
come visitors to the door with exquisite courtesy. They explained
that the experiment would have no meaning unless it were conducted only by young musicians. Since the objective was to prove
that acoustical and electrical recording techniques were enough to
provide the foundations of a tradition, the presence of older musicians who might have actually taken part in the recordings was not
only superfluous but undesirable. Confronted with an old score,
young musicians would of their own accord recreate the interpretive style of the period, said Doc; they would find a new style, said
Fenimore Winthrop. The two brothers had spoken simultaneously.
They looked at each other in bewilderment. Each thought he had
misunderstood the other's words.

This divergency, which was to have such dire consequences, was
undoubtedly brought about by deep and contradictory musical convictions, but these had purely accidental origins. One day as he
leafed through Feather's encyclopedia, committing an occasional
passage to his amazing photographic memory, Doc's gaze was
arrested by the name of Adolphus Cheatham, a trumpet player in
the old Cab Calloway orchestra; aside from the fact that their first
names had similar endings, Doc was deeply touched to discover that
the musician's nickname was the same as his. And thus it was that
Doc Cheatham determined the fate of Doc Aldebarran. Henceforth,
he would refuse to listen to recordings from any period other than
that in which his semi-namesake had won renown. This marked the
beginning of a very strict musicological specialization. Meanwhile,
Fenimore Winthrop, who was jealous of his brother's popularity in
jazz circles, spent all his nights at Birdland; his resemblance to Doc
helped him to make many acquaintances and soon, he too was well
known. As it happened, the musicians with whom he became most

intimate were suspected by the police of drug addiction. The treacherous smiles of marijuana prepared the way and the elder of the Aldebarrans promptly gave in to crueler enticements. At the same time, he acquired an increasingly exclusive taste for modern jazz.

The dissension between the brothers became evident at rehearsals. Doc invariably brought a phonograph with him and played originals by Cab Calloway, Chick Webb, and Bennie Moten, the very recordings whose scores had been the object of the Group's sagacious efforts. However, Fenimore Winthrop demonstrated, by an outrageously disrespectful attitude, that he regarded listening to these records as a waste of time. Part of the band went along with him in his contempt for the playing of old time predecessors, but the others were susceptible to his brother's impassioned speeches and did their best to remain faithful to tradition. What with these two opposite poles of attraction, one could hardly expect the ensemble playing to be particularly homogeneous. In point of fact, the orchestra had a rather strange sound and it is a pity that some of the performances of that period were not recorded; they would have provided material for many a band leader in search of a "new sound."

The date of the Group's first concert was drawing near. The atmosphere at rehearsals was no longer so friendly. There were violent arguments, as though a virgin with shining eyes had brought discord between the two brothers. One day on Times Square at rush hour, their shouting and gesticulations were such that the pedestrian traffic around them was slowed for a moment. Fenimore Winthrop made sly attempts to bring musicians he could rely upon into the orchestra. Doc combed the studios to find some trombone player who might happen to be an advocate of swing. The break finally came over the matter of a drummer's foot. Latent hatred became patent because Fenimore Winthrop had convinced that artist that a more sparing use of the bass drum would increase the flexibility of the rhythm section. This time Doc did not waste time appealing to the authority of Charlie Johnson or the example of Elmer Snowden the Elder. He gave a signal and eight musicians stood up, packed their instruments and left the hall in the wake of their mentor. Fenimore Winthrop made an excited speech stigmatizing this premeditated desertion, but deep in his heart he was delighted. The very next day, eight new musicians, recruited on suspiciously short notice, joined the orchestra. The results were admittedly more balanced and coherent. When the day came for the concert, Fenimore Winthrop's fifteen musicians had put together the following program:

The Stampede (1926)	by Fletcher Henderson
Misty Mornin' (1928)	by E. K. Ellington
Six or Seven Times (1929)	by Benny Carter
Double Check Stomp (1930)	by E. K. Ellington
Chant of the Weed (1931)	by Don Redman
Lazy Rhapsody (1932)	by E. K. Ellington
Fanfare (1933)	by Spike Hughes
Reminiscing in Tempo (1935)	by E. K. Ellington
Christopher Columbus (1936)	by Fletcher Henderson
Clarinet Lament (1936)	by E. K. Ellington
Organ Grinder's Swing (1936)	by Sy Oliver
The Gal from Joe's (1938)	by E. K. Ellington
Blue and Sentimental (1938)	by Eddie Durham
A Portrait of the Lion (1939)	by E. K. Ellington

In front of Hunter College, members of the Group handed out a manifesto which, according to Sir Stephen, was beautifully written. An audience, which can only be described as sparse, discreetly applauded the musicians' entrance; dressed all in white, they were introduced by a smiling and eloquent Fenimore Winthrop in evening clothes. The concert was quite commendable. While the orchestra was not always at home in the written sections, a number of soloists brought off brilliant improvisations in a staunchly modern style which elicited from the back rows a number of sarcastic remarks no doubt inspired by Doc and his friends.

Oddly enough, it fell to the younger brother to publish, pseudonymously, the only article on the concert to appear in a major newspaper. He wrote:

> The modernist perversion has killed a great idea. According to a manifesto issued by the Group for Historical Experimentation, its objective was "to establish in jazz that essential discovery of the Western world: the interpretive performer." Such a transposition would have been conceivable only on a basis of absolute respect for the original works. For although the manifesto is rather vague on this point, the notion of works as such is the interpretive performer's sole justification. It is an aberration to think otherwise, and a heresy to act on such thinking. Yet this is just what the Group has done, for though founded under auspicious circumstances, it has been led astray by harmful initiatives. On the pretense of "bringing works back to life by integrating them into an evolving tradition" (sic),

a Don Redman piece conceived in 1930 was entrusted to musicians who play the trumpet like Miles Davis and the tenor like John Coltrane. You might as well ask Thelonious Monk to record Schubert's *Impromptus*! As a matter of fact, it is a pity that Monk and Coltrane were absent from this festival of errors; their solos would have further emphasized the absurdity of the situation, enough so perhaps—who knows?—for that docile audience to have become aware of it. As it was, the only opposition came from a handful of courageous and clear-sighted youths. However, it is more than likely that jazz musicians of that quality would have correctly assessed the dangers of such an undertaking and refused to get involved. In the absence of any top-flight artists, there were nevertheless enough musicians on stage to play old-time arrangements, scrupulously transcribed from records, in the most unscrupulous way. As for the shockingly "modern" improvisations which replaced Jimmy Harrisson's and Dicky Wells's lovely variations—even though these had been transcribed as well—not only did they suddenly seem out of place, but even the allegedly "faithful" ensemble passages were "interpreted" in a spirit of sheer vandalism, which disfigured them even more than if the rhythms and changes had been altered. Thus, certain saxophone ensembles, originally conceived to display a warm vibrato and a brisk attack, were rendered with a colorless, transparent sound and without any attack at all; this tended to emphasize the naïveté of the phrasing and the simplicity of the voicing, and ultimately held them up to ridicule. An architect who imagined that he could improve on a Romanesque church by rebuilding it in reinforced concrete would not be making a graver error. Thanks to the current fashions which tend, as we all know, toward harmonic sobriety, we were spared the thirteenths and the passing chords which a few years back would have inflicted an even further outrage on our ears. This is possibly the only positive aspect of an undertaking which was doomed to be characterized by the stamp of betrayal. It will be up to other artists, more respectful and more lucid, to build up a repertoire and perform it in a true spirit of fidelity.

Doc's intellectual honesty would not allow him to stop at this purely destructive piece of work, no matter how certain he was of being right. Patiently, he set about building another orchestra that could function according to his directives at last. Some months later, Washington Square was plastered with posters that read:

LITTLE GREENWICH THEATER

AN EVENING OF ANCIENT MUSIC

B Y

The Golden Nights of Swing Orchestra
Master of Ceremonies: Dr. Aldebarran

Programme:

ELLINGTON: *Reminiscing in Tempo*
Clarinet Lament
Misty Mornin'
Double Check Stomp
A Portrait of the Lion
Lazy Rhapsody
HENDERSON: *The New King Porter Stomp*
Christopher Columbus
The Stampede
DURHAM, OLIVER, REDMAN, CARTER, etc.

The Golden Nights of Swing Orchestra took the stage wearing tuxedos and red carnations in their buttonholes. Doc, who allowed his musicians to improvise only in strictly defined and limited cases, launched into a long and brilliant improvisation of his own. This was the part of the performance which elicited the loudest applause, even though this display of undeniable encouragement included sounds of sirens and rattles which might have been regarded as heckling elements; later on, it became quite clear that this was what they were when they mingled with the instruments of the orchestra, producing an effect that seemed all the more offensive as nothing in the musicians' very respectable performance justified such a reception. Among the packed audience, which turned out to be no larger than the one at Hunter College, considering the smaller seating capacity of the hall, were several of Fenimore Winthrop's most biased partisans. And he himself, sitting in the front row with his arms crossed, stiff with contempt, was no doubt already composing the article which the director of a weekly that thrived on polemics and scandals had promised to publish unedited. And indeed, it read as follows:

The experiment which we were invited to attend yesterday evening was a very interesting one. A band made up of young jazz musicians gave a public performance of works conceived by their elders; one might almost say "by their fathers," so intent were they on identifying themselves with the image that the old-timers have left behind. The conscientious efforts of these young men to recapture the sound, the accents, and even the blunders of the old-time performances were touching indeed. Their objective —or rather the objective which has been assigned to them —is to create a museum orchestra capable of perfectly reconstituting the jazz of the Prohibition and New Deal eras in order to perpetuate, through live concert hall performances, music that can be found today only on records of the period. However, one may well wonder whether records, even when their grooves creak with old age, are not more "live" than anything we heard at the Little Greenwich Theater. Ellington's *Clarinet Lament* was played very correctly. I can guarantee that all the notes were there; the only thing missing was Barney Bigard's passion. Similarly, Henderson's *King Porter Stomp* was played with paleographic minuteness, for want of any jazzmanship or musicianship, which Fletcher's real admirers were not expecting anyway. The implications of such a concert are evident not on the musical plane, since these stereotyped renditions are meaningless, but from a sociological and historical standpoint. Undertakings of this sort, on the assumption that there will be more of them, may well be a sign that the world of jazz is inevitably going bourgeois. In the name of fidelity, a machinery has been set in motion which can only lead to the ultimate form of bourgeois art, i.e., the pastiche. And this indeed is the result when you require a young saxophonist to forget the attainments of Charlie Parker, Lee Konitz, and Ornette Coleman in order to produce a carbon copy of Johnny Hodges's vibrato and tone quality. An attempt was also made to give certain soloists "an opportunity for creation," with the proviso that they remain faithful to the style of the period; no one, however, seems to have been aware of the ultimate contradiction involved. As was to be expected, the best that any of the poor improvisers could manage was an involuntary pastiche, tantamount to a twenty-fifth Chopin prelude, or a forty-ninth prelude and fugue from the Well-Tempered Clavier. Conditioned as they were, what else could they do except fall back on a whole set of all too time-worn devices? I must admit that I have doubts as to the real capacities of young men so insensitive as to lend themselves to this parody of creation. Is it possible that the undeniable talent of these musicians will never find a more appropriate outlet? I hope I am wrong, and that they will, on the contrary, follow in the footsteps of that bourgeois genius Marcel Proust, whose early pastiches, also very brilliant, were perfectly justifiable insofar as they were merely exercises in view of the authentic work of art which made him famous. First, however, they must break with the evil geniuses that hold them in sway and restore creative significance to an experiment which so far is purely negative. We have no possible use for the mummies that are offered to us here. Any respectable composer would be reluctant to allow his works to be perpetuated in such a trivial form. What we must do, taking our cue from classical music, is build a repertoire and protect it against the onslaughts of over-zealous archeologists.

After these concerts, the two groups went back into rehearsal. But they had lost the Faith. The two performances had left deficits which the Aldebarran twins, neither of whom was anxious to bear the full financial weight of his undertaking, hoped to make good by taking up a collection among the members of their respective bands. At the following rehearsals a number of musicians failed to show up for the first time. Doc appealed to his most influential connections to obtain University sponsorship for the Golden Nights of Swing. Unfortunately he made the mistake of sounding out two rival foundations simultaneously so that the very people who had promised him their support turned against the project. Fenimore Winthrop was no more successful in Washington, where he had gone in hopes of persuading a government agency to finance a world tour of the Group for Historical Experimentation. According to Sir Stephen, these financial difficulties were aggravated by the harmful effects of an ostracism that grew increasingly stricter on both sides. Doc excommunicated a trumpet player for having agreed to replace a sick friend at a rehearsal of the rival group. Fenimore Winthrop banished one of his best collaborators because he had seen him talking with Doc in front of Nola's Studios; as it happened, the guilty man was the only member of the group capable of transcribing by ear an arrangement of any complexity. Thus, the elder brother could no longer supply his orchestra with scores, while the younger one could not keep his musicians together, so that both were obliged to suspend their musical activities. If we are to take Sir Stephen's word for it, they felt very bitter about this. For a while, they dropped out of sight. They were no longer seen at the Village Vanguard or the Café Metropole. Finally it was learned that they had left for Europe. They now live in Paris where they are both involved in the art world. Doc, they say, has become a fervent champion of *les abstraits chauds,* while Fenimore Winthrop seems definitely to have abandoned his work on the Avignon primitives in order to devote all his time to a defense and illustration of *les abstraits froids.* It is not known whether they are reconciled.

5

Architect of a Dream

EXPOSITION

The sharpest clashes are not those that occur between artists of the same nature; they take place when two complementary forces, meant to collaborate, are badly matched. A screen writer and a playwright can very well ignore one another; on the other hand, both may have similar difficulties with their actors or directors. Thus, the jazz composer and jazz arranger have more in common than not. Though their aesthetic goals may not be comparable, both profess to write jazz: they both fight in the same arena. They both weave the same fabric: if you snip off a sample, an expert would be hard put to say whether it belonged originally to an arrangement or a composition. In order to identify the latter as such, a somewhat longer sampling must be taken; only then will the intellectual rigor of its structures and the complexity of its form become apparent. It will be easier for our expert to detect the presence or absence of the techniques of written jazz: writing simply does not *sound* like improvising, and the slightest textural difference will be enough to indicate its origin.

"Texture: arrangement of the particles or constituent parts of any material," says Webster's. It is the texture of a polyphonic material that determines its substance; this is where the act of writing, through the devious routes and artifices which it implies, can be superior to spontaneous playing; and it is also in this quest for efficacy that jazz, in its present state, affords the greatest opportunities for experimentation. There is nothing wrong with this, quite the contrary. The concept of experimentation has been discredited only by the abusive use that has been made of it. Purely experimental music might deserve contempt; but the experimental act is fully rehabilitated when it precedes actual conception so closely as to coincide with it, offering the work a fresh scope of potentialities. Once he has given up the security of tried and true recipes, once he has thrown off, to however small an extent, the tyranny of technique and professional know-how, the arranger or composer who sets down two notes on a sheet of music paper is *experimenting*, whether he knows it or not, even as he elaborates his work. It is impossible to evaluate the sum of care, ingenuity, memory, and imagination which these two notes represent; what is characteristically experimental is the risk that the creator is running on their account—and of this he is aware.

This basic risk is a responsibility that must be assumed; it is only normal that he should pay the price of the limits he places on freedom when he restricts metrical fantasy and curtails the variations of timbre inherited from the soloist (only under these conditions can the heavy machinery of the band be set in motion). Having turned his back on all the surprises which a spontaneous work may have in store, having abandoned the naïveté of impromptu creation and replaced chance by self-imposed restraints, the man who writes jazz finds, on the level of texture, a fresh incentive as well as an aesthetic goal. Here, an effort whose ultimate aim is to wipe out all trace of effort sometimes leads to the realization of potentialities which, though they exist in improvised jazz, are not actualized for lack of substantial texture. Let a careful gauging of the ensemble writing produce an effective heightening of dynamic differentiations; let a skillful contrast between tone colors and volumes establish a "deep-field focus"; let a subtle mixture of tone colors combine with the harmonic density of the sound they carry in order to add an element of tension; let the interweaving of parts and the overlaying of rhythms lend vigor to the life of the polyphonic substance; let all the wiles of musical craft be subordinated to indisputably rigorous structures—is this not an initial justification of the composer's and the arranger's undertaking, however restrictive it may be in other respects? By contrast, combo jazz, while it enjoys greater freedom, cannot hope to obtain such a varied and complex texture; its own rests upon the piano-bass-drums entity and its relationships with the solo voice it supports. Thelonious Monk, the greatest background organizer that jazz has known to date, has succeeded in creating, within the rhythm section proper, an articulated space whose perpetually threatened balance effectively underlines the evolutions of the soloist; but the remarkable texture which he obtains through his intelligent, sensitive use of note values, registers, attacks, and intensities does not seem to lend itself to any further development; it is an integral part of a closed system in which the modifications from one performance to the next are still determined by differences in the tempo and other qualities of the chosen theme. In written jazz, on the contrary, the texture must be suited to the life and growth of the particular work, it must adhere to its every intention, in short it must be multiform. It is in this sense that experimentation can coincide with conception; the artist experiments *within the work* and because the work forces him to do so.

This situation, which countless composers have experienced, is further complicated, in jazz, by a significant development. In a field where such great store is set by the performer's collaboration (whether he be soloist or mere desk-man), every experiment which is successful on paper is put to the test all over again in performance. A work of jazz, like a human being, is born prematurely; it is not enough to bring it into the world, it must also be raised. Its gestation goes on even after the problems involved in the actual writing have apparently been solved, but what is its source, its basic motivation? Do composer and arranger stand equally helpless on the same starting line, in the most unknowable region of the human mind?

PERIPATEIA

"Not unlike an architect . . . [who] works only on commission," and "like an architect . . . always free to refuse any offer," an arranger escapes the fate of the hireling who is always ready to hire out his services to the highest bidder. Sometimes an architect who has been unable to build the structure of his dreams, feels the need to express new forms in the shape of a mere model. Sometimes, though less often, it is true, an arranger, in the privacy of his study, may sit down to write a score without knowing whether it will ever be played. Around 1920 Mies van der Rohe conceived several projects which were never executed; he may have regarded them as works, but for the public they are merely sketches and blueprints. So too, an arranger may conceive, but not totally create, a work for an imaginary group; here again the uncertainty he feels is the same as that of an architect setting out to work on his own. Le Corbusier's "living unit" was meant to be built on a certain spot in a huge green park; but the best that hard reality could grant him was a location on the edge of a main highway, surrounded by a few isolated trees. If nature and the whims of city planners are such hindrances to the architect's intentions, what kind of hindrance will be encountered in those men chosen to play the roles of the phantomlike, ideal performers that only exist in the mind of the arranger?

This situation, which an arranger sometimes deliberately chooses and which is known as *working for oneself*, is very familiar to the composer since it is the one in which he lives. Here then, the arranger is on the composer's ground; or more exactly, both are on the ground that is common to them. Indeed, experience shows that an arranger is never closer to the composer than when he must imagine the group that will one day work with him; this effort generally implies that the work under way is not a commission but the result of a personal decision. A true composer, after all, is one who can only be commissioned to write works he really wants to write, or one who knows how to turn an outside opportunity to his advantage and, like Beethoven, write the *Diabelli Variations* on the pretext of a trivial contest. The world of jazz being what it is, an arranger who takes this path without powerful, deep-felt motives, will be tempted to abandon it in favor of pleasanter and easier ones; but he would never have taken it at all if it had not, for a time, been necessary for the development of his creative personality.

How does an arranger come to express himself? Why does he lapse back into silence? The men involved in the Miles Davis–Capitol experiment would probably give different answers to these questions. Yet, Carisi, Evans, Lewis, and Mulligan were all composers by vocation, artists of a different species than Hefti, Strayhorn, or Wilkins, which explains the special nature of their experiment, its commercial failure, and their temporary retirement. They had found the strength within themselves to conceive the collective projection which was Miles Davis's band; they could survive its downfall only by withdrawing into themselves for a time. However, this public failure, preventing them as it did from drawing on a vein which would have brought them that dangerous combination, fame and fortune, may have been the origin of the full-blown achievements which two of them at least ultimately arrived at. The long retirement of Gil Evans, who spent several years doing obscure hackwork, may have allowed him to regenerate creative powers that a life of too many easy opportunities might have stripped him of; and though it is probably a pity for the history of jazz that for seven years he had next to no opportunities at all, this bleak period may have contained the seeds for the creative explosion of *Miles Ahead*. Moreover, who knows whether Evans would not have kept silent voluntarily, for while social stimuli did prevail behind this pattern of advance and withdrawal, there is no doubt that reasons of an aesthetic order also motivated his behavior. When the arranger adopts the composer's role, or the poet's for that matter, when he closes himself to any outside suggestion and listens only to the fluttering of his innermost being, he asserts himself, in one way, as a composer, for even though he is working on borrowed material, he encounters the same musical necessities and has to face the same human problems.

The first of these, and the most important, is the problem of the group, that single mirror in which both arranger and composer will contemplate his own image. [*Who speaks? What image?*] The jazz composer is blood brother to that arranger-composer who justifies his desire to write by being so foolish as to imagine a group which he knows may never exist outside his own mind; he is only a distant cousin to the composer of European tradition who writes for anonymous orchestras from which he expects no real collaboration, if he is lucid, but which he hopes will transmit to other, unborn orchestras an Ariadne's thread enabling them to reveal, long after the composer's death, perhaps, the work's intimate splendor.

We admit for a fact that neither jazz composer nor arranger can be conceived of independently of the group, real or imaginary [*Who speaks?*], which is to play the fruit of his work. Do we do so because—as might be suggested by Evans's strange remark, "I'm not sure of anything until I've listened to it"—we are afraid he may not be able to blend with precision the tone colors and the harmonic progressions which the mind's ear can sense but has difficulty defining? In Evans's case these are merely the scruples, the quaint modesty of a self-taught man, for his writing has long been remarkably deft; for many others, though, the terror is all too real, as has been confirmed by sad experience. However, the consequences of certain technical deficiencies, widespread though they may be, must not be raised to the dignity of a universal principle; and while the laws governing the relationship between those who play jazz and those who write it need to be defined, this cannot be done on criteria of minor relevance. The risk of experimentation is a reality; the work's own dynamics may lead to a complexity of writing which temporarily escapes the creator's grasp, no matter how experienced he may be; but not one iota of his responsibilities can be shifted onto the shoulders of another. Far from being a precision instrument designed to let composers know whether they are on target, the performer may, through his inability to adapt himself, warp a project which is basically valid. Since control over the sound phenomena is supposed to be achieved *before* the first reading of the new work, how can the work take account, in advance, of its performers?

A certain concept of architecture, as embodied by Wright's notion of the poet-architect, holds it impossible to imagine a structure without having first reconnoitered the location on which it is to be built. Possibly the arranger's or composer's relations with the group are similar, possibly the group is his building site. [*Who speaks of building?*] Indeed, should he not be familiar with its orientation, its direction, evaluate its resistance and malleability, grasp, in short, the *real* limitations of the entity which he is working for? By neglecting this information, he places himself at the mercy of chance, knowing that its effects will be directly proportional to the originality of a work that is supposedly determined once and for all on paper. It seems that no man who writes jazz can escape this dilemma. He is denied the classical composer's serene approach, the certainty that time will bring forth the as yet undiscoverable performer of any work of quality, and it would be unrealistic of him to hold any such aspirations.

A jazz work must be composed with the flesh of the performers [*No!*] it has selected at the very moment of its emergence from nothingness. Its genesis is simple, its heredity multiple. The creator writes it with his hand, but he imagines and tests it with the wind of the trumpet player, the fingers of the pianist, and the feet of the drummer. [*No!*] His own creation is a perpetual borrowing and lending. This or that inflection of Miles Davis is that artist's personal property. No other performer could have drawn the same effect from a Flügelhorn; but it was Gil Evans, seizing on this element which existed prior to his work, who gave it musical meaning by the way he appropriated it and the role he assigned it [*No!*] in the organization of a universe born of his inner vision.

Thus, a man who writes jazz, unlike the traditional composer, cannot feel that when the last double bar is written, the work is finished. Confident in their genius, Wagner or Debussy can wait for the verdict of posterity; the jazz composer must make certain that the result of his labors will be crystallized before the group it was written for has ceased to exist. To dissociate himself from the apparently finished work is to send it to the slaughter, doom it to be forgotten, or abandon it to the unfortunate enterprises of the Aldebarran brothers and their like. A race against time begins, one so depressing that it is impossible to blame the musician who prefers to abstain from writing unless he has the assurance that his work will be crystallized within a reasonable lapse of time. How could any architect who has imagined a house in relation to a particular location, and lovingly built it on paper, not be furious to see his chosen site put to some other purpose?

Prior to its execution, the written work—composition or arrangement—should be designated as a *project*, a term which it seems fair to borrow from the architect's vocabulary. The transition from project to work through performance and the permanent crystallization of the latter through recording are, for the creator, the most delicate stages; then he relaxes his grip, then the work may escape from his control. *"Ma pièce est écrite; je n'ai plus qu'à la faire. . . ."* The construction of a building he has designed may be a painful experience for an architect; yet with caution and courage he can now at least secure his work against defects due to bad workmanship; we may assume that if he supervises the construction closely enough, the finished work will comply with his inner vision. The jazz arranger or composer can scarcely have any such certainty: his ground is a man, his glass is a man, his concrete and steel are men, and so are his stone and wood. The site is unsound, the materials unreliable. [*Does a site have a voice? Does a material have a voice?*] If he had an unlimited amount of time at his disposal, he might be able to meet the challenge; but when it comes to crystallizing a work, the race against time sometimes takes a form which is as petty as it is compelling. A difficult arrangement or unusual composition which has been submitted to the pressure of the group and is slowly beginning to take shape after a few rehearsals has to be recorded the very next day. Often courage and caution are not enough to estimate the amount of time necessary to bring a work to maturity. A thousand extramusical imperatives, which are the rules of the trade, almost inevitably bring about a premature birth. Men who work for regular bands sometimes manage to avoid this accident; but it is the constant dread of freelance composers and arrangers, for it has ruined some of their most beautiful dreams.

In 1957, George Avakian considered rerecording some of the arrangements written for Miles Davis's band in the Royal Roost days; some of them had not been played as well as they might have been during the 1948–1950 sessions—*Moondreams* is often cited as an example. This "rerecording" session never took place. A few months later Avakian sponsored the timely revival of Miles Davis's fruitful partnership with Gil Evans. This astute producer [*Charles Lloyd! Charles Lloyd!*] undoubtedly spent as much as he possibly could on *Miles Ahead*, for he was fully aware of the musical importance of the experiment. In spite of this, the final recording— the fixing of the work in its final truth—though more satisfactory than *Moondreams,* is not a perfect rendering of Gil Evans's conception, and Miles Davis, in more than one instance, might have played better. Now, it is highly improbable that another version of *Miles Ahead* will ever be recorded. Occasionally, Hollywood does a remake of a film, scene by scene, spending as much as a million dollars on what is almost an archaeological reconstruction; a disappointed arranger or composer, however, can never entertain the illusion that a record company will spend two or three thousand dollars to bring back to life a work of jazz which a mediocre performance has put to sleep forever. Bad fairies do exist. There are many in the world of jazz, for it is also the world of profit and loss, and a Prince Charming has yet to appear. Once the error has been made it remains. [*Who speaks? That is not where the error lies!*]

This process is as relentless as disease, since it is not enough that a work should be played by the group it was written for; it must also be crystallized in some way or other. On the face of it, this is not a basic necessity. The composer has composed, the group has played; the interchange might end there. Why must a work be crystallized on records or tape, as though it were indispensable for future generations to hear it? What perverse urge drives the artist to publish it, as if the world could not go on without it? A long chain of complicated machinery is set in motion, involving producers, company directors, sound engineers, recording engineers, business managers, publicity agents, and salesmen, so that the whole world will be sure to know that Mr. Z has written a few minutes of jazz, that group Y has played it and that company X has made it into a black circular wafer; but also—and here we might encounter an ambition that would be more human and hence more deeply moving

—in order that the creator may be outlived by the echo of a dream that was his alone.

CATASTROPHE

In order for a work to live, in order for a project to be embodied, in order for it to be crystallized without the slightest adulteration, and in order to be sure that it will reach the public, now or in the future, undistorted by errors of execution which are more permanent than wrong colors or cracked walls, a man who writes jazz needs something more than caution and courage; his genius as a composer must be completed by another form of genius, totally at odds with the first: he must be a leader of men. [*Who would lead whom?*] So long as the world of jazz still fails to produce that mythical being, the conductor, the men who write jazz will have to do without the aid of a Furtwängler; like Mahler or Boulez, they will have to rehearse and conduct their own works. Now, however significant these two examples, there would seem to be an insuperable contradiction between the conductor's temperament and the composer's. It would no doubt be an over-generalization to define the conductor as an extrovert and regard introversion as the composer's prerogative. Yet, the fact remains that the one must be capable of imposing his will on his fellow men, must know how to talk to them, while the other thrives on silence and solitude. One of the more distressingly ironic aspects of the world of jazz is that a number of musical thinkers, woefully unprepared for the struggle, were forced into the arena to face that wild beast, the musician. [*That wild beast with his sharp claws will attack you! That wild beast thirsting for the love of other beasts will wound you! That wild beast drunk with freedom will rend you limb from limb!*]

With a few rare exceptions, the collaboration between the leader of a regular band and an arranger, or even a composer, is conceivable only in professional terms. The creator who is too impatient to wait for commissions and too independent to comply with them, who needs room for his revolutionary ideas to explode, can hardly hope to find an attentive listener in a man dominated by his social responsibilities. More than one leader who is capable of clear-sightedness in aesthetic matters will deliberately blind himself if he senses that his band's very existence is at stake; and it would be at stake if he imposed upon his public musical innovations for which it was unprepared. There is only one thing that sells worse than ugliness and that is true beauty—hard, ruthless beauty.

A less deceptive opportunity might be available to the composer or arranger in the guise of a group devoted to a given aesthetic conception. Certainly not an official institution or a state orchestra. A nonpermanent, flexibly constituted group, in spite of its fragility—how do you replace an Eric Dolphy?—would be better suited to the personalized nature of the jazz work. At times, such a group forms spontaneously around a man whom his fellow musicians recognize as a creator; more often, since the mountain rarely comes to Mohammed, it is the creator, weary of waiting for an opportunity which never comes, who takes the initiative of gathering musicians around him to form a group or even a regular band. In both cases, he must assume the spiritual as well as the musical direction of his team. John Lewis and Mulligan both know this well. More recently Gil Evans and George Russell were led to try the same experiment. Necessity was pressing in from all sides and they were forced to claim a leadership for which they may have been very badly suited; they had to interrupt their solitary meditation and learn to communicate, persuade, and model. The prime importance of the human factor in these creator-group relationships is due to the fact that the one must bring the other to create as well. In this type of collaboration, a subtle exchange is established, a fusion begins, and it is up to the leader to keep it under control so that the group will not overstep the rights which it has been granted by the composer. This situation is a source of constant danger: if the leader exerts too much pressure on his musicians, their contribution to the work will be merely passive; if he lets them dominate him, he may find himself unable to preserve its poetic essence. In this case, the work's character may change: what was once meant to be underlying tenderness, refined sensibility, may become gushing sentimentality; a spasm of violence may turn into a barbarous outburst. [*Be afraid lest other outbursts, more barbarous by far, annihilate your precious ideas!*] In the past, particularly coherent established groups have proven capable of collective creation, not only on the interpretive level but in the elaboration of the work itself. In the Ellington and Basie bands everyone did or could participate in putting a piece together, anyone could change a detail or suggest an addition. This type of collaboration seems quite inconceivable today; the stylistic perfection which one may hope will ensue is invariably obtained at the expense of form. For formal inventiveness, a gift which is the prerogative of only a very few artists, also demands, in order to be fully exercised, the abstractions and meanderings of meditation. There is no example in musical history of a collective work's having achieved any real architectonic unity. [*Unity is not in the form! It is in the hearts! In the raging hearts!*] The joys of collective creation are gone forever from orchestral jazz; all the composer may expect from a group is the return of an incomplete thought, the palpable expression of an abstract form, a veil and a color to dress his dreams, an unforeseen fluctuation, a rigorous gentle plasticity, a *rendering*. If he knows not how to shape this appeal, extend his creative act, the work will be compromised, lost altogether perhaps. How many irretrievable failures have been due not to the fear of solitude, of Time, of oneself, which is the cancer of the orthodox artist, but to the feeling of utter impotence which often assails the meditative mind when it must get outside itself and be embodied in others, as jazz demands!

There is no reason to lament the fate of individuals so badly adjusted to their vocation: failure has always been a constant in every form of human endeavor. Évariste Galois, the mathematician, did not live long enough; that was why he never became Einstein. Statesman Pierre Mendès France is unfortunate enough to be a Jew in a country where the ruling bourgeoisie is still anti-Semitic; this is why he can never become a Clemenceau. A champion athlete may miss a record because he is too heavy; a general may lose a battle because a piece of information on which his plans were based was false. If the jazz composer, harassed by Time, decides to fill the shoes of the conductor he cannot find—so that his project may become reality while it is still possible—he must *also* invent the words and gestures that the conductor would have had to find had he existed. [*Those gestures will be in vain! Those words will go unheard!*] In addition, he must maintain, through frequent or continual contacts, a living relationship with his group, for a creator changes more swiftly and deeply than other musicians; but what good will it do him to evolve if, at the end of a long journey, he finds himself alone? [*Loneliness was the lot of the maker of history! Loneliness is the lot of the exile of history! Alone and without slaves—powerless forever!*]

In this head-on conflict between two nearly opposite forces—the man who writes jazz and the man who plays it—it has always until now been the soloist who, with a few exceptions, has predominated over the arranger. He has been the more inventive of the two: in almost every case he has been the one to set a style which an arranger has subsequently taken up, reconsidered, and transposed to the band. Guiffre and Mulligan conceived orchestral extensions of the poetic universe created by Lester Young; they expressed certain undoubtedly minor aspects of it in terms of refined harmonies and a deft use of tone color; similarly, Foster, Hefti, and Wilkins organized the new Count Basie band on the basis of a *sound* which the old one had produced without the help of an arranger. However, if a new jazz is to be born, this balance of power will have to be reversed. The example of Ellington—another precursor—is significant. With the appearance of the composer, an unquestionably exceptional being if he is also gifted with the persuasive powers of a group leader, it will be the soloist's turn to be influenced: he will not be able to resist the ascendency of a world born of deeper experience and longer reflection than his own. The fact that this influence may not give birth to a school or classifiable style is of no importance; what can be expected of it instead is a new approach to the phenomenon of improvisation. While he may sometimes think for the soloist, dictating every note he plays—Jelly Roll Morton already made use of this privilege—the jazz composer will accomplish an act of genius only if he manages to place the improviser in situations such that it is impossible, so to speak, for the soloist not to exhibit genius in return. [*What genius would want to owe his genius to another genius?*] This process of osmosis must reveal two things: the potential contained within the work but which is beyond the composer's grasp because of his inability to take the place of the soloist whom he calls upon to play it; and a potential within the soloist which he could not have discovered alone had the work not forced him to rise above himself. In order for this exchange to be productive, a certain number of rare qualities will have to be combined: the man who writes jazz must have a clear imaginative vision of the man who plays it; the man who plays it must be attentive and receptive, with a musical intelligence capable of embracing an unexplored world of formal situations in which the backgrounds will no longer have a merely decorative function but a structural one and in which the ensemble passages, far from being reduced to an elementary antiphony, will have the power to heighten the tension as the solo approaches in order to provide the improviser—who played no part in the work's inception or elaboration, but who will now contribute to its further development and final explosion—the springboard which he needs. [*Who wants this vice-royalty fearfully granted to the most dangerous subject? What springboard is necessary for thee who needest only the cell, thy mother, and thy nurse? Choose! Choose the world thou wouldst live in! How can thou prefer that stratified society where thou must wait for thy food, to that system in which all are dependent on one, to the egalitarian, fraternal cell in which each thrives on himself and on the others?*]

The danger of such a demanding challenge is that the soloist may be incapable of taking it up; in this case he might, in the long run, be obliged to disappear. This threat, which jazz may succeed in warding off, has a historical precedent; a comparable situation existed in Europe during the preclassical period, when the composer left some creative freedom to the performer and expected a contribution of him, an inventiveness that would parallel his own. Then music gradually evolved toward the composer's complete assumption of creative responsibility, while the performer was stripped of his former privileges and became inept at exercising the minimal rights still granted him. As of several years ago, however, composers of European tradition have begun to invite the performer to participate in the unfolding of the work, and he is now struggling to reinvent the gestures of spontaneous creation. It would be a sad irony if the jazz soloist were to be deprived of his traditional tools just when his "classical" counterpart feels that he is in a position to recover his again at last, after they have lain buried for centuries. Because improvisation is still one of the vital elements of jazz, and because the jazz composer needs active creative collaboration from his soloist, the improviser must learn not to die. [*Who speaks of dying? Who is at death's door? He who has burst the ambiguous bonds forced on him by a contemptible world and who now relies on himself alone? Or he whose sole hope is to be embodied in another? A hope that is perpetually frustrated—why? Fifteen century-years between Bird and total improvisation: should your Messiah not have come? Who is still dreaming? What shade hungry for existence wants to vampirize the living? Why hast thou freed thyself, if thou willst succumb to the charms of this Prince of Darkness, god of his own work and who never tires of gazing on it? What dost thou care for that abhorred object, seething with movement and diversity when thou hast succeeded in doing away with custom and convention and returned to the immobility which prepares for the contemplation of Sameness? Tragedy is communicable; but that which is incommunicable demands the Ceremony!*

Once there was a duke of Mantua, a lord of refined tastes, famous for his sumptuous retinue which included a group of five domestics skilled in playing the trombone. One day the duke sent for his choirmaster, claimed to be versed in the art of writing music, and he said to him, "Composer, see these anonymous faces. This group was mine; now it is thine! 'Tis good enough for thee. Now write for these lackeys!"]

A Sermon
by the Reverend Mr. Sunrise

O f all the arts, brothers, jazz is the most exposed to universal entropy. We play our music, and the music we play is like the water from a spring that runs down to the sea. It wets our shoes, and we've got a little brook; it runs on down a bit and widens into a stream; a bit farther on, it becomes a river. And we'd never see that water again if it wasn't the natural-born symbol of the everlastingness of this world of ours. But if that stream's going to keep on flowing, there's got to be fresh water rising from the spring. We've got to play, brothers, we've got to play on and on, we've got to use our imaginations and play what comes out of them over and over again if we don't want that fountain of creation that God has placed inside of us to dry right up forever.

For a while there, some lucky accidents made people think that no matter what guise the fruits of our imaginations took, they could be saved. As the Almighty willed it, a man-made invention came along just when jazz was growing up, a contraption that saved what we played from vanishing right then and there! But this is all illusion, brothers, nothing but illusion! Man has triumphed over oblivion, but not over entropy! This unnatural pickling of the here and now has simply made it plain as day that spiritual decay is just around the corner! A man's conscience is a magnetic tape on which his sins are recorded one by one, but the magnetic tapes on our machines are mirrors that show us how old we're getting. They're all there, all the notes we blew on our hollow tubes, all the sounds we pounded out on our stretched skins and beaten metal, and every mother's son among us can see that the life has gone out of them. Embalmed corpses, that's what they are; we give them a friendly nod in passing, but they have nothing more to do with the world of the living. Our young folks pay no heed to them at all, they're too busy blowing and pounding for themselves. And we could resign ourselves, brothers, humbly resign ourselves to this state of affairs if we did not know that God has given us another gift—a priceless gift. In His infinite kindness, He wanted us to have a way to create music besides just playing it on the spur of the moment. He wanted us to be able to dream our creations, figure them out ahead of time, crystallize them, and pass them on to others so they'd come back to us sounding even better than they did in our dreams. He wanted those creations of ours to be able to go down through the ages.

God gave us writing, brothers. And when He gave us writing, He wasn't just giving us a handy way of noting down all the little twists and turns of our thoughts so we'd never forget any detail; no, brothers, writing is ever so much more than that, even though it would deserve all our blessing if it did nothing but make up for our bad memory. The Greek Bard, he could rely on the cadence of his verse; that was a mighty powerful memory aid. But what about Saint Augustine, brothers, where would he have been without his goose-quill pen? And in our lowly land of music, writing has an even bigger part to play: it stimulates our thinking powers and it gives them a bigger range. I'm just an ignorant preacher and it's downright presumptuous of me to take a comparison from science and technology, but I say that the real purpose of writing in music is like those space platforms that the space-flight boys are always talking about; it's a relay station that anybody who wants to go on a longer jump just has to have. We'd be making poor use of our God-given capacity for writing music if we deliberately kept ourselves from getting what's most beautiful out of it; and our music paper wouldn't be much good to us if it didn't give our creation a place to rest before it takes off again on a higher and stabler flight into the Unexpected, yes, brothers, into the Unexpected! That is to say toward those indistinct regions where the Almighty works out His designs. Faith! Dedication! Resignation! The truth is that writing has the power to increase our creative capacity, because writing gives us a chance to watch our Work grow, and not just to make a few corrections on it, that would be a pretty poor excuse, but to strip it naked, snatch away its last defenses and reveal it in all its final perfection! There are no limits to writing, brothers, writing is our way of meditating, it's the best prayer we have, writing is the Purgatory of a work of Music, and a Work of Music is a reflection of that Divine Thought which a man who can only play will never attain, and which is the key to the Infinite Universe.

Now, what have we done with this sublime gift, brothers, what have we done with it? Ah, brothers, this is a weighty question indeed and I'm sure it's uppermost in all your minds when you proceed to examine your consciences. Because the gifts of the Almighty fall straight into the crucible of Free Will, where all our passions are boiling away. And Satan knows how to fan the fire; his stinking breath makes truth and lies melt together even faster, and pretty soon the Divine Idea is so horribly transformed that we can't even recognize it! So now what's the good of our fountain pen? We can't use it to ride to Heaven with; all it can do is take us back to Earth. All our best creative energy is spent trying to communicate with our audience. We keep back anything that might upset those people out there, we do everything we can to keep them happy. And we even put part of our consciences into it! That's one of Satan's little ironies! Because I ask you, brothers, when we try hard as anything to do a conscientious job on a page of music that does not shine with the faintest spark of divinity, aren't we playing straight into the hands of the Evil One? This is a very sly kind of trickery that's right up to Old Nick's standards. Here we are, doing our level best, putting our conscience to sleep so it can't tell us that all our careful work just serves to pave the road to Hell! Pharisees! That's what we are, brothers, Pharisees, if we don't ask ourselves in the first place: *why* are we writing? Oh, I know; some of you already ask yourselves questions. Woe unto you, brothers! You live in confusion and you know it! You've lost all hope, you're like those poor mental cases who use up all the energy they've got left just keeping themselves from living. Look at yourselves: you set up your own Inquisition and deprive yourselves of Free Will on the strength of the so-called commandments of some imaginary Brotherhood, and even then you don't do a good job of it!

Amateurs, you are! If you wanted an Inquisition, why didn't you call in experts! Oh, brothers, I'm aware that the path to saintliness is a steep one and that there are plenty of obstacles on the way; but are they really insuperable, as the Evil One seems to whisper in our ears? Ask yourselves! Think to yourselves! Wonder to yourselves, brothers, put the question to your consciences! We brethren who write music, we've all been through that stage and it's the hardest one of all, when scruples are so heavy on our hand as to paralyze it, yea, we've all been through that agonizing stage of looking for a Performer to play what we've written. What? You can't find one? Brothers, do you mean to tell me that not a single one of the six thousand saxophone blowers in the directory is good enough to work with you? Six thousand—and not *one* to suit you? Ah, brothers, if such thoughts ever cross your minds, repent! for such thoughts are dictated by pride! Repent, and learn to have a brotherly relationship with your Performer. Now the Old Gentleman may whisper to you, "Do what your Performer wants, put yourself in his hands!" He'll tell you that there lies the way of true modesty—this is one of those old tricks of his—but if you cater to your Performer's laziness, you'll be catering to your own! I ask you: if we lived in a world in which our only task was to feed and provide for our Performers, where would our trials and tribulations be? No, brothers! We must learn to suffer, we must learn to bear setbacks on the way to holiness; we must learn to accept the fact that our happiest, our most spontaneous, our most beautiful efforts may not succeed all at once. And this suffering is not enough. We must also learn to make others suffer. First we make our Performer suffer, directly at our hands; next it's the audience's turn. Because we're not bringing those people tranquilizers, we're going to upset them even more! We've got to be soldiers of the Faith! Let us accept suffering, brothers, for suffering is Joy when it brings us closer to Heaven. Then our Performer, chosen by us, will suffer for us; and he will bless his suffering, knowing that we will help him find Joy; he will play for the salvation of his soul; and he will play for nothing, he'll ask no wages for this Great Initiation; in fact, he will even pay the rehearsal costs out of his very own pocket (but you, my dear brothers, will give him a hand; when we pass the plate around, remember to be generous: it's for the studio); he'll feel involved in the work of the man who does the writing, he'll even copy out his part and maybe even his neighbor's part! Involvement, brothers, is a holy thing; it can overcome any obstacle! Now, people also say you need a band leader. Let's say that for some unknown reason you can't coach your musicians yourself. How could it be that somewhere in all that faithful flock there isn't one man chosen by the Holy Ghost to be smitten with divine inspiration, a man who will take the podium and find the right words to make music come bursting out of those instruments? Philosophers will argue that this takes more than a smooth tongue, that it takes a technical know-how which performers don't usually have. True enough! So let us build schools, brothers, where we can train learned musicians, scholars radiating the prestige of the expert who can take care of that ticklish job and be qualified to act as a bridge between the man who writes jazz and the man who plays it. And if the audience is hostile or maybe just indifferent to the holy enterprise, don't forget it often comes back to worship what it once burned. Now I know there's a lot of blasphemy around today and it's got lots of de-fenders, but we mustn't let this shake our convictions, brothers. It may be part of the Almighty's plans to let the evils of modern paganism get out of hand and to let that vague, formless protest get bigger and bigger until listeners get sick of it, sick of being frus-trated, until, eventually, they come running back keener than ever to him who embodies Truth. And when that day comes, it will be clear that the Almighty, in his unfathomable ways, only allowed this schism to happen in the first place so that Righteousness would triumph in the end, and that He made sure that the black sheep of today will enter the Kingdom of Glory to come with flying colors. And, brothers, I'm not just talking about the eternal glory that is the reward for the Righteous, I am talking about the worldly glory that will reward him in this life, while the apostles of Sin go down into Death. Haven't you guessed the truth, brothers? Even the most revolutionary forms of improvised jazz are still

exposed to universal entropy! A man plays music and the music he plays is like the passing wind. Somewhere, nobody knows where, a breath of air is born and starts hovering around us; you'd think it was all over the place; but a bit further along, it's already not so strong; and pretty soon it just dies away without a trace. Sometimes impro-vised music leaves a trace, brothers, because by the Lord's will there appeared in the nick of time that little round capsule named Mike that can pick up anything that passes, including the wind. But, brothers, it's precisely on account of that fidelity it's so famous for that our friend Mike makes a valuable tool for the Faithful who want like anything to avoid the pitfalls of Satan. And dear old Mike is going to help us root out all those deceitful memories of ours. We might be feeling sentimental about some chorus we heard forty years ago; but thanks to little old Mike we hear those "never-to-be-for-gotten" thirty-two bars again today and suddenly we see all the terrible things that are wrong with them. Sin was already at work—invisible worm!—in the very bosom of their music! We used to think it could never decay, but now the bandages are coming off and we can see those oozing sores. Behold this huge mass of pus, with boils and stumps and bits of gangrene sticking out, breathe in the poisonous stink that pervades the air! Does this picture shock you, brothers? Don't you think God was shocked by those grunts which we took for sweet warbles, by those jerky syncopations—we didn't realize how much they had in common with Saint Vitus Dance (forgive me, Saint Vitus)—by those old-time clarinet bleatings which sounded like somebody vomiting, by all that musical leprosy which our little friend Mike lays bare so ruthlessly! And yet there was no sacrilege meant, none of those boys was sneezing for the fun of it! Man's fate is all too human and we might have resigned ourselves to our fate, brothers (Resignation is the daughter of Humility), if God hadn't made it possible for what comes out of our imagination to be saved—saved forever!—if He hadn't made it possible for us to give it a lasting form.

Brothers, oh brothers, God gave us writing. Let us give thanks to the Lord. Hallelujah, hallelujah! He wanted us to learn to note down our thoughts so we could create at last, brothers, create Works! Man was brought into the world of jazz to create! Everything is set for the coming of the Work, brothers, everything points to it: the only excuse for the improviser's scales and arpeggios and for the arranger's shamefaced parodies is that they were paving the way for Works. We can never shout loud enough that we have faith in The Work! It is as immortal as the Soul; in fact, it *is* the Soul! By writing, we create Work; in other words, brothers, we give voice to our Soul and our Faith. Rejoice, brothers, for Happiness is near! Sure, we've still got to go on struggling a little longer; we've got to move mountains to get our work played and played again. But not at any cost, brothers, no, not at any cost! We mustn't take the easiest, fastest way. We mustn't give in to our performers' appetites. Instead of using our fountain pen to satisfy his pleasures—Satan might be mixed up in that—our job is to make him hear an echo of the Divine Will so that he will serve the Work. With a little skill, it can be managed. Believe me, brothers. A performer can be molded like clay in a sculptor's hands and made to stop being a futile, egotistical, self-indulgent sensualist; he discovers his true mission—he is the servant of Creation—and also a new life, harder but far more beautiful. We bother him, we worry him, we send him farther along the path of creation than he could ever have traveled on his own. Instead of having him play something he already knows dressed up in fancy clothes to make it look new, we challenge him with the riddles of Knowledge. Oh, divine initiation! So you see, dear brothers, what separated the True Believers from the Unbelievers. Would an Unbeliever ever dare write the second trombone part that his work requires for its inner balance if there is no trombone player around who could play it right? He would not! But a True Believer would! He'd put his trust in the Almighty and he'd write it! "What does it matter if I never hear it?" says he in his simple heart. "God will hear it for me." A man like that is bound to be the laughing stock of philosophers; just because he won't adjust himself to the situation that temporarily prevails in the world of jazz, they jeer at him. "Aren't you writing too much?" they say, "and aren't you writing too well? Aren't you going just a bit too far, aren't you losing touch with concrete reality, aren't you being over-zealous?" But, brothers, how can anyone who's zealous for the House of God *help* going too far? What do we care about flat reality? If our performer doesn't exist, he will someday! And even if we don't find him in this life, it still doesn't matter! The Work will live on after us. What counts is writing it! He who doubts that the Work will survive is refusing to execute it, brothers, and that's playing right into the hands of Satan. Let's create first, and trust in the Almighty for the rest. Be faithful! Be dedicated! Be resigned! The Truth is that we've got no use for the so-called problems that the Devil tries to trip us up with. When we look at our music paper, symbolically ruled with five parallel lines, don't we see between those lines the hallowed faces of the saints that prayed before us: Saint Sebastian, Saint Wolfgang, and Saint Ludwig, the blessed ones. Those were True Believers! I speak their names out loud and clear to drown the sarcastic remarks of that doubting philosopher who thinks he's a better man just because he has doubts. He doubts that Works are immortal, he refuses to conceive of the Work as a thing in itself, regardless of any performance it might get, and he puts a sly question to us which he thinks will baffle us: "What if the performance doesn't swing?" he asks, and we shrug our shoulders with as much charity as we can muster and answer back that all we have to do is change performers. "But," hints the philosopher hypocritically, "what if there is no swing deep down at the bottom of those notes on the paper?" And then a holy fury comes upon us and we answer his infernal question with another question: "What if there's no swing? And what if THERE'S NO MUSIC? BROTHERS!!!"

7

The Last Will of Matti Jarvinen

On October 21, 196– the news reached New York that Matti Jarvinen had died of cancer in Helsinki. "There goes another square!" quipped Ned Thorne, advocate of all "new-things-in-jazz," past, present, and future. "It's a bourgeois disease. Whoever heard of a real dypso or a junky dying of cancer?" The next day, however, *The New York Times* commissioned him to write a long obituary notice on the Finnish composer, and Thorne turned out sixteen enthusiastic pages; the circumstances were so exceptional and the pay so good that he could not decently hand in a disparaging article.

Thorne began by recalling that Jarvinen had been born in Finland thirty-seven years before, that he had studied with a pupil of Sibelius and later in Germany with Furtwängler (this was subsequently proven false). At eighteen, he had begun to earn his living as a dance-band pianist. This was how he had come into contact with jazz. For years Jarvinen had spent most of his earnings on American phonograph records. His library consisted mainly of Duke Ellington, Count Basie, Dizzy Gillespie, and Charlie Parker. One day, after *Metronome* had published a transcription of a Parker chorus done by a well-known soloist, the editor of the magazine was surprised to receive a long letter politely disputing the accuracy of the transcription and listing thirty-two mistakes, most of them rhythmical. The author of the transcription acknowledged twelve of the mistakes, but his explanations were rather confused, so that the editor, who did not read music very well, decided that the other twenty criticisms must be equally well founded. The letter was from Matti Jarvinen.

At the age of twenty-three, Jarvinen set about forming a group composed of the best jazzmen in Helsinki. He wanted them to play a number of pieces that he had written. The undertaking failed, for in those days, with only a few exceptions, Finnish musicians did not possess the very special qualifications needed to play the works of their fellow countryman. The following year, Jarvinen went to Stockholm, but was unable to interest Swedish musicians in what he expected of them. They were too intent on keeping up with the twists and turns of American jazz to pay any attention to an obscure musician from the east. So the timid Matti went back home without having heard a note of his music.

Still he kept writing. He seems to have produced a great deal during that period. Now and then he would make a photostat of one of his manuscripts and send it to this or that American band leader, but there was never any reply. Bop gave way to Cool, Cool to Funky, and Funky to Soul; Norman Granz kept sending Ella Fitzgerald around the world; and no one paid any attention to Matti Jarvinen.

Finally, Matti inherited some money and was able to pay his way to the United States. He lived for a while in New York and his stocky figure became a familiar sight in the various jazz clubs. He met Miles Davis, Sonny Rollins, and John Coltrane. Occasionally he visited Thelonious Monk. They would sit in silence on the floor by a pile of records, between the bedroom door with its sign ("SILENCE! GENIUS ASLEEP") and the piano ("SILENCE! GENIUS AT WORK"), and listen to old Monk records or to a more recent tape. Sometimes Monk would sit down at the piano and Jarvinen, who admired him, would try to understand how the mind of a great improviser works.

One day Quincy Jones took the Finn to a rehearsal of Count Basie's orchestra. The musicians were waiting around for their parts, which weren't ready yet. In his briefcase, Matti was carrying the parts of a score which called for an orchestra of similar composition. For ten minutes, Basie's men sight-read the foreigner's work, not without some difficulty. Intrigued by the disjunctive writing for the brass and the strange way in which the saxes were woven in, Marshal Royal was about to ask for another run-through when the copyist strode in with four arrangements that had to be rehearsed immediately. The next day, the band went on tour.

Another time, at Gunther Schuller's suggestion, Jarvinen was invited to appear on a radio program. It began with an interview. Matti said that Duke Ellington was the greatest arranger in the history of jazz. To everyone's surprise, he stressed the fact that Ellington was an "arranger," not a composer, and added that in his opinion there had been no jazz composers as yet. He also said (and this created a very bad impression) that while from a certain standpoint *Ko-Ko* might be regarded as the work of a jazz musician, *Concerto for Cootie* could have been conceived by a square. After that, a hybrid orchestra rehearsed and performed with a fair degree of accuracy a piece that he had just written. The musicians debated among themselves whether or not Jarvinen had created a new sound; all agreed, however, that he was a good orchestrator. The bass player even pointed out that certain *tutti* passages scored for ten horns conveyed the impression of a much larger orchestral mass.

On the strength of this program Matti was asked by a small company to record a series of arrangements for quintet. He refused, on the grounds that he was not an arranger but a composer. Finally an agreement was reached: Jarvinen would be allowed to record a work for seven musicians provided that he paid for copying and rehearsals. When the record was issued, the critics' attention went to the solo passages which he had set aside for several of his carefully chosen performers. Only one critic praised the piece as such, but for reasons which to Jarvinen seemed completely irrelevant. "I feel as if he were talking about some other record," he confided to his friends.

Some time after that, failing any further commissions, Jarvinen set sail for Europe. Four or five musicians who had become his friends came down to say goodbye. He shook hands with them and in a choked voice uttered a few solemn words that were hard to understand (his accent was atrocious). Stan Getz (or perhaps it was Hen Gates) thinks he remembers them as follows: "I am a man without roots. I have nothing to pursue. Everything still remains to be done. Perhaps I have understood a few things. I came to give you. . . ." But then an expression of doubt—of panic, some say—

crossed his face and he hurried up the gangway without looking back.

The years passed. Concert jazz went through a period of latent crisis. To hear their favorite soloists, people preferred to go to places where they could see them close up, and drink and talk while they listened. There was an obscure feeling of uneasiness in those big halls with their rows on rows of seats. When a large orchestra ventured onto the stage, the arrangements it played sounded like accompaniments for a musical show during a chorus-girl strike. The small combos had a hard time accommodating themselves to the silence of the audience, while the audience had a hard time sitting through programs involving only one range of tone colors. Band leaders reached the point where they were curtailing their concerts in shocking proportions, but the public, far from being grateful, found this solution inelegant. On the other hand, a succession of several orchestras in a single evening produced a hybrid program appreciated by many listeners. Their dulled senses were stimulated by this rapid alternation of styles. The new forms of jazz, with their ritualistic aspects and the qualities of uncertainty peculiar to them, did not seem any better suited to the concert hall. It would have been necessary to find a special setting to exhibit them at their best.

People began to ask questions. Did the ideal conditions for a concert merely consist in placing a handful of musicians face to face with a thousand listeners? Did not a concert as such require a true spiritual communion on both sides? And to achieve this, did not jazz have to outgrow its traditional limitations and strive toward certain architectural qualities which it still lacked? A few astute minds suddenly realized that Matti Jarvinen was a precursor. George Morris, an open-minded critic with a fairly large audience, found Matti's record in the back of a closet. Ignoring a shamefully low sales figure which at that time seemed definitive, perhaps because the record contained no obvious gimmick, Morris wrote a very sober article and sent it to an important high-brow magazine. Conscientiously rewritten by an editor whose talent was equaled only by his hatred for jazz, the article fired the imaginations of those who claimed to be avant-garde. People began talking about Matti. In the absence of any pressure from public opinion, still quite indifferent, it was the curiosity of the intelligentsia that prompted the promoters of a big jazz festival to program a work which Jarvinen had left on deposit with a publisher in manuscript form. The audience was a large one; they applauded and shouted. Carried away by the movement he had set in motion, Morris reported this first performance in terms which were rather impressionistic but fairly enthusiastic:

The first thing that struck us was the huge size of the orchestra. There were more players on the stage than for some symphony concerts. I counted no less than thirteen trumpets divided into three different groups, with a proportionate number of trombones and saxophones, a great many percussion instruments, and an entire small choir from a Harlem church. However, most amazing of all was the way these musicians were arranged: some were grouped together, others were off by themselves, some were on the very edge of the stage, almost in the audience as it were, as though they were not supposed to be taking part in the same performance. It was not until the work was nearly over that I understood the reason for this unusual placing. The music began pianissimo with an indescribable crowd effect; it sounded like a thousand people talking at the same time about different things yet in the same language. Broken down in turn into every possible combination, the whole orchestra seemed to be exuding blues wails at every pore; multiplying endlessly, their apparent number was increased even further by the fact that they were spread through every register, from the lower depths of the double bass to the shrillest heights of the flute. . . . Then that forest of music seemed gradually to fold back and it was suddenly as if it consisted of only one species of tree. The component melodic cells revealed their identities; almost, it seemed, with reluctance they admitted that they were made up of three or four identical notes. Finally, they all came together in a unison as thick as an Oriental carpet, and this served to introduce a melodic line so bare that it was impossible to tell whether it was a theme or simply a motive, the remainder of a long painstaking process of subtraction. At this point we realized that the pulse of the drums had crept stealthily beneath this closing canopy of sound; now it came into the foreground, setting the work's first tempo, a medium tempo sustained by an elegant, bouncing two-beat. Our attention was drawn to the far left side of the stage where some ten instruments, including a trumpet, a Flügelhorn, a flute, and several saxophones, were arranged in a wavy line that stood out from the rest of the orchestra; this was the *concertino*. Far from being fixed, however, this group varied from one section to the next, shifting gradually or suddenly, according to the players' positions; when the piano, located at the back of the stage, came into play, the concertino's center of gravity swung in that direction and the sound seemed to acquire greater depth. Tempos and keys meshed or clashed with the instrumental composition of these little kaleidoscopic groups, whose glittering exchanges were sometimes shaken by the bubbling cries of huge orchestral ensembles, sometimes slowed by their massive weight. More rarely, certain ensemble passages dissolved or broke off to make way for a solo, written or improvised as the case might be; and here and there a voice would rise up in praise or complaint. At other times, near silence, colored only by a shivering cymbal, would prepare the way for some unexpected explosion. I cannot say with certainty that all this luxuriance was held together by an indisputable unity; on the other hand, as a playwright renews the situations around his characters, so too Jarvinen offers the listener fresh aspects of the material which he manipulates, a material which constantly changes shape and color, like the molten lava in Haroun Tazieff's volcano films. And though there were moments when I felt that the work was a bit spotty, this feeling was effaced completely during the last few minutes when all those tempi, all those keys, and all the contrasting faces of the jazz orchestra came together in a single tempo, a single key, a single overall "sound." This convergence took place to the beat of a regular, balanced rhythm reminiscent of the old-time blues. Suddenly a whole group of voices that had been silent until then were laid over and woven into the orchestral fabric, bursting forth in joyous riffs that summed up the thousands of melodic ideas glimpsed earlier and endowed them with a quality of final but multifarious truth, which the vast unison at the beginning of the work had not prepared us to expect. And so, in an orgy of notes from every direction, which seemed to spin wildly in space owing to the stereophonic arrangement of the players—voices and orchestra mingled or separate—in a huge whirling glow, ended a work which in my opinion marks the appearance of a new lyricism in jazz.

Newspaper praise was not unanimous. Some critics, deliberately ignoring the work as such, confined themselves to a description of the musicians' playing; they had noticed that the players were abnormally "concentrated," which "inevitably" led them to "tense up"; moreover, they deplored the "alarming" presence of a "classical" pianist who had had to be brought in at the last minute after several jazz pianists had declared themselves unequal to the task of reading a piano part (deemed "unusually and no doubt unnecessarily difficult") which had finally been played "à la John Cage." The most widely appreciated article, however, was not written by a music critic at all, but by a popular columnist. His angle was humorous; he dwelled with rather heavy irony on the disconcerting effect which this out-of-the-ordinary concert had had on the audience. The very title of the article—"Recipe, or How to Concoct a Name"—gave a clear idea of its contents:

> Take one composer from Europe (the finest grade come from there: beware of American imitations which often look better than they are). Have him put out two or three works of an acceptable length and requiring a fairly large number of pieces. If he puts out more, set aside the excess; it can be served up later and will be all the better for it (the works of European composers always improve with age). Make sure the finished work is rich in syncopations of every kind. If necessary, add a few more; there are plenty of good ones on the market. Empty out the instruments; clean them; give them a polish. If the audience is stiff, it has to be softened. Don't hesitate to shake it up. Choose your musicians carefully; they determine the flavor of your dish (too jazzlike or not enough, as you choose). Pick them preferably young and tender; the older ones are less malleable and more expensive. Set them out around the stage in several groups, leaving an open space in the middle for the aroma to circulate among the groups and permeate them. Carefully fold in the horn parts. Now comes the ticklish part. Still shaking up the audience from time to time, bring the performance to a boil: the work should be served up piping hot. As for bouillabaisse, a "tempestuous fire" is indispensable. Arrange a sizable number of spectators around the podium with a fairly large claque mixed in; let them simmer for fifteen or twenty minutes at the most. If you have been very careful, the Name you have just cooked up

will be a great Name. A moment ago it was completely unknown, but as soon as it has been tasted in concert, it will find its way onto every table and into every mouth.

The columnist's conclusion was perfectly right. A great stir began around Jarvinen. For a few days he was almost famous. Anyone who had heard his music was assailed with questions. Many listeners had experienced a feeling of strangeness; a smaller number had been sensitive to the formal balance; a few had felt that the basic components of jazz had been interpreted too freely. The jaded concert goers, possibly because they were tired of expressing their opinions in the form of ironically ambiguous smiles, insidiously dropped the names of Gershwin and Stravinsky.

Delighted at having unearthed such a controversial musician, the well-meaning Morris, on a trip to Europe, crossed the Baltic for the sole purpose of seeing Jarvinen. However, the interview he hoped to bring back never took place. "It was like a visit to the Kingdom of the Dead," he declared on his return. Jarvinen was emaciated, his face was expressionless and he seemed to have a hard time following the conversation. The news from New York was greeted with indifference. Morris's congratulations aroused no response; but when Morris, mentioning some of the comments he had heard after the concert, associated the words *music* and *beauty*, Jarvinen interrupted him for the first time. "My music was beautiful . . ." he murmured, and he repeated the words over and over, like a litany. Then he fell silent and his eyes filled with tears. When he finally became aware of his visitor's consternation, he smiled sadly. "Forgive me," he said. "It's because my music is getting old. It used to be . . . so beautiful." George Morris was an experienced reporter, but he could get nothing more out of him. The Finnish composer went on talking about his music the way a man talks about a love that has died: "It was so beautiful."

Once again, public interest died down, but no one could have predicted that this perfectly natural ebb of popularity would turn into actual hostility. One day a group of young "beat" musicians rented a little hall in the Village to play Edgard Varèse and Earle Brown, and decided to add one of Jarvinen's works to their program. They gave it very few rehearsals. Scarcely had the first few measures been played when the audience began to react with such surprising gratuitous violence that the performance had to be stopped. In his obituary, Ned Thorne mentions this unfortunate concert, deploring, of course, the lack of preparation and the disastrous reception, but emphasizing, too, the fact that it cost next to nothing (the musicians had taken no salary), whereas the Festival had spent five thousand dollars on the Jarvinen concert alone (obviously too much, considering present-day standards; in fact, had it not been for the contribution of an all but anonymous patron, the resulting deficit would have been serious indeed).

In New York, Jarvinen was regarded as a perfectly well-balanced man. After his death, however, it was learned that he had behaved rather strangely during the last years of his life. From time to time he placed eccentric ads in several Scandinavian newspapers. All began by specifying that he could "read music fluently in the seven clefs," then went on to solicit employment as a gardener, embassy counselor, or whatever else was available. He was also conspicuous for his attire: having heard that dark clothes were a handicap in the event of an atomic explosion, he had ordered a collection of snow-white suits and a white overcoat, and wore them in all kinds of weather. It was also learned that Jarvinen had died at home, without undergoing any kind of surgical treatment. This seemed to confirm the rumor that Jarvinen had not died of disease but had committed suicide—just one more oddity in a milieu in which actual suicide is quite rare. This final eccentricity, however, made very little impression and was already forgotten by the time Jarvinen's last will and testament was made public.

Jarvinen's legacy was a modest sheaf of documents (its relative slenderness seemed to indicate that he had destroyed part of his work) comprising only six scores and a sealed envelope which contained the will. This consisted of three sheets of paper unevenly covered with careful, spidery handwriting. On the first were set forth those famous directives, so provocatively and paradoxically laconic, which probably played a more important part in the Finnish composer's posthumous fame than the works to which they applied. Jarvinen authorized only a single public performance of each of his works and prohibited any subsequent execution; the names of the musicians whom he wished to have play each part were set down meticulously (he allowed for no substitutes); as soon as the performance was finished, both orchestral parts and manuscript were to be destroyed on the spot with no recording or publication rights granted for even the shortest passage. The second sheet contained twelve "propositions" dealing with jazz composition; this was his technical and spiritual bequest. The third sheet bore the title: "Pieces of advice for a young musician tempted to leave the beaten path." However, this plural was belied by the single sentence that followed:

> "If you can,
> create nothing
> but learn life instead."

These words, possibly the last that Jarvinen wrote, fill only a small portion of the sheet on which they were carefully penned. The rest of the page is blank.

Jarvinen's will was variously interpreted. Some saw it as an evidence of fierce nihilism. Others claimed that the last phrase applied to the work of jazz per se which, by its very nature, cannot survive. Still others believed that he was expressing a profoundly pessimistic view of contemporary art. This was not Ned Thorne's opinion. "It is obvious," he wrote, "that these bitter words were prompted by Matti Jarvinen's own wretched fate. They are the words of an artist who has failed to find recognition during his lifetime, a phenomenon which is increasingly rare today; they are the words of a man who was so deeply affected by this lack of success that it disturbed, as we know, his mental balance. It is in the interest of everyone everywhere that Matti Jarvinen's last wishes should *not* be respected, that his works should be played and recorded as much as possible. Personally, I have no doubt but what they will yield sizable royalties which might be used for the benefit of all to found a Jarvinen Institute for the Study of Jazz Composition. May it have many students!"

Just recently, an American musician, who wishes to remain anonymous, has authorized publication of a long passage from a letter which Jarvinen wrote to him shortly before his death. It is perhaps the most significant text written by this artist, who was little inclined to communicate his ideas; in fact, aside from the testament, it is the only one known.

EXCERPT FROM MATTI JARVINEN'S LETTER

Winter flowers . . . will you have time to bloom? Our civilization has invented suicide, it can destroy itself in the space of a second. A mistaken radar reading, a faulty transistor, and twenty-five centuries of humanity will be blotted out. From a mystical point of view, it might be said that the anguish and self-doubts of contemporary artists merely foreshadow the inevitable catastrophe. No future before us. . . . If this be true, a great work now has no meaning; it does not have ten or twenty years to dig its hole and wait for men to unearth it: all its short life it will be alien. Thus, the greatest form of beauty today may not signify a new dawning or even a rebirth; it may be an unheard swansong—a faint voice immediately drowned by the din of the most stupendous man-made spectacle of all time, the world's last splendor, which no man will see.

No future before us. . . . For someone who believes only in his own reality this sentence is scarcely any harder to bear than that of his own death. Still, it is difficult to accept the idea that there may be nothing to transmit, no history to perpetuate. The notion of the end of the world, even if it is only the end of *a* world, seems to multiply by a staggering factor the absurdity of a condition which we had only just begun to accept. For this world is *our* world, and those who have helped build it, in no matter how small a way, cannot imagine its annihilation without a certain feeling of frustration. What is the use of creating something which is doomed to be destroyed when we cannot even save what already exists? Nietzsche's shout rises to our lips with a taste of tears: "Do not ask why!"

The wisest approach is to concern ourselves only with the present, to neglect the threat that hangs over all our peoples and limit ourselves to the day-by-day progression, as yet uninterrupted, of our individual lives. In short, we should act as though we were to have no posterity. Granted this, a work of art can be nothing more than a moment of existence wrested from the contingency and monotony of our days and nights. I created *that:* therefore I existed. But "that" remains; does anyone ever have the strength to destroy it before it can live? And it follows you around; and you cannot help watching it live beside you, outside of you. There are periods in which the lure of something new keeps you awake, in other words, deep in dreams; there are other, often longer periods in which your gaze wanders back and lingers on the monster you once spawned. How could you possibly recognize it? Already it has changed. A barely noticeable blemish, which you had never seen, *which was not there before,* has begun to mar the perfection of a face you once loved, a face you may continue to love in spite of its decay; but now your love will be tinged with despair.

Yes, the wise man should consider a work of art within the limits of his own lifetime, hoping that it will resist the aging process until the artist himself is dead, since he cannot completely forget it or annihilate it. And this attitude might be practical were it not for all the other people to whom the work has been communicated and for whom it lives at a different rate. A listener who took years to grasp the meaning of an early work of yours will describe it as a pure and ageless maiden; but for you, he is talking about a mature woman whose beauty is already fading. You had been growing accustomed to that imperceptible waning away; now you are forced to see it. That moment which seemed to you pure joy, which seemed graven in marble . . . was this all there was to it? And yet, for this other person, that hodgepodge is a poem. Because of this lack of synchronism, points of view cannot be compared, and the artist is doomed to solitude.

Now, the jazz musician would seem not to suffer from this curse. He is almost always an improvisor, he can carry a world within him, though not the work which would embody that world. This difference is quite real for anyone who has experience of one or the other status. When you play a chorus, you do not deliver yourself of a living inner world, you merely project an image of it outward. This is why all the choruses played by a given jazz artist during a given period are in some respects so similar. In time, his inner world may change, and its projected image with it. If an earlier image, preserved on records, happens to show signs of age, the artist is unaffected since he does not recognize it as his child: it is no longer with him. He played it and there's the end of it. I would venture to say that no musician, no matter how great, can detect in a recording of one of his past improvisations the essence of what was once his inner life.

In the world of jazz, only the composer has an intimate understanding of the relationship between an artist and his past works. For the composer has lived with his works, sometimes for a very long period. An authentic creation robs its creator of a part of himself when it detaches itself from him; that is why it is the embodiment, not the image, of his inner world. Months, years of meditations, of struggles and of crises are condensed in a work which lasts only a few minutes of physical time, whereas the improvisor's thoughts can be measured on the same time scale as the listener's impressions. An improvisor may play choruses just as beautiful the very next day; the exhausted composer must patiently rebuild his psyche before he can begin to conceive new forms. However, this suffering is also the composer's pride. The privilege of creating forms enables him to set forth his inner world in all its aspects, whereas the soloist can only express the same aspect over and over. If the composer has a sense of unity, he can create order through diversity; the improvisor has nothing to organize: his realm is that of the act per se.

In the long run a sensitive improvisor will be driven to despair by his inability to transform a world of which he can express only one facet. As a young man, he will spend all his energy repeating a single creative gesture; as he grows older, his enthusiasm will wane and he may begin to doubt the necessity of what he is doing. If he stops believing, he is doomed to failure; in some cases, the pain of failure is alleviated by commercial or social success, which allows him to forget the tragedy of life in the vanities of this world.

It is hard to imagine a composer finding peace of mind so easily as that. Even a famous composer can achieve such a state of beatitude only by abandoning all creative activity. For him, creation is a process of self-questioning—and it is this which brings home most forcefully the haunting faces of his forgotten works. . . .

You, my dear . . ., as one of the most reliable mainstays of the school which fascinated me in my youth, may feel that there is no point to this pondering, that the artist's function is to create, not to exhaust himself in painful introspection. And possibly there would be a certain grandeur in pursuing one's work with the knowledge that it can contribute only an inferior form of beauty. . . . For my part, however, I cannot repress these questions; they rise up to smother me, they chill me to the marrow, they absorb all my strength. Beauty, oh Beauty, you flee him who seeks you with doubt in his heart forever more, with shame in his heart forever more, with anger in his heart forever more! Music, music, you were once pure joy, music, why are you now only sorrow?

M.J.

And so the man from Finland died. Those who are familiar with his works and ideas may wonder how it was possible for him to live. Those who admire his work and respect his ideas may wonder how these can continue to live.

A dream cannot be a work unless it is projected into reality. The undisclosed works of Valéry's Monsieur Teste cannot be regarded as works at all since they were never contemplated by their creator in their vulnerable form; they would have had to become substance and face the hazards of daylight. Wrapped in darkness, they may appear more beautiful, but they deceive their creator; and weak indeed is the artist who prefers never to see his work actualized rather than risk laying its secret beauty out for all to see. Perhaps a sonnet can exist in the mind; but a sculpture? a building? And if an architect cannot bring himself to build that splendid arch whose huge span soars before his closed eyes, perhaps deep in his heart he dreads the dire collapse of his dream, should it prove unable to stand the test of reality.

Jarvinen seems to have possessed every form of courage short of carrying his works with him into death, preserving them forever from decay, denying them any chance of being transmitted. Yet this last-minute weakness was, in fact, his most courageous act of all. For he himself knew that this would have meant denying the arch its unborn splendor, only faintly indicated by the abstract signs which, though couched on paper, do *not* crystallize the work, any more than the architect's blueprint *is* the arch; and Jarvinen knew that an arch can collapse.

Jarvinen was a jazz composer who was in part foreign to the world of jazz; as a result he had to dream his own world of jazz, then confront it with that of others. He made one attempt at this during his lifetime. The resulting failure does not imply that his conception was lacking in genius, but rather, as Jarvinen himself seems to have been painfully aware, that its realization was lacking in love. Alain Resnais brilliantly integrated Delphine Seyrig's beauty into his film *Last Year at Marienbad*, possibly because he was in love with her; Jarvinen's attitude toward his performers was one of respectful indifference. How can a man have others play the substance of his soul except through an act of love?

Yet although Jarvinen's relations with his musicians never went beyond the stage of mutual esteem, although he never succeeded in sharing with them the intimate secrets of his inner self, and although these remained hidden away, like a subterranean plant that still fears the light of day, he did make one last courageous attempt to assume the risk of total failure, making it possible for *all* his works to collapse or, perhaps, for one of them to live on.

A posthumous achievement—truly posthumous. . . .

However, Jarvinen placed remarkably strict limitations on this postexistence. His last wishes are an insult to common sense. One might be tempted to go along with certain commentators and interpret them as an act of revenge, a cry of hatred flung in the face of humanity. It is as if Jarvinen, by this rather theatrical annihilation of his work, were trying to destroy the world. For despite the fact that he selected each musician individually, it is unlikely that the conductor whom he chose to rehearse and perform his posthumous scores should be more fortunate, granted only this single opportunity, than the composer himself had been. Why then did Jarvinen refuse to give his music a chance to resuscitate again one day, a chance to appear at last under the direction of a more skilled or more convincing conductor with its true face unveiled, free from the stigmata of well-meaning incompetence? And, on the assumption that this goal is attainable, why did Jarvinen refuse to give his works a second chance? Why did he deny them immortality?

Jarvinen's last wishes are outrageous in many respects; moreover, they seem to contradict the status which he conferred upon himself: that of a composer, *a maker of works*. He must certainly have judged himself, seen his own place in history. He was the first composer of jazz, an artist without precursors, a man "without roots" who has "nothing to pursue," in a world in which "everything remains to be done." Here was a man for whom Duke Ellington, hitherto regarded as the jazz composer par excellence, was merely "the greatest arranger." What, then, did he "come to give"? Jarvinen made no statement concerning the significance of his work; yet we can easily guess the significance that the works of his predecessors held for a mind as rigorous as his. With his keen awareness of musical form he was bound to gather an impression of coherency from the crude succession of choruses in *Ko-Ko*, because these form a line of tension which leads boldly up to a breaking point implicit in the language of the work itself; conversely, he would regard the apparently richer *da capo* which channels the lyricism of *Concerto for Cootie* as a conventional mold devoid of any relationship with the work's poetic substance. A musician who assigns prime importance to the form-language relationship may consider that *Concerto for Cootie* does not derive from a purely jazz conception and that, as Jarvinen bluntly put it, that "masterpiece" might have been "composed by a square." Viewed from so lofty a standpoint, Ellington's entire production reveals its limitations. The powerful musician who wrote *Saddest Tale* invented a technique of writing, developed a language and created a style, but not a poetics of form; this is no doubt why Jarvinen denies that he or any other jazz artist is a composer.

Implicitly, then, *a composer is a man who, even using a language which is not his own, is capable of guiding the musical flux in terms of a formal balance (space-time relationship) determined, among a thousand possible determining factors, by the material born of that language.* Short of this, there is no *composition*, no *work of music*, in the modern sense of the word. A theme maker who imagines a melody, no matter how well constructed, an arranger who builds a series of choruses on a given theme and unless he endows them with a specific relationship, do not *compose;* in a sense, they do not even create works. The one weaves a piece of cloth and the other embroiders on it. Neither cloth nor embroidery have the power possessed by the sound alone of Miles Davis's horn: that of creating a world.

Now, when a composer writes a work, does he not hope that it will last? Should his prime concern not be to preserve it against the erosion of time? Beethoven or Wagner would have answered these questions without a moment's hesitation, but certain contemporary composers prefer to elude them. This is because they no longer feel the necessity of communicating with others. Some of them are so contemptuous of the world around them that they claim the right to silence; and yet from time to time they seem almost to be forced out of their silence, entrusting to the uncertain winds of chance a triumphant or a trembling sail that may bear some tribute of which they vaguely hope future generations will be worthy. Jarvinen's attitude is not entirely devoid of this metaphysical implication: he sees himself as an end-of-the-world artist. And yet, at the same time he hopes that the world will survive: why else does he wear white? He agrees to go through the motions, to give birth to an "inferior beauty." He advises young musicians to shun creation and "learn life," yet he holds creation up as an example. After all, his twelve propositions are an approach to creation. Such minor contradictions are in the nature of the man but foreign to the artist. Jarvinen's last wishes have a deeper significance. They express the intensity, the authenticity with which he, as a jazz composer, experienced his work.

Once it is granted that in jazz a written work can only be a blueprint, it is necessary to reappraise the notions of stability and permanence traditionally associated with the idea of composition. Jarvinen was perfectly well aware that his works, couched in a language as mature and complex as that of European classical music, worked out on paper in every detail, were written jazz, and therefore essentially unfinished blueprints. He undoubtedly took into consideration the possible end results of his blueprints and weighed the chances for their potential beauty's being actualized. This is where an effort must be made to understand his strange gesture. In a universe in which beauty is fleeting and difficult to achieve, the "wisest" approach would be to afford as many opportunities as possible for the blueprint "to become what it is." If it is played a thousand times, it may ultimately find its true identity, reveal itself as a work. This attitude would seem all the more reasonable as a jazz orchestra is basically a society in constant evolution. Its motto is "play it the way it feels, tomorrow it may be better." How can such a free-and-easy approach be reconciled with Jarvinen's requirement that the work be performed only once, unless one admits that he was aware of the all but inhuman situation thus created and that he deliberately increased the scope of his challenge to staggering proportions? To achieve ephemeral beauty in a world of instability, and to achieve it only in and through contingency: this goal may have fascinated Jarvinen. Yet in all justice to him it must be admitted that above and beyond this Promethean gesture he did succeed in bringing new meaning to contemporary creation in its most tragic sense, for he assumed the fate of the work of jazz before the world as a whole; he proclaimed the impossibility of such a work by condemning his own music to an existence even shorter than that of those world's fair pavilions that are demolished at the end of summer but remain at least in photographs.

"The work of jazz is an impossibility. . . ." This would seem to be the meaning of Matti Jarvinen's testament. The same idea is implied in more personal and, therefore, more emotional terms, in the letter written shortly before his death. The world being what it is, jazz being what it is, and the world of jazz being what it is, a work inevitably grows old, loses its freshness, slips slowly into death. So Jarvinen invented suicide. He had the courage to imagine an uncertain work, of a limited life span, which at worst might be a sham and at best a flash of lightning, a burst of fireworks, vanishing almost as soon as it appeared, fated to live on only in the clouded distorting mirrors of memory. Perhaps he also invented euthanasia. It is said that on the cover of his most important score he penned these sardonic words: "Not to be opened after July 1st, 197–," thus painlessly eradicating a dream which would in any case have been mutilated by society, contemporary relativism, and the sensibility peculiar to any given period.

Bach, Mozart, and Beethoven forged tools which were equal to their integrity. Though constantly betrayed by countless well-meaning performers, their work has never lost its essential beauty, preserved as it is by powerful technical qualities whose perfection has not yet been impaired by time in any way. The work of jazz, on the other hand, dies each time it is played, for it does not involve the composer's soul alone, it also involves the performer's. Tomorrow the performer will not be the same and, accordingly, the work itself will be different. One may accept these successive births and deaths as a natural phenomenon: one may greet them with enthusiasm. Jarvinen experienced them as so many impingements on the purity of his dream (perhaps because they could not go on forever, because he lived in dread of the unbearable moment of final, irreparable death). Successive executions—all of them right, all of them wrong—struck him as impure, but no more so than the unending sameness of a recording. A thousand lying smiles; or what was meant to be a fleeting glance frozen for all eternity. . . . To escape from this dilemma, Jarvinen created the potentially multiform work *which has no future;* he thus succeeded in conveying, possibly for the very first time, that undefinable feeling which an artist has toward his past work; his irremediably past work.

JARVINEN'S PROPOSITIONS
TOGETHER WITH A COMMENTARY

The most reliable approach to the musical thinking of Matti Jarvinen would have consisted in reproducing fragments of his works and analyzing them. Unfortunately this is impossible under the terms of the Finnish composer's testament. However, this testament includes a set of aphorisms which do provide a basis for study. Those who are lucky enough to have actually heard a work by Jarvinen may examine the impression it produced on them and their memory of it. As guides, these are no doubt misleading, yet they may help to clarify certain propositions that are difficult to interpret. Jarvinen does not seem to have deliberately sought to be esoteric, but his ideas are expressed in such condensed form as to make them ambiguous and to require a commentary.

It is very unlikely that he composed his works according to a priori principles. On the contrary, these aphorisms are quite certainly the results of his meditations on the finished works; he was looking back at his past. In them, Jarvinen summed up the essence of his experience as a musician; but he did not feel it necessary to take account of the many successful exceptions to the rules set forth here that can be found in his own work. A brilliant ironist could play very prettily with the contradictions in which a creator entwines himself when he attempts to theorize, but these do not prove that his theoretical contribution is absolutely useless.

"Creation," says Pierre Boulez, "can exist only in the unforeseeable's becoming necessity." If the unforeseeable is to appear at all, a scope of foreseeables must first be defined. This is the purpose of these propositions. They do not tell us how the rarest flower may sprout, but they do describe the soil that will, perhaps, nourish it.

1) *Modern jazz writing is the key to a re-creation of the tonal system, whose coherency is then assumed by controlled dissonance.*

Establishing in this first proposition a distinction between all the characteristic traits which writing has the power to crystallize and those elements which cannot be noted down (swing, the plasticity of the sound tissue), Jarvinen defines the written language of jazz as a transcendental attainment by virtue of the equation: *modern jazz writing = re-created tonal system.* To his mind, the sum of possibilities evolved by jazz composers and arrangers forms a coherent whole, a specific entity. However, he does not seem to regard it as an essential attribute (which would be tantamount to adding a third term to the dyad suggested some years ago by André Hodeir: *an inseparable but extremely variable mixture of relaxation and tension*). Jazz writing is essential only to the written forms of jazz; these forms might be said to constitute a province whose laws do not apply to the rest of the country. Later on we shall see that writing does nevertheless partake of the essence of jazz, expressing as it were through this basic dualism, new aspects of tension and relaxation. Moreover, we must not lose sight of the fact that this part of the testament is dedicated exclusively to the man who writes jazz. We must therefore guard against over-generalizing the first part of this aphorism, in which even the word "modern" must be interpreted in a restrictive sense. Jarvinen refuses to set himself up as an historian; he means to consider his own period to the exclusion of any other, and to limit himself to his own experience as a contemporary composer. Thus, the fact that in his eyes written jazz has created a new kind of tonality does not necessarily imply a belief that this creation involves jazz as a whole. True, some of the constituent elements of this phenomenon were born in improvised jazz; but only some of them, and they are not enough to form that coherent whole to which Jarvinen is referring. Yet he considers it an established fact that written jazz has succeeded in giving tonality a true meaning once again. His choice of the term "re-creation" will probably for a long time give rise to discussions both in and out of jazz circles (some feel that jazz has not re-created the tonal system, but merely *adapted* or *rearranged* it); perhaps it will be replaced by the word *reform* or *reconstruction*. The fact is that among other wreckages, the twentieth century has been characterized by the destruction of the great art of tonality which had been raised by the German Classics and Romantics to its highest peak of perfection. Questioned by Wagner and Debussy, suspended by Schönberg, disregarded by the serial musicians, the tonal system has been even more mistreated by those who still claim to be its faithful guardians, for they have brought to it only confusion and disorganization. Now contemporary jazz, through its first really composed works which, together with all the other works and arrangements related to them, serve to define "contemporary jazz writing," constitutes a regeneration of the tonal concept. It will depend entirely on the value of these works and of all the others that jazz can produce, whether this resurgency turns out to be a momentous or a trivial event, whether it will establish an unprecedented phenomenon: the coexistence of two parallel forms of music within a single civilization, or whether it will merely be a spurious contestation of the serial idea, with no possibility of real development, doomed to early oblivion. However, we are probably trying to see too far into the future. It might be wiser to base our commentaries on the assumption that far from being irresponsible, Jarvinen's bold expression, "the re-creation of the tonal system," is an apt way of summing up an historical reality. If such is the case, it describes a major transformation, the end-result of a long period of gestation. From eighteenth- and nineteenth-century European music, jazz has appropriated that extraordinary musical rhetoric based on the organization of the tonal areas, but its interpretation of this rhetoric is entirely different. From its own traditional source—the blues— jazz draws a seminal element which gives new meaning to the system: the tonic-subdominant relationship (as against the tonic-dominant relationship on which classical music was based). Yet, although Jarvinen was almost certainly aware of the importance of this point of departure, he regarded it merely as a preamble to *written* jazz, his sole concern. Writing is a projection, but also a structural reconsideration of the harmonic relationships conceived by the modern jazz pianists, principally Monk; as such it serves to organize complexity and to expand musical space with no loss of coherency, a fact which Jarvinen ascribes to the *implementation* of a concept which he regards as the basis of the unity of the discourse and which he calls "controlled dissonance" (probably as opposed to the anarchic role assumed by dissonance in Western post-tonal music). Has he hit upon one of the keystones of the language of orchestral jazz? Possibly. The failure of consonant writing in jazz is not due to any "lack of modernity" experienced as such by the listener; it has a more deeply musical cause. The reason why dissonance has gradually asserted itself in jazz writing, so much so in fact that we may regard written jazz as inherently dissonant, is that it corresponds to a real necessity. It creates a parallel tension, quite distinct from the basic underlying tension, "the pole around which the electricity of jazz is concentrated," but which helps to strengthen it. Just as the syncopated rhythms of written jazz favor swing and consequently convey the dimension of relaxation, while at the same time retaining a structural autonomy which makes it possible, as the phrasing evolves, to shift from tension to relaxation and back again,

so too the existence, on the harmonic level, of an underlying permanent tension produced by the language of dissonance (and which
acts as a tributary to the main stream of tension, directly issued, that
one, from the sound-components) does not prevent the simultaneous manifestation of a phenomenon of a different order: a *tonal*
dialectics of tension and relaxation due to the influence of the
harmonic degrees and tonal areas, and to the chord structures and
their inversions. This secondary set of dialectics is not to be neglected; in particular, it can be expected to produce, in view of the
tonal perspectives defined by Jarvinen, an expansion of musical
space. Implicit in the idea of controlling dissonance is the idea of
dosing it; the concept of uneven degrees is the basis of any tonal
organization. In the tonal hierarchy, a chord of the first degree does
not exert a tension comparable to that of a subdominant; nor is a
seventh chord equivalent to a thirteenth. Moreover, these various
natural forces may combine, they may accumulate, or they may
destroy each other. The existence within a syncopated context, of a
phrase that is fluid enough to have its own independent accentuation; the existence, within a dissonant context, of a harmonic regime
treated with enough finesse to establish a stimulating relationship
with the melodic line; the interplay of secondary tensions and
relaxations that are laid over the basic tension-relaxation; the fruitful
musical paradoxes which occur when the phenomena of rhythm
combine with harmonic accidents—all of these elements go to make
up the language of modern jazz. This is where the composer's
domain begins. As the constant development of Jarvinen's work
demonstrates—and this also is the meaning of this aphorism—it is
useless to imagine an authentic jazz form if one has not acquired a
total command of the language.

2) *Motion cannot replace mass, nor mass motion; but they can
compensate for one another.*
   In this second proposition, Jarvinen is referring to a dual type of
writing which he had learned to handle masterfully. He makes an
implicit distinction between mass writing, with its precise, heavy
phrasing, and the figures reserved for small group writing, suppler
and, of necessity it seems, more mobile. An ensemble consisting of
three, four, or five melodic parts should thus be able to "compensate" for its relative frailty by a greater mobility of the phrase, or
even—and this is strongly suggested in the word "motion"—by the
greater independence of the separate voices within a given sound
structure. Thus, Jarvinen recommends that the use of counterpoint
vary as an inverse function of the mass of polyphonic forces

brought into play. Jarvinen applied this law of compensation to his own work; the brilliant virtuoso passages are almost always assigned to small ensembles, in which each voice achieves a kind of autonomy, even when the writing is not purely contrapuntal, while the large ensembles evolve along more rigid lines. In these latter passages, the phrasing is determined by the succession of vertical blocks; monotony is avoided by the variations of intensity which this kind of writing favors. In the small ensemble passages, the style of the discourse is determined by the successive overlaying of various voices whose accent patterns sometimes coincide but more often clash. In a few instances, Jarvinen has demonstrated that there can exist a middle term. His "half-mass" writing, which is in no sense an attempt to reconcile incompatibles, retains some of the fluidity of the small orchestra without sacrificing too much of the weight and impact peculiar to the large orchestra.

3) *No one who does not write for the fun of the instrumentalist can hope to receive from him any joy in return.*
This aphorism seems merely to be the corollary of the previous one. Indeed, when Jarvinen maintains that in medium and small ensembles the voices must be relatively independent, he is proclaiming the necessity for an individualized style of writing in which each instrument is assigned an interesting and well-defined melodic line. Here, he goes along with the conception, at once communalistic and individualistic, which culminated in the work of the Renaissance madrigal composers, who sought to persuade each singer that his part was of prime importance; moreover, he fulfills the listener's expectation that each voice in a small ensemble should have its own, easily perceptible, internal coherency. And yet, this third proposition carries with it a fresh imperative. Jarvinen grants that every musician in every jazz band, big or little, is entitled to the "instrumentalist's fun." Thus, he extends to the domain of mass-writing, in which each voice seems satisfied with an anonymity that listeners accept as such, the requirement that each musician be provided with a part both rhythmically and melodically coherent. In this respect, jazz orchestral writing is completely at odds with post-Webernian serial writing, in which the principle of timbre-osmosis and the emphasis placed on discontinuity have given birth to a highly complex, systematically dispersive scoring which, from the standpoint of the performer—unable as he is to grasp the totality of the context in which he moves, unless he is a soloist himself— may seem absurd. In this way, Jupien the waistcoat maker was an

artist; as for his successors, who divide up the sixty-five pieces that go into today's vest between them, are they any more alienated than the successors of Morel, the violinist, when faced with their bits of artfully divided quintuplets? While the musician who plays contemporary music in the European tradition can derive no "fun" from his playing unless he understands the whole work at all times—obviously a rare occurrence—the jazz musician recovers this lost pleasure at the price of coping with the only slightly greater complexity which Jarvinen introduces into jazz writing, the general principles of which are relatively simple. It is not altogether un-interesting to note that he is guided by no philanthropic intentions: the last part of the aphorism clearly shows that he means to be paid in return. This is the only time Jarvinen ever referred, and indi-rectly at that, to his relationships with musicians, which were, as we know, often rather strained.

4) *If you do not want beauty to foster ugliness, find out what your performer is capable of and do not expect from him miracles that only you can conceive.*

The chief merit of this splendid aphorism, a harmonious comple-ment to the previous ones, is to show its author in a revealing light. Here we see Jarvinen in all his complexity, yet in all his naïveté as an artist as well. Here the creator steps back and views that collabo-rator of his, the "performer," glimpses his limitations, then with-draws into himself and seems to gaze proudly at his own genius as reflected in those "miracles" of which he knows himself capable. There is something pathetic in this gesture when we consider the anguish which Jarvinen experienced toward the end of his life, when it seemed to him that all the freshness and luster had gone forever from works which he had once hoped were untarnishable, and which, to be sure, still were so in the eyes of the rest of the world. The first part of the aphorism also conveys something of the "wisdom" which Jarvinen bitterly refers to in his letter. Indeed, it would be useless to write trills for the trumpets, no matter how perfectly the composer hears them in his mind's ear, if the trumpet players for whom they are written are to prove incapable of execut-ing them correctly. Then too, this fourth proposition defines the relationships which a composer must have with his performers. "Find out . . .": the implication here is that the composer knows them directly. This confirms that Jarvinen did not regard the work of jazz as a gift to posterity, a virtual entity which might have to wait a quarter of a century or more for the opportunity of a performance worthy of its merits, but as something to be actualized immediately and—this is an important factor—with the means at hand.

5) *Using twelve instruments where ten would suffice is a fault in the exercise of one's profession.*

In his writings, P. L. Nervi defines the contemporary architect's need for economy of means. He considers that building correctly implies, above all, building without useless expenditures. In this respect the architect's concerns coincide with those of the great classical composers. Mozart's orchestration is a model of economy; its effectiveness on the sound level is not obtained by the number of instruments, but by the perfection of the writing. In jazz, too, the great orchestrators are noted for their skill at limiting the number of musicians; it has often been pointed out that masters like Duke Ellington or Gil Evans manage to get a rich sound out of four horns in instances where others would have scored for six or even eight to no better effect. In Jarvinen's view, this kind of achievement need not be the monopoly of a few exceptional talents; he regards it quite simply as a technical fact, a basic skill "of one's profession." However, better than anyone else, Jarvinen knew that it is hopeless to expect an arranger or composer, no matter how perfectly he had mastered his trade, to produce in any and all circumstances the best possible sound with a minimum of means: he also needs some imagination. His meaning becomes clearer when we recall that he used to say, borrowing an idea from Bergson, that "no one is obliged to write music." Thus, to avoid a "fault in the exercise of one's profession," the man who writes jazz—and this is a truism often ignored—must know how to write and have something to write.

6) *The orchestra is no longer that cake that was always cut up in the same direction.*

In this sixth proposition, one of the most ambiguous of all, Jarvinen seems to be protesting against the routine method of orchestrating "by sections" which tends precisely to divide the orchestra up in uniform slices of trumpets, trombones, or saxophones. True, there is no denying that this conception is indeed part of jazz tradition. After all, it probably originated in a mode of musical thinking—antiphony—shared by African music and Protestant hymns and which naturally survived in the church music of the American Negro. We know that the tradition of the blues song with accompaniment thrived on this elementary form of musical discourse, based on an alternance of parts, in which question calls for answer and antecedent for consequent; we know that later on the dance band used a similar contrast between brass and reeds. The necessities of harmonic development eventually split the brass family into two subdivisions, and there are now three sections to be heard successively or simultaneously; the double choir has become a triple choir, but the principle has scarcely evolved. Jarvinen's work provides examples of far more subtle methods of dividing up the orchestra, which is no longer "that cake. . . ." In one instance, writing for a Basie-type orchestra, Jarvinen boldly opposes two groups made up as follows:

—A: flute, two muted trumpets and a muted trombone, alto, baritone
—B: two trumpets, two trombones, alto, tenor.

Nor is this more than an example of simple antiphony, a technique to which he rarely resorted. Most often, he divided up the orchestra "diagonally," tending to disrupt its unity, then reestablish it partially or totally through a relentless process of acoustical chemistry (which, needless to say, can thrive only within a very advanced musical conception). The principle of freely contrapuntal writing, advocated by Jarvinen for small ensembles, with its interweaving voices and perpetually changing instrumental combinations, already seemed to provide a solution to an essentially orchestral problem.

7) *If the voice is an instrument, it has no words to sing.*

Here Jarvinen touches on what he regarded as a vital problem: the integration of the human voice into instrumental ensembles. In private conversation, the Finnish composer never hid his contempt for pop singers of both sexes, nor his hatred for their repertoire of ballads. He called Sinatra "an Yves Montand with a sense of timing, an ear and a voice." As for blues singers, he was less sensitive to the literary and musical form of their complaints than to their spirit and style. During his stay in the United States, he seems to have considered putting various instrumental combinations together around a vocal soloist who would have sung—or perhaps declaimed in a lyric style—a specially written text. Either because he never found the voice he had in mind, or because no poem ever lived up to his expectations, he gave up the project. Today, however, we have reason to believe that Jarvinen's decision was not taken for want of these missing elements, but as the result of a mental itinerary which led him to give up of his own accord the idea of using any form of text. Indeed, while his last works make increasing use of the voice, it is cast in a role which is increasingly instrumental. The soundness of this approach has been disputed; some even felt that it was clumsy. The seventh proposition proves that it was the result of a deliberate choice: "If the voice is an instrument . . ."; Jarvinen refuses to entertain the idea that it could be anything else. The conclusion of the aphorism is therefore perfectly logical and explains why there is not a trace of any known language in the works of the Finnish composer, whereas on the other hand, he treated every type of vocalizing and most particularly the *scat chorus* in all its forms. Moreover, he did not hesitate to blend one or more voices into an instrumental ensemble, letting them carry the treble or bass parts as often as the less important intermediary parts. We may therefore safely say that in Jarvinen's world, the voice is part of the orchestra. It is more than a mere coloristic trait; it introduces a new organic substance.

8) *Reading—not writing—is too heavy a burden to bear for anyone who wants to go through the comedy of written improvisations.*

With this aphorism, Jarvinen tries to sum up the problem of the nonimprovised solo. Implicitly, he seems to admit the compulsion under which the composer is to *write* certain solos, and to write them in the style of improvisation. The latter proviso is not dictated by a desire to deceive the listener, but by an urgent stylistic necessity: the jazz tonus of a solo instrument is best conveyed, he believes, by the free sweeping lines of improvisation. Now, in practice, the performer will find that this approach ultimately obliges him to deceive the listener. His task is to ensure that this false improvisation, conceived for him by someone else, sounds like a real one; hence the expression "comedy of written improvisations," hence also the role of actors which Jarvinen assigns to the composer as well as the performer. In writing the supposedly improvised passages, the composer must imagine to himself the comedy which the soloist must later enact before the public; then, transcending this factitious situation, he must set down on paper the elements of an authentically experienced improvisation (which may, in a certain sense, imply the capacity to think as fast as the fastest soloist). Jarvinen does not altogether seem to regard this procedure as excessively complex, since he maintains that it is not "too heavy a burden to bear." Paradoxically enough, reading is the burden. While the soloist is bound to be somewhat hampered by a score which he reads, he can, on the other hand, enjoy complete freedom in his interpretation, "faithful" as it may be, of an "improvisation" that he has learned by heart. What Jarvinen expects of him is an effort of memorization which will also, he vouches, be a step toward liberation.

9) *Stereophonics is a studio art, and conducting is a studio art; a jazz composer must learn the studio arts.*

This ninth aphorism does not deal merely with the minor responsibilities of a composer; in a paradoxical way, it challenges certain stereotypes which are generally taken for granted. The assertion that "conducting is a studio art" will shock many a musician; as for stereophonics, it is generally considered to be a means of reconstituting in a living room the listening conditions of the concert hall (even though an exaggerated panoramic distention of the sound source too often tends to destroy the global aspect of auditory perception). Now, Jarvinen's attempts to use the stereophonic principle in his works lead us to believe that the first part of the aphorism concerns stereophonics not only as a recording technique but as a means of creation. It goes without saying that if a composer came to feel that the "stereophonic dimension" was essential to his work, and therefore acquired through study the technical means to conceive and implement it, he would find it an easy task to verify the quality of the sound and the spatial balance in a recording session of any music whatsoever, whether stereophonic in its conception or not. The paradox here does not lie at the end of the aphorism, in Jarvinen's demand that composers acquire a technical education that few today possess even superficially, but rather in the implications of the first part, in the explosive potentialities which Jarvinen only scarcely hints at and which he leaves to the commentator to develop. If stereophonics "is a studio art" and only that, and if, on the other hand, it is essential to the musical accomplishment of all future works (Jarvinen does not say this, but does seem to imply it), then the jazz concert is doomed. Does this mean that every manifestation of the stereophonic dimension in a concert hall is bound to fail? Must we consider that Jarvinen's experiments in this area fall into the cone of error which invariably accompanies every original work? Although he never attended a performance of any of his stereophonic works, Jarvinen may have sensed in advance that the effect which he sought through specific writing techniques could never be fully achieved unless the audience sat in the middle of the hall and was *surrounded* by the orchestra. Now, except for a nightclub performance at which the musicians would outnumber the audience, such an arrangement means an extreme scattering of the musicians; and while this may be suited to Stockhausen's triple orchestra led by several conductors, it could never do for the blind jazz orchestra, whose internal respiration requires the placing of all the melodic elements near the rhythm section. It is probably this powerful argument which, in the last analysis, led Jarvinen—possibly at the cost of repudiating, in part, his own works—to advocate only the artificial stereophonics of the studio: if this dimension is prepared for by the composer during the writing stage and controlled by him during the recording session, it will be possible for the performers to experience collectively the music that they play, though they will perhaps not have full cognizance of the stereophonic dimension. However, Jarvinen is not setting himself up as an implacable adversary of concert jazz, no more so than when he suggests that conducting is also "a studio art." The conductor of a jazz orchestra, in contrast with that of a symphony orchestra, scarcely intervenes during the actual performance; most of his work is done in rehearsals. Jarvinen, it seems, identified rehearsals with the studio in which they take place. But for once he was somewhat timid in his prediction: there is no reason why the conductor's role should not evolve. (Or else perhaps Jarvinen felt that this evolution would be nipped in the bud by the disappearance of the jazz concert, and simply refused to take it into account.) Whatever the case, the ninth proposition unequivocally asserts that composers no longer have the right to be ignorant of any aspect of conducting and recording techniques. Whether or not the stereophonic effect is to become an essential part of tomorrow's jazz, whether the conductor's role is to remain passive or become active, Jarvinen wants the final responsibility for the work's actualization to be assumed by one person only: the man who conceived it, the composer. Must he play an executive role? Or can he simply be a witness? Must he intervene directly? Or should he merely advise engineers and conductor? Jarvinen expressed no opinion one way or the other and it may be assumed that he leaves an open choice. However, he obviously believes that a performance must be prepared in the composer's presence, and that this presence must be effective and efficient.

10) *One must guard against manufacturing "jazz forms" which would inevitably be carbon copies of the cantata and the concerto.*
Jarvinen's work as a whole is a model of formal diversity: no two scores have a common pattern. This tenth aphorism expresses, rather deviously, it is true, his contempt for preexisting forms. It is generally agreed, of course, that the fugue and the sonata form are too foreign to the spirit of jazz to be transplanted into it; however—

and this is a truth which is harder to grasp—any attempt to conceive forms specific to jazz would be equally specious. In the name of the new-born art of jazz composition, Jarvinen steadfastly rejects the notion of "formal families"; related as they would "inevitably" be to the great classical forms, they would simply lead to the rediscovery of all the formal situations which the great European art of tonal music brought forth two centuries ago; the bridge, reexposition, or stretto would appear one by one as chance variants under the pens of different composers. It is important for the jazz composer to be alone in front of the blank sheet of paper, so that no preconception, no privileged itinerary can divert the growing work away from the form that it carries within itself: here Jarvinen refers to, and adopts the great contemporary idea that the *material should determine the structure.* Only this creative open-mindedness can engender a form that is specific not with regard to jazz in general, but to the particular work; genuinely experienced by an original creator, only this attitude can produce a work that is not "a carbon copy of the cantata or the concerto." However, it can only be experienced by a composer endowed to some degree with a genius for forms; other musicians, though they may be gifted with melodic inventiveness or orchestral imagination, will still have to fall back on set forms. Moreover, it is only at the cost of much effort and energy that the composer can compel himself to invent the formal progression of his work on the basis of his material. Jarvinen's career is proof of this. Anyone who accepts this limitation, while it will enable him to set his sights high indeed, must resign himself to producing little.

11) *If a tradition is to be destroyed, we must know why, and if we wish to replace one of its elements, we must know with what.*
    If we examine it in the light of the previous one, this proposition may seem paradoxical: however, in spite of its faintly sarcastic tone, it nicely completes the tenth. True, respect for tradition is a strange virtue in a musician who has just forcefully rejected any reference to the greatest of all musical traditions. Isolated and "rootless" as he was, hopelessly alien to the community in which he would have had to live, was Jarvinen trying, until the very last, to create some tie that would bind him to it? As a composer, did he feel so ill at ease in the world of jazz (where, as he himself said, there had never been any composers before him) that he could not help asserting, in terms of certain basic choices, his right to be a citizen of that world? If this was how he felt, his aesthetic motives for rejecting the forms of the past and his determination to guard jazz against any

classical influences must have been all the stronger. The real paradox is that it should be a European-trained composer who rejects the European influence more rigorously than anyone before him. Yet, when we come right down to it, is this really a contradiction? Perhaps it was easier for a man who was brought up on the fugue to avoid the fascination that the fugal style has held for less educated jazz artists. Thus, it is the jazz tradition with which Jarvinen is concerned. Far from regarding jazz as a lowly form of music with which any liberties might be taken, Jarvinen tried to establish its autonomy. In composing his works, he was guided by this same concern. It has been said that he changed jazz more than anyone else by his new techniques of writing and the formal developments which he evolved; but it has also been emphasized that these changes were conceived in a spirit of absolute respect for the stylistic purity of jazz and the originality of its materials. His genius for assimilation spared him superfluous scruples; his lucidity saved his pen from corruption. Countless quotations have been found in his work and traced back to the recordings of the great soloists. He was familiar with the art of integrating the ideas of others: he wrote them, he wrote them all, he wrote them all down. Every pore of every stone that enters into Jarvinen's aristocratically personal architectures owes allegiance to the nation of jazz. A few great jazz artists—the later Parker, the declining Ellington—have yielded to the lure of the rich masses of the string section and accepted a fatal transplantation of certain inviolable stylistic components. Jarvinen's sense of orchestration was too rigorous to let him fall into such an obvious error. He was acutely aware of the antagonism that exists between a given family of timbres and a given type of writing which, derived as it is from a harmonic style of opposite nature, is designed to show off a completely different family of timbres. Thus, while the violin sometimes appears in his music, it is always as a solo instrument. Nevertheless, even though his written improvisations, his vocal-instrumental amalgams, his formal innovations, and his deliberate borrowings remain stylistically faithful to the jazz of his time, Jarvinen never regarded the jazz tradition as a corpus of sacred laws. The eleventh aphorism accepts the idea that tradition is meant to be destroyed. But the foreigner Jarvinen did not feel he had the right to make a clean sweep of the customs of the world in which he had come to live. "If there is a tradition to be destroyed . . ."; it may be a necessity, but it must never be iconoclasm for its own sake. He expects any man who sinks an ax into the edifice to be perfectly lucid. "We must know why." Now it may come about that formal innovations, conceived in a spirit which is respectful of tradition, ultimately lead to unforeseeable upheavals in tradition. A clear-sighted creator may immediately glimpse the long-term consequences of an apparently insignificant disturbance in the existing balance. Jarvinen's destruction of the four-bar pattern in the written improvisations of his early works was not the result of a gratuitous decision devoid of compensating factors; like the "destruction of the box" advocated by Frank Lloyd Wright at the turn of the century, it derived from a previous acquisition (the enjambments of the regular patterns in the work of the great bop improvisers), and carried within it the seeds of the reorganizations and even the new formal organizations later conceived by Jarvinen. There can be no doubt but what he had a premonition of the developments implicit in this act, nor that even as he "replaced one of the elements" of that tradition which he so deeply revered, he knew "with what" it was going to be replaced. Thus, for anyone who proposes to study Jarvinen's work, the eleventh proposition may be the most important of all; it defines the limits of his historical role. If Jarvinen was the first jazz composer, it was because he was the first who dared claim all of the composer's privileges, while at the same time he did not, like some of his predecessors who originated in jazz, yearn for a fruitless escape into the unknown.

12) *How can jazz be diversified without being murdered, and how can it fail to die if it is not diversified?*

The need for diversification, the subject of this last aphorism, is the most ambiguous of all the requirements expounded by Jarvinen. Moreover, it creates a dilemma which is but imperfectly conveyed by the interrogative form in which the proposition is couched. Many a jazz artist among Jarvinen's contemporaries felt that it was imperative to blaze new paths for jazz; as proof of this, we have the diverging conceptions of Ornette Coleman and Charlie Mingus, as well as the appearance of a movement like the Third Stream, not to mention Max Roach's experiments in 3/4 and 5/4 time. Other efforts have been motivated by nothing more than a frantic search for a gimmick; yet the best of them were born of an awareness that jazz urgently needs to reinvent itself, as it did in the days of be-bop. Jarvinen recognizes the self-evident cogency of this drive; had he doubted the necessity for a diversification of jazz, the question contained in this aphorism could never have been expressed in these terms. In phrasing it, perhaps he was placing himself on the plane of the individual. Perhaps he was addressing each man who writes jazz singly, asking him if he is capable, all by himself, of diversifying jazz through the contribution of his own work. Jarvinen undoubtedly believed that it was henceforth up to the composer to supply the greatest efforts to renew jazz. Perhaps he also felt that a given improvisor could never conceive more than a single contestation of the existing order, and that his universe, being necessarily closed, did not lend itself to this diversification from within. The examples of the greatest improvisers (Armstrong, Parker, Monk) prove that until now the jazz soloist has always evolved within a clearly circumscribed sphere, which he at times succeeded in enlarging but never in breaking out of. Of course, one may maintain that this is not a sign of weakness but of strength. Commenting on the "characteristic phrases" which he ascribes to Monsieur Vinteuil, Marcel Proust states that "the great writers have always written one, single work"; the equivalent of these phrases, "would be, for example . . . in the work of Barbey D'Aurevilly, a secret reality revealed by a material trace" or "that stone-carver's geometry in the novels of Thomas Hardy." The names of César Franck and Gabriel Fauré—two artists who never ceased writing, under various guises, the same work constantly shot through with the same phrase—might be added to those cited by Proust as similar examples taken from the world of music. And one could name offhand several famous painters whose life's work can be summed up in a single canvas. However, none of these examples is really convincing. Neither Fauré nor even Franck was a very great musician; and we can scarcely claim that either Hardy or Barbey towered over the literature of his period. Perhaps, on the contrary, the concern for diversity provided European art with a healthy stimulus, without which many masterpieces would never have been produced. Diversity constitutes a staggering challenge to unity; when they exist together, the first reveals the most secret and precious aspects of the second. This is as true of a single work as it is of a body of works. The greatest composers—Bach, Beethoven—unconsciously cultivated diversity, by the mere fact of their development as individual creators. A score like *Don Giovanni* owes its perfect stylistic unity to the extraordinary economy of means which it employs; but its most splendid beauty is due to the fact that this economy does not prevent diversity from flourishing in aria after aria, scene after scene, bringing forth the most harmonious variety of colors. This is a far cry from the "characteristic phrase" which, in the output of an uninspired composer, moves endlessly from one work to the next, as its counterpart moves from one chorus to the next in the output of an improviser, no matter how inspired he may be. Borrowing, for once, a constant of European art, Jarvinen demands that jazz possess a double diversity: that of the single work with respect to other works, and that of the work with respect to itself. (We may assume that he takes for granted the creator's diversity with respect to other creators: if Bud Powell had not diverged from Monk, and Stan Getz from Lester Young, would they ever even have existed?) In an age which Paul Valéry described as an age of "moving structures," an art which is incapable of achieving this stage of development is condemned to waste away. "How can it fail to die if it is not diversified?" asks Jarvinen. But at the same time, he wonders whether diversity is conceivable, whether every effort designed to "open up" jazz will not ultimately destroy jazz, if jazz is not, in its essence, more limited than he believes. Is this an inextricable dilemma, or the anguished expression of a dilemma which he simply could not solve by himself?

PART FOUR

ETHURE AND CULTICS

A Play in One Act

Acted narrated sung
In theatrical habit
Sect and Society
Heart, ethure and cultics

Night, Washington Square park. On a bench, dimly lit by a streetlamp, sits DIMITRI *(badly dressed, long hair). He is reading a book. Enter* LAUREL *(same appearance), playing distractedly on a tenor saxophone:* E – E – D C E – D C – .

LAUREL: What are you reading?
DIMITRI *(without looking up from his book)*: What, you're here? I was dreaming.
LAUREL: So you weren't reading?

DIMITRI: When I read, I dream.

LAUREL (*looking at his saxophone*): That never happens to me.

DIMITRI: You never dream?

LAUREL: I never read.

DIMITRI: If you never read, I guess you dream faster.

LAUREL: I don't know, I've no way of comparing.

DIMITRI: You're right.

LAUREL: What were you dreaming about?

DIMITRI (*dreamily*): I was dreaming . . . what should I say? I was just dreaming. (*As a statement of fact.*) It's always hard to explain.

LAUREL: You ought to see an analyst. I know analysts who've made a mint just explaining other people's dreams.

DIMITRI: Those aren't the same kind.

LAUREL (*interested*): You mean you know other kinds of analysts?

DIMITRI (*stung*): I mean it was a poetical dream. You can't explain that kind medically.

LAUREL (*doubtful*): Who did you go to?

DIMITRI (*calmer*): You know, I was wondering why the great musicians of the past didn't conceive music the way we do.

LAUREL: Is that quite sure?

DIMITRI: Believe it or not, what counted most for them wasn't this, that, or the other thing, believe it or not, it was Form.

LAUREL (*yawning*): What did you say?

DIMITRI: Form. Musical flux. Why are you leaving?

LAUREL (*coming back toward Dimitri*): You should watch your language . . .

DIMITRI: Sorry to use dirty words. They're in this book.

LAUREL (*impatiently*): You might at least have the courtesy to replace them with words I can understand.

DIMITRI: Well . . . (*pause*) you might say . . . (*pause*) for example . . . (*pause; he hands the book to* LAUREL) why don't *you* read it?

LAUREL: I told you: I never read.

Pause. LAUREL *sits down on the bench next to* DIMITRI.

DIMITRI (*dreamily*): I've always been gone on the great musicians of the past . . . especially the Germans. Their music wasn't cast in rigid molds. They modeled it like a sculptor does clay. They were architects of space-time.

LAUREL (*suddenly getting up*): I don't know that I want to see you again.

DIMITRI: I'm awfully sorry. It's this damned book. A European wrote it. Over there they think you have to use a metaphysical language to talk about jazz.

LAUREL: About music.

DIMITRI: About jazz.

LAUREL: About music. About music.

DIMITRI: As if that were culture. Are you a man of culture?

LAUREL (*proudly*): Of course I'm a man of culture.

DIMITRI (*doubtfully*): You are? Well, then how about telling me about your problems?

LAUREL: My problems?

DIMITRI: You aren't a man of culture unless you've got problems.

LAUREL (*stung*): Of course I've got problems.

DIMITRI (*treacherously*): Mind mentioning one?

LAUREL: Not at all. Let me think . . . Well, as it happens, I was on my way to get my tenor repaired.

DIMITRI: Oh, really? Nothing serious, I hope?

LAUREL: A twisted key. I can't hit low B-flat.

DIMITRI: That's your tenor's problem, not yours. Haven't you got any others?

LAUREL: You took me by surprise. Think I carry my problems with me? I've already got my tenor.

DIMITRI: Think hard. (*Pause.*) Mind you, you've got an excuse. Your specialty doesn't lend itself to problems. If you played the alto instead of the tenor, you might wonder whether you actually oughtn't to play the baritone.

LAUREL (*sudden illumination*): That reminds me! Last year my cousin wanted to sell me his soprano. The very idea of blowing a horn straight as an arrow just makes me sick to my stomach. (*With enthusiasm.*) I like the haughty, feminine curves of my tenor.

DIMITRI (*pompously*): In other words, you almost became a man of culture . . .

LAUREL (*modestly*): Do you think so?

DIMITRI: . . . but you refused to cope with the problem and didn't buy the soprano.

LAUREL (*indignant*): I did too!

DIMITRI (*disappointed*): Oh . . . Did you learn to play it?

LAUREL: No, I sold it again. With a five dollar profit. I forgot to tell you it was a real bargain.

DIMITRI (*ironically*): Maybe a man of culture bought it.

LAUREL (*getting up*): Don't try to insult me. I'm as much a man of culture as you are.

DIMITRI: Of course you are, because I'm not.

LAUREL: You're not a man of culture?

DIMITRI: No!

LAUREL (*sitting down again*): You haven't got problems?

DIMITRI: Oh yes, but they're not the right ones. A man of culture has problems of an ethical order.

LAUREL: You mean like the Chief Justice of the Supreme Court?

DIMITRI: Let me finish. Of an ethical order but of an artistic nature. Do you know a man of culture?

LAUREL: Wait a minute. You say a man of culture is somebody who has problems of an ethical order and an artistic nature?

DIMITRI: Do you know any?

LAUREL: Of course I do.

DIMITRI: Who?

LAUREL: Billy Strayhorn.

DIMITRI: Billy Strayhorn?

LAUREL: And Duke Ellington. They both have problems of an ethical order and an artistic nature.

DIMITRI: In connection with which art?

LAUREL: The art of music . . .

DIMITRI: Jazz?

LAUREL: The art of music.

DIMITRI: Be more precise. Problems about what?

LAUREL (*gossipy tone*): You mean, you don't know? It's the talk of the town! About their jazz version of *The Nutcracker Suite*.

DIMITRI: Ethical problems about *The Nutcracker Suite*?

LAUREL: They wanted to know if they had the right to do their version.

DIMITRI: There's no law against it. Tchaikovsky's music is public property.

LAUREL: That's what most people would think. But they're men of culture.

DIMITRI: What's a man of culture?

LAUREL: Somebody who asks other people what he has the right to do or not to do.

DIMITRI: So they asked other people's advice.

LAUREL: According to what I've heard, they asked them what Tchaikovsky would have thought of their idea.

DIMITRI: Why didn't they ask themselves?

LAUREL: That's a tall order!

DIMITRI: Would it have been dangerous?

LAUREL: Suppose they hadn't gotten the answer they were hoping for?

DIMITRI (*realizing the horror of the situation*): Oh!

LAUREL: Whereas, by acting as men of culture, they got what they wanted.

DIMITRI: People told them Tchaikovsky would have been delighted.

LAUREL: Of course that's what people told them.

DIMITRI: So they did their jazz version of *The Nutcracker Suite*.

LAUREL: And recorded it.

DIMITRI: Is it any good?

LAUREL: I don't know, I'm not a man of culture.

Pause. LAUREL *lays his tenor on the bench next to him.*

DIMITRI: Do you think Ralph Burns is a man of culture?

LAUREL: Why do you ask?

DIMITRI: Because he did a jazz version too.

LAUREL: Of *The Nutcracker Suite?*

DIMITRI: No, *A Night on Bald Mountain.*

LAUREL: Is it any good?

DIMITRI: I don't know.

LAUREL: You're not a man of culture.

DIMITRI (*getting up and taking a few steps with a meditative air*): I wonder what they've got against the Russians.

LAUREL: I guess they want to put pressure on Moscow. On account of the royalties.

DIMITRI: Develop, develop.

LAUREL: Development is a bourgeois notion.

DIMITRI: I'm sure they despise the Russians: Slavs, slaves!

LAUREL: You're way off the beam. They love Russia.

DIMITRI (*theatrically*): They love her so they can rape her.

LAUREL: But since other people said that Tchaikovsky . . .

DIMITRI: What about Moussorgsky? Did other people also say that Moussorgsky . . .

LAUREL: I don't think Burns asked them.

DIMITRI: So you see.

LAUREL: But what could they have said? Just think! Moussorgsky! An alcoholic!

DIMITRI: Who knew nothing about jazz!

LAUREL: So you see.

Pause. DIMITRI *sits down again.*

DIMITRI: Just the same, I'd like to know for *sure* whether Burns asked other people before he went to work.

LAUREL: He ought to have.

DIMITRI: He ought to have indeed! Whereas Ellington didn't ought to have.

LAUREL: You mean Ellington oughtn't to have published that jazz version of *The Nutcracker Suite?*

DIMITRI: On the contrary. I mean Ellington didn't have to ask other people about a thing like that.

LAUREL: And Burns ought to have?

DIMITRI: He ought to have.

LAUREL: Why? Because Burns isn't as great an artist as Ellington?

DIMITRI: Because Tchaikovsky isn't as great an artist as Moussorgsky.

LAUREL: Is that quite sure?

DIMITRI: It's clear as day. For example, in this particular case, *Bald Mountain* is unquestionably a greater work than the *Nutcracker.*

LAUREL (*thoughtfully*): I've got a question to ask you.

DIMITRI: Then ask it yourself.

LAUREL: I'll do no such thing.

DIMITRI: Please, I insist.

LAUREL: You're very kind. Here it is: *Where* exactly is the dividing line?

DIMITRI: What dividing line?

LAUREL: Just how great a work by how great a composer can't be put into jazz without other people's permission?

DIMITRI: Provided you get it.

LAUREL: Let's assume you do.

DIMITRI: No, we've got to be rigorous about this; first let's assume that we ask other people's permission to do a jazz version of the finale of the *Jupiter Symphony*, for example.

LAUREL: Who's it by?

DIMITRI: That's immaterial. What I wanted to show was that nothing proves they'll give it to us.

LAUREL: Who?

DIMITRI: The people we ask for it.

LAUREL: The *Jupiter?*

DIMITRI: No, the permission.

LAUREL (*reproachfully*): You haven't answered my question.

DIMITRI: Really? What did you ask me. Oh yes! You want permission to do a jazz version of the finale . . .

LAUREL: No, I don't, I asked you where the dividing line was.

DIMITRI: That's right, the dividing line, of course. I remember distinctly.

LAUREL: Well?

DIMITRI (*dreamily*): Well, to begin with I imagine it'd be rather high. I'd probably put it somewhere between Chopin's nocturnes and Schubert's impromptus.

LAUREL: I see. . . . In other words if I wanted to arrange one of the nocturnes, I'd have to ask . . .

DIMITRI: You've got it all wrong. If you wanted to arrange Schubert, then you'd have to . . .

LAUREL: Who can decide such a serious issue?

DIMITRI: Other people. Men of culture.

LAUREL: Didn't you just tell me that it's men of culture who ask other people?

DIMITRI: Those aren't the same men of culture.

LAUREL: Nor the same other people, I would surmise.

DIMITRI: I would surmise so, too. They're *other* other people.

LAUREL: Why don't we try to decide for ourselves?

DIMITRI: That's pretty daring.

LAUREL: So be daring; *please* be daring.

DIMITRI: All right. Let's think of a favorable case, an easy case.

LAUREL: Ask me a question.

DIMITRI: What did you do yesterday?

LAUREL: I did a paraphrase on the *Moonlight Sonata*.

DIMITRI: In jazz style?

LAUREL: In jazz style.

DIMITRI: Delightful! What a subtle, refreshing idea!

LAUREL: What about you?

DIMITRI: I did a paraphrase on Beethoven's Opus 27, No. 2.

LAUREL (*threateningly*): In jazz style?

DIMITRI: In jazz style.

LAUREL (*violently*): Horrible! Abominable! How could you dare!

DIMITRI: But you wanted me to be daring!

LAUREL: You could have picked something else! Beethoven! Opus 27! And Number 2 at that!

DIMITRI: You don't think that Beethoven . . . ?

LAUREL (*contemptuously*): No, I'm afraid not. Have you asked other people at least?

DIMITRI (*shocked*): You think I'd embark on anything like that without asking other people?

LAUREL (*unctuously*): So you know them?

DIMITRI: Who?

LAUREL: Other people. The ones we're supposed to ask.

DIMITRI: Oh, well, we don't know exactly who they are.

LAUREL: Actually, we don't know much of anything.

DIMITRI: We don't even know if Burns asked them. He ought to have, that's sure. There's no doubt about Ellington and Strayhorn; we know they asked. As for Burns . . .

LAUREL: Yet these other people do seem to have been men of culture.

DIMITRI: Aren't they jazz artists?

LAUREL: I would surmise so.

DIMITRI: Then they're men of culture by definition. Today, jazz artists are cultivated.

LAUREL: They know all about literature.

DIMITRI: Classical.

LAUREL: Modern. Mostly modern.

DIMITRI: Butt and Jif.

LAUREL: Mutt and Jeff.

DIMITRI: Mick and Nick.

LAUREL: Hic and Nuc.

DIMITRI: Zig and Zig.

LAUREL: And they know music! Brookmeyer recognized the original row of Alban Berg's *Violin Concerto* in a jazz arrangement.

DIMITRI: But he was wrong. It wasn't there.

LAUREL: That makes no difference. He recognized it anyway.

DIMITRI (*admiringly*): That takes culture, all right.

LAUREL: And there's Miles Davis! Know what he listens to on his phonograph?

DIMITRI: Let me guess! Mozart?

LAUREL: Nonsense! Too romantic.

DIMITRI: Monteverdi?

LAUREL: Bel canto.

DIMITRI: *The Twelfth String Quartet?*

LAUREL: Academic.

DIMITRI: Wagner?

LAUREL: Classical. He listens to Ravel and Rachmaninoff. Two hip cats who are really way out.

DIMITRI: Are they really?

LAUREL: That's what he said. Or it's what people say he said. But if so, he didn't say anything.

DIMITRI: You just said he said it.

LAUREL: He didn't say anything when people said he'd said it. Which means he said it.

DIMITRI: Rachmaninoff?

LAUREL: And Ravel. That's culture for you, isn't it?

DIMITRI: If it isn't, what is it?

LAUREL (*indignantly*): I didn't know you could be so crude.

DIMITRI (*snobbishly*): You misunderstand. I meant, if Ravel's music isn't culture, then what is culture?

LAUREL: *La Mer?*

DIMITRI: Pedagogical.

LAUREL: *The Art of the Fugue?*

DIMITRI: Descriptive.

LAUREL: Bellini?

DIMITRI: Which one?

LAUREL: You mean there're more than one?

DIMITRI: You see, you're not a man of culture.

LAUREL (*in preaching tone*): Your culture is merely a catalyst of error. Don't you think you and your kind are making an irreparable mistake with this fuss about Form?

DIMITRI: What sort?

LAUREL: You mean there are more than one?

DIMITRI: I mean, what sort of mistake am I going to make?

LAUREL: You and your kind.

DIMITRI: Are we going to make?

LAUREL (*with an accusing finger*): You and your kind are doing your best to deprive the masses of something they're going to need just when they're going to need it most.

DIMITRI (*sententiously*): As the situation develops, it creates new needs.

LAUREL (*over* DIMITRI'*s last three words*): . . . creates a mode of expression.

DIMITRI: What did you say?

LAUREL: I said the masses are going to need a mode of expression.

DIMITRI: But the masses have pop music!

LAUREL (*decisively*): Not any more. Pop music has become a consumer product.

DIMITRI: Who produces it?

LAUREL: Specialists.

DIMITRI: Don't they belong to the masses?

LAUREL: Sometimes they come out of the masses. (*Confidentially.*) You know how it goes: consumer products make good profits. Pretty soon you've got a swimming pool in your garden and a Cadillac in your garage. (*Bitterly.*) And you stop belonging to the masses.

DIMITRI: What about the consumers?

LAUREL : They pay.

DIMITRI (*disgusted*): The consumers always pay. There's no justice.

LAUREL (*lyrically*): In the society of the future, the one that will be born, painfully, I'll admit, of today's automation . . .

DIMITRI: Revolution?

LAUREL (*cuttingly*): I said cybernation. (*Lyrical again.*) In that society, everyone will lead a life of leisure. Mankind will learn how to create again. (*Accusingly.*) This fuss about Form is obsolete, in fact it's criminal, all it can do is murder a mode of expression which jazz could pride itself on having made available to everybody: the chorus.

DIMITRI (*impressed*): You mean tomorrow everybody'll have (*he picks up* LAUREL'*s tenor from the bench*) a saxophone?

LAUREL (*taking back his tenor*): As sure as they'll have a swimming pool and a Cadillac.

DIMITRI: And time to play it?

LAUREL: Yes, plenty of time to kill.

DIMITRI: So what will people do?

LAUREL: They'll piss.

DIMITRI: They'll piss?

LAUREL: Face to face with the audience.

DIMITRI: But I thought there wasn't going to be any audience left?

LAUREL: No audience left?

DIMITRI: If everybody is both artist and spectator . . .

LAUREL: You're right. You can't piss in your own face.

DIMITRI: You see?

LAUREL (*needling him*): So what *will* people do?

DIMITRI: I don't know. Make popular music.

LAUREL (*annoyed*): That's out of the question. Popular music is just a consumer's product.

DIMITRI: That's true. There's no point in having two swimming pools.

LAUREL: Or two Cadillacs.

DIMITRI: Or two books.

LAUREL: I never read.

DIMITRI: Or two saxophones.

LAUREL: Or two TV sets.

DIMITRI (*getting his bearings again*): Ah, no! That's different. I maintain that two TV sets can be quite useful. It's much easier to keep track of all the different shows. There've been times when I was so captivated by one commercial that I missed another one, which was actually much more important.

LAUREL: What if there were no more advertising?

DIMITRI: No more advertising? You're out of whack.

LAUREL: In an affluent society, what purpose *could* advertising serve?

DIMITRI: If there were no more advertising, what purpose could television serve?

LAUREL: And who'd sponsor the jazz shows? You're right, it wouldn't work.

DIMITRI: That's not the worst part. After all, if everybody is going to have a saxophone (*he tries to take back the tenor but* LAUREL *shoves him away*) they won't have to watch jazz on TV. They can play it for themselves.

LAUREL: That's true. But they have to have something to play. (*Angrily.*) And you've taken the chorus away from them!

DIMITRI: I have?

LAUREL: You and your kind.

DIMITRI (*in a conciliatory tone*): They could play written music.

LAUREL: It's not the same thing.

DIMITRI: Or play recorded choruses over again.

LAUREL: Doc Aldebarran says it's wonderful to play the old-time choruses over again.

DIMITRI: You see?

LAUREL: But his brother says that's nonsense.

DIMITRI: You've got to believe them. They're men of culture.

LAUREL: They have problems.

DIMITRI: But we don't know what problems.

LAUREL: No, we don't.

DIMITRI: Culture is like a good education: it shouldn't show.

LAUREL (*aggressive again*): Then why are you wearing that obsession on your face?

DIMITRI: What obsession?

LAUREL: The one you were talking about a minute ago: Form.

DIMITRI: I and my kind.

LAUREL: When you've given form to your jazz, it'll sound even a little more like old-time European music. Where will that get you?

DIMITRI: But what if it's a specific form?

LAUREL (*sarcastically*): You know perfectly well that contemporary music has abolished fixed forms.

DIMITRI: You mean the fugue and the sonata form?

LAUREL: Finished, dead, done with!

DIMITRI (*in anguish*): Architects of Time! Sculptors!

LAUREL: Electricians! So either your specific form will be a stereotype, or else it'll simply join the indeterminate forms of modern music.

DIMITRI (*clinging to his line of thought*): Gentle landscapes of Sound and Silence!

LAUREL (*pursuing his demonstration*): Then jazz will sound like the new European music instead of the old.

DIMITRI (*getting his second wind*): That's better than sounding like religious music!

LAUREL: I can't follow you there!

DIMITRI: Is the ground marshy here, too?

LAUREL: We're digressing.

DIMITRI: I would surmise so.

LAUREL: You're not somebody who goes to mass . . .

DIMITRI: . . . unless it's in B-minor.

LAUREL: Now don't tell me you're not just a little open to the extraordinary echo you hear in modern jazz.

DIMITRI: Echo of what?

LAUREL (*solemnly*): Of church!

DIMITRI (*also solemnly*): Soul jazz, spiritual music.

LAUREL: Devotional.

DIMITRI: Canonistical.

LAUREL: Sacralistical.

DIMITRI: Brim full of religiosity.

LAUREL (*with satisfaction*): You can't hear a plagal cadenza without immediately thinking, "Yes, Lawd!"

DIMITRI: Let's digress a bit more, shall we?

LAUREL: What about preaching? Doesn't jazz return to its source through preaching?

DIMITRI: Expression! Drama!

LAUREL (*irritated*): Preaching fills a theatrical need neglected in modern jazz.

DIMITRI: You just said modern jazz . . .

LAUREL: It's not the same modern jazz. There's our modern jazz, and there's yours, the sort that belongs to you and your kind.

DIMITRI: What about you?

LAUREL: Pardon?

DIMITRI: Don't *you* have a kind?

LAUREL: There are more of us than you think.

DIMITRI: All lovers of plagal cadenzas and preaching?

LAUREL: Every one! Plagal cadenzas are ritualistication.

DIMITRI: Liturgicalistication.

LAUREL: Nonprofanitization.

DIMITRI: Religiosonation.

LAUREL: And preaching embodies the sense of ceremony.

DIMITRI: The appeal to the showman that sleeps in every man.

LAUREL (*piqued*): At least it's a show without any business.

DIMITRI: Is it?

LAUREL: Shut up! (*Almost screaming.*) How can you dare talk that way about Jommy Smith!

DIMITRI: Did I say anything about Timmy Smith?

LAUREL: No! Don't say a word about him!

DIMITRI: But Jimmy Smith is . . .

LAUREL: Stop! Anything but that!

DIMITRI: . . . a musician . . .

LAUREL: NOOOOO!

> *He falls to the ground and rolls about in a fit. While* DIMITRI *goes on with his speech,* LAUREL *alternately utters incomprehensible shouts and blows screaming notes on his tenor saxophone.*

DIMITRI: . . . a very fine one . . . who's produced a sizable body of works . . . no less than thirteen thousand . . . five hundred and fifty-three blues choruses . . . plus two thousand one hundred and twenty-seven . . . ballads . . . not counting the introductions.

LAUREL (*sitting up suddenly like an acrobat*): You see?

DIMITRI (*scrupulously*): But should we count the introductions?

LAUREL: What about the times when there's no introduction?

DIMITRI: There's always an introduction. It's as if you told me this book had no preface. (*He leafs through it.*) This book has no preface.

LAUREL: What purpose would it serve?

DIMITRI: It would provide an opportunity to speak of culture.

LAUREL: Culture speaks for itself.

DIMITRI: Astronomy, then. Or gastronomy. I like turkey.

LAUREL: I like lamb better. The culture of Panurge.

DIMITRI: What about quotations? Should we count quotations?

LAUREL: Not mine.

DIMITRI: You mean what you quote from others or what I quote from you?

LAUREL: You've no right to quote me.

DIMITRI: But what if I quote your quotations?

LAUREL: And you've no right to say that I told you that you've no right to quote me.

DIMITRI: You must be a man of culture.

LAUREL: I'm a man of my era. (*He gets up, walks over to the edge of the stage and stands holding his tenor before him like an object of worship.*) Anyway, it's time.

DIMITRI (*looking at his book*): It's nineteen minutes past two.

LAUREL: That's what I said.

DIMITRI: Nineteen minutes and twenty seconds.

LAUREL (*ceremoniously*): At this very moment, in all public and national parks, the members of the Sect dedicate their Nocturnal Invocation to the powers that govern the world.

DIMITRI: Can I help you in any way?

LAUREL: Simply by being quiet. (*He starts to play. Sequence of sounds as "unmusical" as possible; crescendo. Then, without looking at* DIMITRI) Did you hear that dissonance?

DIMITRI: Don't play so loud! It's late!

LAUREL: I'm only playing (*he waves toward the audience*) to wake all that up. What time have you got?

DIMITRI: Two twenty-two, twenty-four.

LAUREL: Thanks. (*He plays again.*)

DIMITRI: Faker!

LAUREL (*still playing*): Ritualization is not faking!

DIMITRI: I wonder what school that can be associated with. (*A pause.*) They say Mulligan began that way.

LAUREL (*screaming*): I've got it! I've got it!

DIMITRI: Got what?

LAUREL: My low B-flat! I hit it!

DIMITRI (*coldly*): I'll wire you my congratulations.

LAUREL: Thanks. What time did you say it was?

DIMITRI: A little after fifty-two. Make it fifty-five. (*Suddenly holding his nose.*) Oh! You modulated!

LAUREL: Is that quite sure? I beg your pardon.

DIMITRI: Please wait till you're alone to do that.

LAUREL: One is never alone, because . . . (*He plays again; his speciality is now ear-splitting harmonics.*)

DIMITRI: What a tempo! That's what you call being with it. (*As if assailed by a doubt.*) And what if he really *were* a man of culture?

LAUREL: You sure you've got the right time?

DIMITRI: Do they ever answer?

LAUREL: Not so far. (*He dangles his tenor at arm's length.*) It seemed to me unusually long today.

DIMITRI: The nights are getting shorter.

LAUREL: Well, there goes another one. (*He lays the tenor on the bench and sits down.*) Today, you have to know how to play an invocation. Go on, try it. Try it!

DIMITRI (*getting up with an inspired look*): Pharaoh!

LAUREL (*chanting*): He has second-sight.

DIMITRI: Solar. (*He sits down.*)

LAUREL: Go on.

DIMITRI (*getting up with a less inspired look*): Sun Ra!

LAUREL (*chanting*): He has second-sight.

DIMITRI: Amon. (*He sits down.*)

LAUREL: Go on. It takes three.

DIMITRI (*getting up with a completely uninspired look*): I don't know . . . Zarat'stra!

LAUREL: He has second-sight. But that's a little beside the point.

DIMITRI: I'm not Köxal, you know. (*He sits down.*)

LAUREL: Knock off the masonry.

DIMITRI: I wonder if it will follow you all your life.

LAUREL: What?

DIMITRI: The trail of your false notes.

LAUREL: Anyone who's heard my false notes is dead. And since I've never made any records . . .

DIMITRI: You're leary of Edison.

LAUREL: I'm leary of Karl Cros.

DIMITRI: Edison.

LAUREL: Karl Cros. Karl Cros.

DIMITRI: But recording started with Edison. It's a recorded fact.

LAUREL: The idea belonged to Cros. He was a jewel.

DIMITRI: Ideas have a bad smell.

LAUREL: Yes, but they make things grow.

DIMITRI: What if nothing grows?

LAUREL: Then you make a facsimile.

DIMITRI: Like Wells?

LAUREL: Dickie?

DIMITRI: I said "like Verne."

LAUREL: He was a Jules.

DIMITRI (*solemnly*): You have to make a show!

LAUREL : That's a truism.

DIMITRI: No, it's an exorcism.

LAUREL (*pointing to the book*): What! That thing?

DIMITRI: You have to make people believe.

LAUREL: What if they don't believe you?

DIMITRI: Then your career's a fizzle.

LAUREL (*with a superior air*): Some wouldn't stoop to making the Carrère scene.

DIMITRI: Spare me your biography.

LAUREL: It's not mine. It's someone else's.

DIMITRI: If you don't make the career scene, you're cooked.

LAUREL: Like Caraceni?

DIMITRI: Like Careri. His gallinaceans were half-cocked.

LAUREL: Karl Ieri didn't have a feather in his cap.

DIMITRI: No. Ieri was one of the jewels.

LAUREL: Wasn't Paul?

DIMITRI: Or Jack?

LAUREL: The Fatalist?

DIMITRI: No, the other one, the one who wouldn't submit.

LAUREL: So, it wasn't the nephew?

DIMITRI: Whose?

LAUREL: Rameau's.

DIMITRI: No, Karl was the nephew.

LAUREL (*dreamily*): Simon . . .

DIMITRI (*imitating him, through cupped hands*): Simoone! . . .

LAUREL: Simonin . . .

DIMITRI: Siimooonet! . . .

LAUREL (*looks inside his saxophone*): All is fleecing and pigeon plucking.

DIMITRI: And turkey plucking. (*He looks for something in his book.*) But where are the turkeys?

LAUREL: In the farce! In the farce!

DIMITRI: They can't be seen.

LAUREL: You see?

> Pause; DIMITRI *leans slowly forward and stares at* LAUREL *from close up and from below.*

DIMITRI: You know what? I recognize you now.

LAUREL: Is that quite sure?

DIMITRI: It wasn't before. But that sound of yours!

LAUREL: Where did you hear me?

DIMITRI: At the Jarvinen concert last winter.

LAUREL: What a concert! (*Proudly.*) We played so badly the audience booed.

DIMITRI: Were they booing *you?*

LAUREL: No, not us: Jarvinen.

DIMITRI: I remember.

LAUREL : They screamed!

DIMITRI: The whole audience was shouting: El-ling-ton!

LAUREL: We couldn't hear ourselves playing. And it was just as well.

DIMITRI: El-ling-ton!

LAUREL (*joining in*): El-ling-ton!

TOGETHER (*stamping their feet and rhythmically syncopating the name*): El-ling-ton! El-ling-ton!

LAUREL: For once, the public was right. Did you ever hear musicians sound like that? We didn't even play the notes.

DIMITRI: I went to Jaime Xanadu's last recital. Mozart's sonatas. You can't imagine.

LAUREL: Didn't he play the notes?

DIMITRI: Only just.

LAUREL: Did you boo him?

DIMITRI: Who?

LAUREL: Mozart.

DIMITRI: No, we booed Xanadu.

LAUREL: You're right. Mozart can't go wrong.

DIMITRI: Whereas Jarvinen is in the wrong.

LAUREL: Of course he is.

DIMITRI: Why?

LAUREL: Because he's not Mozart.

DIMITRI: You see?

LAUREL: He's bound to be in the wrong.

DIMITRI: Necessarily.

LAUREL: Definitively.

DIMITRI: Obligatorily.

LAUREL: Definitively.

DIMITRI (*viscously*): I'd like to ask you a question.

LAUREL: So would I.

DIMITRI: Then ask it yourself.

LAUREL: I'll do nothing of the sort.

DIMITRI (*simple and direct*): What were you doing at that Jarvinen concert?

LAUREL (*touched*): How did you guess?

DIMITRI: Guess what?

LAUREL: The question you just asked is the very same one I wanted to ask myself.

DIMITRI: That's no reason not to answer it.

LAUREL: Would you mind repeating it once or twice?

DIMITRI (*implacably*): You took part in that concert, and yet you're a member of the Sect?

LAUREL: It's funny, I didn't recognize it that time.

DIMITRI: It's the same one.

LAUREL: Are you sure?

DIMITRI: You're averting your ears.

LAUREL (*panic-stricken*): Well . . . some confessions traumatize me . . . in those days I didn't belong to the Sect.

DIMITRI (*admiringly*): You were a free man.

LAUREL (*modestly*): I was a free lance.

DIMITRI: Like Mezz?

LAUREL: Like Prez.

DIMITRI: Like Bud?

LAUREL: Like Bird.

DIMITRI: You're not going to compare yourself with Bird!

LAUREL: All my life I've . . .

DIMITRI: But in those days, they worked, they earned money!

LAUREL: They got screwed.

DIMITRI: But they played.

LAUREL: You see?

DIMITRI: And now.

LAUREL: Now? (*He bursts out sobbing.*) Why are you torturing me like this?

DIMITRI: Don't try to wriggle out of it.

LAUREL: Inquisitor. (*He sobs some more.*) You knew all along?

DIMITRI: What?

LAUREL (*in a whisper*): I've lost faith.

DIMITRI (*incredulously*): Permanently? (LAUREL *motions with his hand.*) But what about that invocation you just played?

LAUREL (*looking around him*): I'm being watched.

DIMITRI: The Sect?

LAUREL: It might even be you.

DIMITRI: Get that out of your head. I don't belong to anything.

LAUREL (*admiringly*): You're a free man?

DIMITRI: I've got so much freedom I don't know what to do with it.

LAUREL: There's always free jazz.

DIMITRI (*with hostility*): You can't convince me.

LAUREL (*suspiciously*): I see. You aren't a composer?

DIMITRI (*with a gesture of distaste*): I'm not even a terrorist.

LAUREL: But you believe in Form.

DIMITRI: I can't help it. It's hereditary. My father believed in form, my grandfather . . .

LAUREL: We'll study your family tree later. For the moment, let's feed us!

DIMITRI: You're hungry?

LAUREL (*urgently, almost begging*): Give us something to play!

He holds out his tenor like a child. DIMITRI *tries to take it.* LAUREL *resists. They struggle violently in silence. Eventually* LAUREL *keeps his tenor.*

(*Hatefully.*) Now I know who you are.

DIMITRI (*shrugging his shoulders*): Tell me.

LAUREL: You're one of those other people!

DIMITRI (*indignantly*): What's gotten into you? You're out of whack!

LAUREL: If you weren't one of the other people, you'd feed us.

DIMITRI: I haven't brought anything with me.

LAUREL (*calmer now*): It wasn't for me, it was for my tenor.

DIMITRI: It's fed up with improvising?

LAUREL: I don't know, it's gotten so cranky.

DIMITRI: That's your fault.

LAUREL: My fault?

DIMITRI: You and your kind. Your tenor was well fed. It never complained before. (*Indignantly.*) And you've taken the chorus away from it!

LAUREL: It was getting pimples.

DIMITRI: You should have gone to an analyst.

LAUREL: A what?

DIMITRI: Pimples are psychosomatic. The idea of not letting it have any choruses!

LAUREL (*overcome with grief*): Me and my kind.

DIMITRI: Don't try to put your responsibilities off on anyone else. You have tremendous responsibilities. Not only to your tenor but to the whole world.

LAUREL: Which one?

DIMITRI: We, the people on the outside, we used to be able to follow you, we knew more or less where you were at. We used to be able to say: he's coming to the twenty-second bar, twelve more beats and the bridge will be over, only eight more bars till the end of the chorus. Everything was articulate. Order prevailed.

LAUREL: But what about freedom?

DIMITRI (*pompously*): To free man is to enslave him. (*Paternalistically.*) You ought to go back to the Sect.

LAUREL: Do you think so?

DIMITRI: Or else to a new one. One Sect drives out another!

LAUREL: But it's still a Sect.

DIMITRI: What's more, you're lucky with your Sect. The Brotherhood, you know . . .

LAUREL: I know.

DIMITRI (*sadly*): We killed it. At least that's what they say.

LAUREL: Not so loud! (*Pointing to the audience.*) Somebody might hear you.

DIMITRI: It doesn't matter. I won't be punished. Will you?

LAUREL: My future's pretty grim.

DIMITRI: How can we justify a thing like that? We'd have to think up some extenuating circumstances.

LAUREL: We're not men of culture.

DIMITRI: That's true. . . . That might do for a start.

LAUREL: Wait . . . I think I see a possible line of defense. Since we're not men of culture, but nevertheless feel the need for renewal . . .

DIMITRI: Too weak! They'll just say you should have invented the happening.

LAUREL (*perking up*): That's just it! They stole it from us!

DIMITRI: Who?

LAUREL: Them. The men of culture. I'd almost invented it.

DIMITRI: Oh, I understand. It must be awful to have one's own property stolen.

LAUREL: Didn't even have time to register it with ASCAP.

DIMITRI: With BMI.

LAUREL: With ASCAP, with ASCAP.

DIMITRI: And now.

LAUREL: I have to look elsewhere.

DIMITRI: Why not look among men of culture?

LAUREL (*vindictively*): If only I could steal it back from them!

DIMITRI: What?

LAUREL: The happening.

DIMITRI: Forget about it. That's already been done.

LAUREL: Then something else. The sonata form.

DIMITRI: Out of the question.

LAUREL: Why?

DIMITRI: You just told me it was dead.

LAUREL: Then what about the fugue? No, you're right. (*Pause.*) What if we asked them?

DIMITRI: Asked who? Men of culture?

LAUREL: No, other people.

DIMITRI: But I thought we didn't know who they were?

LAUREL: You see?

DIMITRI (*sudden inspiration*): Why not look in this book?

LAUREL: Written by a European?

DIMITRI: That's just it. Those people don't know where to draw the line.

LAUREL : You mean they don't know how to beat time.

DIMITRI: It might give you . . . oh, I don't know, an insight, an impulse!

LAUREL (*suspicious*): The author is a man of culture, I would surmise.

DIMITRI: Yes, but his is a sad culture.

LAUREL: I feel sad too. Give me the book. (*He lays his tenor on the bench between* DIMITRI *and himself, takes the book which* DIMITRI *is urging on him, sniffs at it, cautiously opens it and pretends to read. Immediately.*) That concert really was terrible, wasn't it?

DIMITRI: Atrocious. And what was the composer's reaction?

LAUREL: I don't know. Nobody saw him. (*He looks down at the book. Immediately.*) How did the man next to you like it?

DIMITRI: I don't know.

LAUREL: What about the critic, what did he write about it?

DIMITRI: I don't know. Do you think I read the critic?

LAUREL: When you know how to read, you read. Is he a friend of yours?

DIMITRI: I have nothing to do with that set.

LAUREL: Then I can tell you what I think of him.

DIMITRI: Me first! He's a . . .

LAUREL: Yes. And a . . .

DIMITRI: In fact, he's a . . .

LAUREL: And a. . . .

DIMITRI (*gesturing toward the audience*): You shouldn't talk so loud.

LAUREL (*loudly*): I never miss one of his articles.

DIMITRI (*wooden tone*): They're so subtle . . .

LAUREL (*the same*): So sound . . .

DIMITRI: His style is equalled only by . . .

LAUREL (*more naturally*): So far, the immediate future has always proved him wrong.

DIMITRI: Shhh! Maybe that's so the distant future can prove him right.

LAUREL (*more softly*): But why does he always talk about other people? (*He yawns; returns to his reading, without conviction, while* DIMITRI *grows impatient and casts longing, sidewise glances at the tenor. Pointing to the book.*) What about this? Can it be sung? No? Then what's it got to do with music?

DIMITRI: Read! Go on and read! Why aren't you reading?

LAUREL (*putting the book aside*): Horrible. A horrible thought just came back to me.

DIMITRI: Keep it to yourself!

LAUREL: "Every reader, as he reads, is reading himself."

DIMITRI: That's silly. So what?

LAUREL: I'm afraid of reading myself.

DIMITRI (*encouraging him*): Maybe you won't understand. That takes culture.

LAUREL: You admitted I was a man of culture.

DIMITRI: Maybe you haven't got the right one. There're lots of lies in there.

LAUREL: What if that were the only one I did have?

DIMITRI: Try anyway. Perhaps you have to have them all. (LAUREL *hesitates. Exasperated.*) You're not universal, you know!

LAUREL (*bending over the book and starting to read; between his teeth*): Forgotten had you forgotten could you have forgotten . . . (*Without letting go of the book, he falls asleep.*)

DIMITRI: At last! (*He straightens up, but remains seated; silently he picks up the tenor, slowly raises it to his lips and blows. No sound comes out.*) They say night is a good time for inspiration. Let's try to find it. (*He looks up in the air, to his right, to his left, behind him.*) Night! (*He blows; no sound.*) The moon shines bright: in such a night as this, when the sweet wind did gently . . . (*He blows.*) Night! (*He blows.*) I'll get the hang of it eventually! (*He blows.*) Oh, unjust destiny! My head is on fire, it's exploding with ideas, they're more and more beautiful, this is genius! and this horn won't play! (*Blows.*) Filthy instrument! (*Blows.*) Cerberus! (*Blows.*) Nothing gets through. (*Pause.*) Maybe if I wiggled my fingers . . . (*Blows.*) This must be that low B-flat. (*Blows desperately, gets a squawk.*) Ah? (*Tries again; same result.*) Night! (*Squawk.*) Night! (*Squawk.*) What a hymn to the Night! (*Squawk.*) But the repertoire's a bit limited. (*Glances at LAUREL sleeping.*) You palmed your stereotype off on me, you beast! (*Pause.*) Tense my muscles. (*He swells his chest.*) Concentrate my willpower. (*He knits his brows.*) Rise above myself. (*He half stands, raises the tenor above his head with difficulty.*) Now! (*He blows furiously, gets no result at all.*) I can't! I can't . . . (*He sits down again. Pauses. Looks at LAUREL still asleep.*) And there he lies, asleep, never suspecting that . . . He's smiling! Perhaps he's being visited by a dream of inspiration? If only I could sleep! (*Very softly; this is the beginning of a long crescendo.*) Or die. Live a second time. A wise choice might be possible. The planets circle around his birth. He's an exuberant child, and the bands sometimes shed a tear for him. (*Just a bit louder.*) The hair on his body is organizing, proclaiming his virility to the surface of the world. Originality comes to him. See how he diversifies himself: one of his thoughts might be called this, another that, and yet he has plenty left, plenty left! He doesn't know he's still in adolescence. No responsibilities! They'll come soon enough. Well, what do you know; poets are taking an interest in him. He's exotic enough to bother the conformists. (*Louder.*) But the signs of the adult world are already there, the madness that comes before wisdom. The rib cage will expand no further. Now he is living the life of a full-grown man. Starts worrying about his future. (*Louder. Panting delivery.*) Has changed syncopations again. Hard to be faithful! Now he attracts philosophers? Oh, no! It's not going to happen all over again! . . . (*He gets up.*) He's accepted, he's been accepted, and he wants to live! Invent his own madness, invent his own impossibilities! Why did he choose this path? Doesn't he know where it leads? All the routs, all the . . . Untarnishable! Won't accept the whitening hair, the falling teeth. That son, who grew up too fast and summons him now to step aside. One moment more! Let's talk this over. But already it's the seventh time around. Survival? Who speaks of survival? (*Screamed.*) Jericho! Your walls are tumbling down! (DIMITRI *plugs his ears and remains motionless for a moment; then, holding the tenor like a machine gun, slowly comes toward the audience.*) And now what? (*Sarcastic smile.* DIMITRI *takes aim at the audience and sweeps it with a few bursts.*) Ratatatatatatata!

In the meantime, the sun has risen. It is daylight. LAUREL *wakes, yawning and stretching.*

DIMITRI (*bitterly*): What were you doing while . . .
LAUREL (*emerging*): I was reading. Slowly, very slowly.
DIMITRI: That never happens to me. Were you reading or dreaming?
LAUREL: When I dream, I read.
DIMITRI: So you weren't dreaming.
LAUREL: I was reading. I was reading. What, you're here?
DIMITRI: What were you reading?
LAUREL: I don't know. (*Slowly the curtain starts to fall.*) I don't know. I've forgotten.

END